DUE DATE

IMMIGRATION

OPPOSING VIEWPOINTS®

Other Books in the American History Series:

IMMIGRATION

OPPOSING VIEWPOINTS®

David L. Bender, *Publisher*
Bruno Leone, *Executive Editor*

Teresa O'Neill, *Series Editor*
John C. Chalberg, Ph.D., professor of history,
   Normandale Community College, *Consulting
   Editor*

Teresa O'Neill, *Book Editor*

AMERICAN HISTORY SERIES

Cover photos: The Bettmann Archive, top left, top right, bottom; National Archives, middle. The following copyrighted material has been reprinted in this volume: **Chapter 1:** From *The Rise of the Unmeltable Ethnics* by Michael Novak, © 1971 by Michael Novak. Reprinted by permission of Sterling Lord Literistic, Inc. **Chapter 5:** From *The Transplanted: A History of Immigrants in Urban America* by John Bodnar. Bloomington: Indiana University Press, 1985. Reprinted with permission. From *The Uprooted*, 2d ed., by Oscar Handlin. Copyright 1951 by Oscar Handlin, © renewed 1973 by Oscar Handlin. By permission of Little, Brown and Company.

Library of Congress Cataloging-in-Publication Data

Immigration : opposing viewpoints / Teresa O'Neill, book editor.
    p.   cm. — (American history series)
    Includes bibliographical references and index.
    ISBN 1-56510-007-7 (lib. bdg. : acid-free paper) — ISBN 1-56510-006-9 (pbk. : acid-free paper)
    1. Minorities—United States—History—Sources.
2. Immigrants—United States—History—Sources. 3. United States—Emigration and immigration—History—Sources.
I. O'Neill, Terry, 1944-   . II. Series: American history series (San Diego, Calif.)
E184.A1I444   1992   92-21794
304.8′73—dc20   CIP

© 1992 by Greenhaven Press, Inc., PO Box 289009,
San Diego, CA 92198-9009
Printed in the U.S.A

Contents

Foreword

Aboard the *Arbella* as it lurched across the cold, gray Atlantic, John Winthrop was as calm as the waters surrounding him were wild. With the confidence of a born leader, Winthrop gathered his Puritan passengers around him. It was time to offer a sermon. England lay behind them, and years of strife and persecution for their religious beliefs were over, he said. But the Puritan abandonment of England, he reminded his followers, did not mean that England was beyond redemption. Winthrop wanted his followers to remember England even as they were leaving it behind. Their goal should be to create a new England, one far removed from the authority of the Anglican church and King Charles I. In Winthrop's words, their settlement in the New World ought to be a model society, a city upon a hill. He hoped his band would be able to create a just society in America for corrupt England to imitate.

Unable to find either peace or freedom within their home country, these Puritans were determined to provide England with a living example of a community that valued both. Across the hostile Atlantic Ocean would shine the bright light of a just, harmonious, and God-serving society. England may have been beset by sin and corruption, but Winthrop and the colonists believed they could still save England—and themselves. Together, they would coax out of the rocky New England soil not only food for their tables but many thriving communities dedicated to achieving harmony and justice.

On June 8, 1630, John Winthrop and his company of refugees had their first glimpse of what they came to call New England. High on the surrounding hills stood a welcoming band of fir trees whose fragrance drifted to the *Arbella* on a morning breeze. To Winthrop, the "smell off the shore [was] like the smell of a garden."

This new world would, in fact, often be compared to the Garden of Eden. In it, John Winthrop would have his opportunity to start life over again. So would his family and his shipmates. So would all those who would come after them. Victims of conflict in old England hoped to find peace in New England.

Winthrop, for one, had experienced much conflict in his life. As a Puritan, he was opposed to Catholicism and Anglicanism, both of which, he believed, were burdened by distracting rituals and distant hierarchies. A parliamentarian by conviction, he despised

Charles I, who had spurned Parliament and created a private army to do his bidding. He believed in individual responsibility and fought against the loss of religious and political freedom. A gentleman landowner, he feared the rising economic power of a merchant class that seemed to value only money. Once Winthrop stepped aboard the *Arbella*, he hoped conflict would not be a part of his American future.

But his Puritan religion told Winthrop that human beings are fallen creatures and that perfection, whether communal or individual, is unachievable on this earth. Therefore, he was presented with a dilemma: On the one hand, his religion demanded that he attempt to live a perfect life in an imperfect world. On the other hand, it told him that he was destined to fail.

Soon after Winthrop disembarked from the *Arbella*, he came face-to-face with this maddening dilemma. He found himself presiding not over a utopia—an ideal community—but over a colony caught up in disputes as troubling as any that he had confronted in his English past.

John Winthrop, it seems, was not the only Puritan with a dream of perfection, with a vision of a heaven on earth. Others in the community saw the dream differently. They wanted greater political and religious freedom than their leader was prepared to grant. Often, Winthrop was able to handle this conflict diplomatically. He expanded, for example, participation in elections and allowed the voters of Massachusetts Bay greater power.

But religious conflict was another matter because it was a conflict of competing visions of the Puritan utopia. In Roger Williams and Anne Hutchinson, two of his fellow colonists, John Winthrop faced rivals unprepared to accept his definition of the perfect community. To Williams, perfection demanded that he separate himself from the Puritan institutions in his community and create an even "purer" church. Winthrop, however, disagreed and exiled Williams to Rhode Island. Hutchinson presumed that she could interpret God's will without a minister. Again, Winthrop did not agree. Hutchinson was tried on charges of heresy, convicted, and banished from Massachusetts.

John Winthrop's Massachusetts colony was the first, but far from the last, American attempt to build a unified, peaceful community that, in the end, only provoked a discord. This glimpse at its history reveals what Winthrop confronted: the unavoidable presence of conflict in American life.

American Assumptions

From America's origins in the early seventeenth century, Americans have often held several interrelated assumptions about their country. First, people believe that to be American is to be free.

Second, because Americans did not have to free themselves from feudal lords or an entrenched aristocracy, conflict is often considered foreign to American life. Finally, America has been seen as a perpetual haven from the troubles and disputes that are found in the Old World.

John Winthrop, for one, lived his life as though all of these assumptions were true. But the opposing viewpoints presented in the American History Series should reveal that for many Americans, these assumptions were and are myths. Indeed, for numerous Americans, liberty has not always been guaranteed, and conflict has been a necessary, sometimes welcome aspect of their life. To these Americans, the United States is less a sanctuary than it is one more battleground for old and new ideas.

Our American landscape has been torn apart again and again by a great variety of clashes—theological, ideological, political, economic, geographical, racial, gender-based, and class-based. But to discover such a landscape is not necessarily to come upon a hopelessly divided country. If the editors desire to prove anything during the course of this series, it is not that America has been destroyed by conflict but rather that America has been enlivened, enriched, and even strengthened by Americans who have disagreed with one another.

Observers of American life, however, often see a country in which its citizens behave as though all of the basic questions of life have been settled. Over the years, they see a generation after generation of Americans who seem to blithely agree with one another. In the nineteenth century, French traveler Alexis de Tocqueville called the typical American a "venturesome conservative." According to Tocqueville, this American was willing to risk money in the marketplace but otherwise presented the drab front of someone who thought, dressed, and acted just like everyone else. To Tocqueville, Americans were individualistic risk takers when it came to playing the game of capitalism but were victims of public opinion (which he defined as the "tyranny of the majority") when it came to otherwise expressing themselves.

In the twentieth century, sociologist David Riesman has registered his agreement with Tocqueville. He has defined the modern American as "other-directed." Perhaps willing to leap into the economic arena, this American is unwilling to take risks in the marketplace of ideas. The result is either silence or assent, either because this person is unsure of his or her own beliefs or because the mass media dictate beliefs—or a bit of both. The other-directed American is fearful of standing apart from the crowd.

The editors of this series would like to suggest that Tocqueville and Riesman were too narrow in their assessment of Americans. They have found innumerable Americans who have been willing to take the trouble to disagree.

Thomas Jefferson was one of the least confrontational of Americans, but he boldly and irrevocably enriched American life with his individualistic views. Like John Winthrop before him, he had a notion of an American Eden. Like Winthrop, he offered a vision of a harmonious society. And like Winthrop, he not only became enmeshed in conflict but eventually presided over a people beset by it. But unlike Winthrop, Jefferson believed this Eden was not located in a specific community but in each individual American. His Declaration of Independence from Great Britain could also be read as a declaration of independence for each individual in American society.

The American Individual

Jefferson's ideal world was composed of "yeoman farmers," each of whom was roughly equal to the other in society's eyes, each of whom was free from the restrictions of both government and his fellow citizens. Throughout his life, Jefferson offered a continuing challenge to Americans: advance individualism and equality or see the death of the American experiment. Jefferson believed that the strength of this experiment depended upon a society of autonomous individuals and a society without great gaps between rich and poor. His challenge to his fellow Americans to create—and sustain—such a society has itself produced both economic and political conflict.

A society whose guiding document is the Declaration of Independence is a society assured of the freedom to dream—and to disagree. We know that Jefferson himself hated conflict, whether personal or political. His tendency was to avoid confrontations of any sort, to squirrel himself away and write rather than to stand up and speak his mind. It is only through his written words that we can grasp Jefferson's utopian dream of a society of independent farmers, all pursuing their private dreams and all leading lives of sufficient prosperity.

This man of wealth and intellect lived an essentially happy life in accord with his view that Americans ought to have the right to pursue "happiness." But Jefferson's public life was much more troublesome. From the first rumblings of the American Revolution in the 1760s to the North-South skirmishes of the 1820s that ultimately produced the Civil War, Jefferson was at or near the center of American political history. The issues were almost too many—and too crucial—for one lifetime. Jefferson had to choose between supporting or rejecting the path of revolution. During and after the ensuing war, he was at the forefront of the battle for religious liberty. After endorsing the Constitution, he opposed the economic plans of Alexander Hamilton. At the end of the century, he fought the infamous Alien and Sedition Acts, which limited civil liberties. As president, he opposed the Federalist court, conspiracies to divide the union, and calls for a new war against England.

Throughout his life, Thomas Jefferson, slaveholder, pondered the conflict between American freedom and American slavery. And from retirement at his Monticello retreat, he frowned at the rising spirit of commercialism that he feared was dividing Americans and destroying his dream of American harmony.

No matter the issue, however, Thomas Jefferson invariably supported the rights of the individual. Worried as he was about the excesses of commercialism, he accepted them because his main concern was to live in a society where liberty and individualism could flourish. To Jefferson, Americans had to be free to worship as they desired. They also deserved to be free from an over-reaching government. To Jefferson, Americans should also be free to possess slaves.

Harmony, an Elusive Goal

Before reading the articles in this anthology, the editors ask readers to ponder the lives of John Winthrop and Thomas Jefferson. Each held a utopian vision, one based upon the demands of community and the other on the autonomy of the individual. Each dreamed of a country of perpetual new beginnings. Each found himself thrust into a position of leadership and found that conflict could not be avoided. And each lived long enough to face and express many opposing views. Harmony, whether communal or individual, was a forever elusive goal.

The opposing visions of Winthrop and Jefferson have been at the heart of many differences among Americans from many backgrounds through the whole of American history. Moreover, their visions have provoked important responses that have helped shape American society, the American character, and many an American battle.

Is the theme of community versus the individual the single defining theme in American history? No, but it is a recurring theme that provides us with a useful point of departure for showing that Americans have been more rambunctious and contentious than Tocqueville or Riesman found them to be, that blandness has not been the defining characteristic for all Americans.

In this age of mass media, the danger exists that the real issues that divide Americans will be, at best, distorted or, at worst, ignored. But by thinking honestly about the past, the real issues and real differences have often been of critical, even of life-and-death, importance to Americans. And they continue to be so today.

The editors of the American History Series have done extensive research to find representative opinions on the issues included in these volumes. They found numerous outstanding opposing viewpoints from people of all times, classes, and genders in American history. From those, they selected commentaries that best fit the nature and flavor of the period under consideration. Every attempt was made to include the most important and relevant viewpoints in each chapter. Obviously, not every notable viewpoint could be included. Therefore, a bibliography has been provided at the end of each book to aid readers in seeking out for themselves additional information.

The editors are confident that as this series reveals past conflicts, it will help revitalize the reader's views of the American present. In that spirit, the American History Series is dedicated to the proposition that American history is more complicated, more fascinating, and more troubling than John Winthrop, Thomas Jefferson, Alexis de Tocqueville, or David Riesman ever dared to imagine.

John C. Chalberg
Consulting Editor

Introduction

"Just as the stream of immigration has continued, so has the old debate, a debate over the meaning of immigration for the American present and future."

Oscar Handlin, famed scholar of American immigration, wrote, "Once I thought to write a history of the immigrants in America. Then I discovered that the immigrants *were* American history." He and many historians since have discovered that to fully understand America, the historian must consider the experiences, adaptations, and conflicts of its immigrants. America was formed by those persecuted Puritans who fled their English homes in the seventeenth century; by those other English, Scots-Irish, and Spanish who left their homes seeking economic opportunity; by the Irish who fled from their native land's famine in the 1840s and the Germans who left behind political change and economic depression; by the Mexicans who crossed the new border for better jobs; by the Italians, Slavs, and Greeks who flooded into the United States in the decades around the turn of the century; and by the Russian Jews who fled czarist purges. Today, immigrants continue to shape the nation.

The immigrant experience embodies any number of confrontations and conflicts. At one level, discord and tension is personal and internal. In pulling up the roots of the old environment and struggling to put them down in the new, each immigrant has had to struggle with questions of personal identity and with how this person, formed in another country, fits into a new world. Immigrants also face inevitable tensions between the first generation and succeeding generations. Parents, their children, and their children's children have waged many a battle over the use of English, the costs and opportunities of Americanizing, and the retention of the mores and traditions of the Old Country. There have also been conflicts between immigrant groups. Turf battles involving various ethnic groups have dotted the urban landscape since immigrants have arrived and established their Little Italies,

Chinatowns, and Spanish Harlems, and since new immigrants have arrived to supplant the old in their struggles to achieve acceptance and success in America.

But the most critical dividing line in the history of American immigration has been that sometimes porous, sometimes impenetrable line between the immigrant and the host culture. This volume will concentrate on the dissension in that century of American history, from the 1820s to the 1920s, when thirty-five million immigrants entered the United States, kindling dramatic tensions between those immigrants and the dominant culture.

Why Emigrate?

Why does any immigrant choose to leave his or her homeland? Students of immigration have developed a few key words to describe the major reasons for immigration. Chief among these are *push*, *pull*, and *means*. *Push* refers to forces at large within one's place of origin. They may be catastrophic, such as the Irish potato famine; political, such as czarist repression; or economic, such as a depression. *Pull* refers to those economic and political forces that operate like a magnet drawing immigrants to the United States. For example, job opportunities in an industrializing America produced periodic jumps in the graph of post-Civil War immigration. Finally, *means* describes the ability to immigrate. This might include the availability of cheap transportation for the migrant or the absence of strict barriers at either the point of departure or arrival. Of course, all three factors may be a part of any single emigrant's decision to emigrate.

The first wave of non-English immigrants to be "pushed" out of Europe and attracted to America were the Irish and Germans who began to arrive in significant numbers in the 1840s. Between 1820 and 1830, 54,338 Irish and 7,729 Germans came to the United States. Between 1840 and 1850, the corresponding numbers are 780,719 and 434,626. In the ten years immediately preceding the Civil War these two immigrant groups constituted over 70 percent of the total immigration to the United States. For this ten-year period, the Germans barely supplanted the Irish as the largest single immigrant group, 951,667 to 914,119. Never again would two ethnic groups so dominate American immigration.

But numbers reveal only a part of the story. Irish immigration gradually changed the face of Yankee-dominated New England. By the end of the nineteenth century, Irish-Americans had altered the composition of the American work force and rewritten the history of urban politics. Both the impulse to unionize and the growth of big-city political machines were significantly attributable to the efforts and ambitions of Irish-American immigrants. From Terence V. Powderly, head of the Knights of Labor, to James ("Honey Fitz") Fitzgerald, mayor of Boston and grand-father of John Fitzgerald Kennedy, Irish-Americans were challenging and becoming part of the American elite.

By their sheer numbers, the Irish, nearly all Catholic, also added a new dimension to American religious life. Their presence and that of their Catholic counterparts from Germany provoked the first intensely anti-immigrant mood since the charged anti-French atmosphere surrounding the passage of the Alien and Sedition acts of the 1790s. Americans feared that these papists would maintain stronger loyalties to the pope in Rome than to America and would attempt to turn the United States into a papal satellite. In fact, the great numbers of Irish and German Catholic immigrants in pre-Civil War America led to a significant nativist movement. Convents were burned to the ground. Priests were hounded from their pulpits. The anti-Catholic Native American party briefly became a political force in the early 1850s. There were even serious questions as to whether the founding principle of the Republican party would be its opposition to slavery or its animus toward immigrants.

The overall German migration to the United States resulted in a somewhat different story. To begin with, the Germans spoke a language other than English. They also represented three religious groups—Catholic, Protestant, and Jewish. Finally, unlike the Irish, German immigrants tended not to congregate in cities but to distribute themselves widely across the urban and rural American north. This broader distribution hastened the entrance of many German immigrants into the American mainstream, the language barrier notwithstanding. They were forced by proximity to interact more with the "native" Americans they lived among, while the Irish and other later immigrants often clustered in "ghettos," where their time was spent primarily with members of their own groups.

But tensions between the German past and the American present did not disappear quickly. As Mack Walker, a prominent historian of German immigration, has put it, Germans came to the United States "not to establish something new, but to reestablish something old." German-Americans were predisposed to take great pride in their German heritage and its accomplishments. Many established what were essentially "little Germanies" in the American heartland. Many also tried to hang on to their language in the face of the efforts of native-born Americans, as well as English-speaking Irish-Americans, to force them to abandon it. Once allies against the dominant Protestant culture, German and Irish immigrants and their descendants gradually found themselves at odds over the question of language. Irish-American bishop John Ireland of St. Paul, Minnesota, for one, waged a personal war against the German tongue as spoken by German Catholics within his diocese. He insisted that his Catholic subjects become "Americanized," the first step of which was to learn the American language.

In sum, within little more than a decade of this sudden surge of immigrants from Ireland and Germany, the United States had become a political and cultural battleground over issues of ethnicity. In all of American history up to that point, nothing could rival the ethnic wars of the 1840s and 1850s. But the ethnic issue was to heat up even more as the nature of immigration changed following the Civil War.

After the war, new immigrant groups began arriving in the United States in significant numbers. And with these new immigrants came calls for restrictions on immigration and new forms of anti-immigrant protest. Joining the Irish and Germans were immigrants from China and Japan, Poland and Italy, Norway and Sweden, Greece and Turkey, as well as Jewish and non-Jewish refugees from the Russian and Austro-Hungarian empires. The presence of these immigrants led some native-born Americans to redouble their efforts at restricting the flow of immigrants to the United States.

Because most of the new immigrants did not look or talk like either the native (white, Anglo-Saxon, Protestant) American *or* the previous waves of immigrants, many nativists assumed that they were not assimilable. And because they were not assimilable, they were not welcome. Here irony intrudes. The 1880s saw both the dedication of the Statue of Liberty and the first dedicated efforts to keep members of this and succeeding generations of "huddled masses" from America's shores. The issue was not merely one of speeding the assimilation process by halting the use of languages other than English. Instead, efforts were mounted to block the entrance of immigrants to the United States.

In the case of the Chinese, Congress did just that in 1882. For the first time in American history a potential supply of future immigrants was banned solely on the basis of its race. For other immigrant groups, Congress moved gradually to restrict "undesirables," on the basis of their criminal, health, political, or job-prospect status. Ultimately literacy became the device most favored by the power elite—those uppercrust wealthy and intellectual members of society who largely ran the country—for reducing the immigrant waves to a trickle. Through the efforts of the Immigration Restriction League and its most visible and powerful voice, Senator Henry Cabot Lodge of Massachusetts, a plan was devised to exclude all male adults unable to read and write their own language.

On the other side of the debate over immigration restriction was a curious amalgam of idealism and self-interest comprised of those who wanted America to remain a nation of immigrants no matter the source and those who wanted a steady supply of cheap labor. For better than two decades idealism and self-interest combatted the advocates of a literacy requirement. Finally in 1917, Congress managed to override a third presidential veto (Presidents Cleveland, Taft, and Wilson had all vetoed the plan) and pass the law that made literacy a requirement for immigration into the United States.

In many respects 1917 was a climactic year in America's immigration history, both because of the passage of the literacy test law and because of the American decision to send an army to Europe. The former gave the anti-immigrant forces a new tool with which to achieve their larger goal, namely an America ruled culturally and politically by white Anglo-Saxon Protestants. American participation in World War I also contributed to that end. Former president Theodore Roosevelt, among others, railed against the "hyphenated-American" whose loyalty was suddenly under scrutiny. Wartime is never a good time for dissenters, ethnic or otherwise. In fact, war can provide a convenient excuse for suppressing those who are different.

Nonetheless, the harassment and jailing of German-Americans and immigrant radicals opposed to American participation in the war did little to deter the stream of postwar refugees into the United States. Henry Cabot Lodge, among others, was convinced that something had to be done. Lawmaking is seldom a rapid process, but the restrictive legislation of the early 1920s was a fairly rapid response to the anticipated postwar flood of immigrants into the United States. In 1921 Congress passed the Emergency Quota Act, which stipulated that the annual immigration of any nationality could not be greater than 3 percent of the number of immigrants from that nation residing in the United States as of 1910. This law did not fully satisfy the aims of the restrictionists, so Congress replaced it in 1924 with the National Origins Act. This law reduced the quota to 2 percent and employed 1890 as the base year thereby further discriminating against the new immigrants who came from places other than northern and western Europe and who tended to arrive in great numbers after 1890.

Finally, in 1927 Congress moved the base year to 1920 but fixed a limit of 150,000 immigrants per year, of which approximately 90,000 places were reserved for immigrants from Great Britain and Germany. All three of these laws excluded Asian immigrants but set no quotas on peoples from the Western Hemisphere. As a result, immigrants from Canada, Mexico, and Puerto Rico rapidly came to comprise the largest group of newcomers to the United States.

Restrictive immigration laws, the Depression, and World War II all worked to dramatically reduce the flow of immigrants into the United States. But the passage of the 1965 Immigration Act quickly ended better than four decades of relatively limited immigration. After an emotional debate, Congress moved to create a worldwide quota system that no longer favored immigrants from northern and western Europe. As a result, between 1970 and 1990, 85 percent of the 11.8 million legal immigrants came to the United States from what are often characterized as Third World countries. Forty-four percent were from Latin America and the Caribbean (with Mexico alone supplying 20 percent of the 11.8 million total), while 36 percent were from Asia.

One result of this new influx of immigrants has been renewed calls for immigration restriction and further reform of immigration laws. Toward those goals, Congress in 1986 passed the Immigration Reform and Control Act. The purpose of this legislation was to discourage illegal immigration by placing sanctions on employers who hired undocumented workers. At the same time, the law granted amnesty to any undocumented foreign worker who had entered the United States prior to 1982. Good intentions aside, the law failed to significantly slow the flow of illegal immigrants, particularly Mexicans in search of better jobs.

And just as the stream of immigration has continued, so has the old debate, a debate over the meaning of immigration for the American present and future. This debate has not produced clear divisions between liberals and conservatives. Geographic, ethnic, and class differences are not readily discernible either. But what is discernible is the rumbling of what might be yet another titanic struggle over what to do when immigrants seek to cross American borders and what it means to be an American once those borders have been crossed. The viewpoints that follow aim to lend some perspective to the rumbling, the struggle, and the debate. After all, the United States, this nation of immigrants, has fought this battle many times before.

John C. Chalberg
Consulting Editor

CHAPTER 1

Is America a Melting Pot?

Chapter Preface

Until the eighteenth century, the land we call the United States was an immense, mostly empty continent populated only by sparse groups of native peoples, themselves once immigrants from Asia. With the coming of Europeans, the land started to fill and become a distinct nation.

In the seventeenth and eighteenth centuries, immigration was encouraged. The new land needed laborers to make the most of its rich resources. The first immigrants were mainly English and Scots-Irish and the African slaves they imported to work on labor-intensive cotton plantations and other agricultural pursuits. The free men and slave owners—mainly Anglo-Saxon and

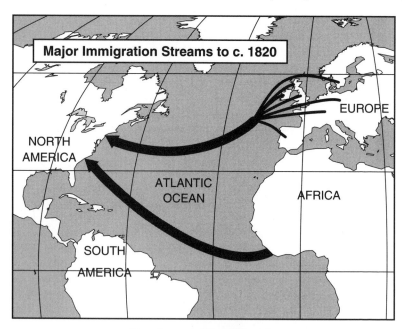

Major Immigration Streams to c. 1820

EUROPE

NORTH AMERICA

ATLANTIC OCEAN

AFRICA

SOUTH AMERICA

Numbers of Immigrants

From Africa c. 400,000   From Europe c. 600,000

Main groups

English c. 350,000   Irish c. 60,000
Germans c. 50,000   Scots c. 50,000

Source: Roger Daniels, *Coming to America*.

Protestant by descent—were the people who shaped the character of the new nation.

By the 1820s, immigrants began coming in significant numbers from countries other than England. Although those who had already settled in America had continued to encourage immigration, they now became alarmed at the large numbers of Germans and Irish who were arriving. As a result, the first cultural conflicts began to arise. The non-English newcomers spoke a different language, in the case of the Germans, and the Irish (and a good many Germans as well) were profoundly steeped in the Catholic religion—the very faith the Protestant settlers' ancestors had rebelled against. Many of those already living in the United States deeply feared the impact of these foreign immigrants. Fueling their fears was the tendency of both Irish and Germans to congregate with their compatriots, living in communities filled with fellow immigrants and participating in German and Irish organizations that appeared to many Americans to be nationalistic, favoring their countries of origin. Many Americans feared that these two groups of interlopers would try to make America into a new Germany or a new papist state.

The immigrants, on the other hand, most in the new land because of the dearth of economic opportunity in their homelands, wanted to take advantage of the benefits America offered, maintain some if not all of their old traditions and their contacts with their old country, and live in peace with their newfound American neighbors.

Both immigrant and established American had to decide how to relate to one another. It seemed impossible to simply live and let live, for in the course of making a living the immigrants and the Americans were forced to interact. Problems of language, religion, and lifestyle constantly reminded each of the differences between them.

When later in the century immigrants began arriving from even more alien lands, the problems of living together multiplied. These same conflicts have occurred continuously throughout American history. For no other country has been created by the members of so many different nations. No other country has continuously been the recipient of new residents from so many other countries.

To illustrate the timelessness of the issue of America and its immigrants, the editors have chosen four viewpoints from widely spaced time periods. They enunciate a perpetual issue in American history: whether the melting pot is truly possible.

*"Here individuals of all nations are melted into a
new race of men."*

America Welcomes and Assimilates People of All Backgrounds

J. Hector St. John de Crèvecoeur (1735-1813)

Born Michel-Guillaume Jean de Crèvecoeur to an upper class family in Normandy, France, the author of *Letters from an American Farmer* took the name J. Hector St. John early in his life as an immigrant to America. He first arrived in Canada, where he briefly fought with the French army against the British. After France's defeat, he moved south and eventually settled in New York, where he became a naturalized American citizen and a prosperous farmer. After nearly two decades, he revisited his homeland and was appointed consul-general to the United States from France. At the time of the French Revolution, he retired from diplomacy and spent his remaining years in study and writing.

Crèvecoeur's best known work, *Letters from an American Farmer*, (London: Thomas Davies), published in 1782, purports to be a collection of letters to his former friends in France, glorifying the wonders of the American countryside and the unique American character. It was published in the United States, England, and Europe. Among the best remembered "letters" today is his essay "What Is an American?" from which this viewpoint is excerpted. In it he claims that the American is a "new man," an amalgam of the many races that have emigrated to the New Land.

Crèvecoeur's ideas about the nature of America and Americans influenced the people of his time and are still read today.

I wish I could be acquainted with the feelings and thoughts which must agitate the heart and present themselves to the mind of an enlightened Englishman, when he first lands on this continent. He must greatly rejoice that he lived at a time to see this fair country discovered and settled; he must necessarily feel a share of national pride, when he views the chain of settlements which embellishes these extended shores. When he says to himself, this is the work of my countrymen, who, when convulsed by factions, afflicted by a variety of miseries and wants, restless and impatient, took refuge here. They brought along with them their national genius, to which they principally owe what liberty they enjoy, and what substance they possess. Here he sees the industry of his native country displayed in a new manner, and traces in their works the embryos of all the arts, sciences, and ingenuity which flourish in Europe. Here he beholds fair cities, substantial villages, extensive fields, an immense country filled with decent houses, good roads, orchards, meadows, and bridges, where an hundred years ago all was wild, woody, and uncultivated! What a train of pleasing ideas this fair spectacle must suggest; it is a prospect which must inspire a good citizen with the most heartfelt pleasure. The difficulty consists in the manner of viewing so extensive a scene. He is arrived on a new continent; a modern society offers itself to his contemplation, different from what he had hitherto seen. It is not composed, as in Europe, of great lords who possess everything, and of a herd of people who have nothing. Here are no aristocratical families, no courts, no kings, no bishops, no ecclesiastical dominion, no invisible power giving to a few a very visible one; no great manufacturers employing thousands, no great refinements of luxury. The rich and the poor are not so far removed from each other as they are in Europe. Some few towns excepted, we are all tillers of the earth, from Nova Scotia to West Florida. We are a people of cultivators, scattered over an immense territory, communicating with each other by means of good roads and navigable rivers, united by the silken bands of mild government, all respecting the laws, without dreading their power, because they are equitable. We are all animated with the spirit of an industry which is unfettered and unrestrained, because each person works for himself. If he travels through our rural districts he views not the hostile castle, and the haughty mansion, contrasted with the clay-built hut and miserable cabin, where cattle and men help to keep each other warm, and dwell in meanness, smoke, and indigence. A pleasing uniformity of decent competence appears throughout our habitations. The meanest of our log-houses is a dry and comfortable habitation. Lawyer or merchant are the fairest titles our towns afford; that of a farmer is the only appellation of the rural inhabitants of our country. It must take some time ere he can reconcile himself to our dictionary, which is but short in words of dignity, and names of honour. There, on a Sunday, he sees a congregation of respectable farmers and their wives, all clad in neat homespun, well mounted, or riding in their own humble waggons. There is not among them an esquire, saving the unlettered magistrate. There he sees a parson as simple as his flock, a farmer who does not riot on the labour of others. We have no princes, for whom we toil, starve, and bleed: we are the most perfect society now existing in the world. Here man is free as he ought to be; nor is this pleasing equality so transitory as many others are. Many ages will not see the shores of our great lakes replenished with inland nations, nor the unknown bounds of North America entirely peopled. Who can tell how far it extends? Who can tell the millions of men whom it will feed and contain? for no European foot has as yet travelled half the extent of this mighty continent!

Asylum for All

The next wish of this traveller will be to know whence came all these people? they are a mixture of English, Scotch, Irish, French, Dutch, Germans, and Swedes. From this promiscuous breed, that race now called Americans have arisen. . . .

In this great American asylum, the poor of Europe have by some means met together, and in consequence of various causes; to what purpose should they ask one another what countrymen they are? Alas, two thirds of them had no country. Can a wretch who wanders about, who works and starves, whose life is a continual scene of sore affliction or pinching penury; can that man call England or any other kingdom his country? A country that had no bread for him, whose fields procured him no harvest, who met with nothing but the frowns of the rich, the severity of the laws, with jails and punishments; who owned not a single foot of the extensive surface of this planet? No! urged by a variety of motives, here they came. Every thing has tended to regenerate them; new laws, a new mode of living, a new social system; here they are become men: in Europe they were as so many useless plants, wanting vegetative mould, and refreshing showers; they withered, and were mowed down by want, hunger, and war; but now by the power of transplantation, like all other plants they have taken root and flourished! Formerly they were not numbered in any civil lists of their country, except in those of the poor; here they rank as citizens. . . .

The New Race

What attachment can a poor European emigrant have for a country where he had nothing? The knowledge of the language, the love of a few kindred as poor as himself, were the only cords that tied him: his country is now that which gives him land, bread, protection, and consequence: *Ubi panis ibi patria*, is the motto of all emigrants. What then is the American, this new man? He is either an European, or the descendant of an European, hence that strange mixture of blood, which you will find in no other country. I could point out to you a family whose grandfather was an Englishman, whose wife was Dutch, whose son married a French woman, and whose present four sons have now four wives of different nations. *He* is an American, who, leaving behind him all his ancient prejudices and manners, receives new ones from the new mode of life he has embraced, the new government he obeys, and the new rank he holds. He becomes an American by being received in the broad lap of our great *Alma Mater*. Here individuals of all nations are melted into a new race of men, whose labours and posterity will one day cause great changes in the world. Americans are the western pilgrims, who are carrying along with them that great mass of arts, sciences, vigour, and industry which began long since in the east; they will finish the great circle. The Americans were once scattered all over

Europe; here they are incorporated into one of the finest systems of population which has ever appeared. . . .

There is no wonder that this country has so many charms, and presents to Europeans so many temptations to remain in it. A traveller in Europe becomes a stranger as soon as he quits his own kingdom; but it is otherwise here. We know, properly speaking, no strangers; this is every person's country; the variety of our soils, situations, climates, governments, and produce, hath something which must please everybody. No sooner does an European arrive, no matter of what condition, than his eyes are opened upon the fair prospect; he hears his language spoken, he retraces many of his own country manners, he perpetually hears the names of families and towns with which he is acquainted; he sees happiness and prosperity in all places disseminated; he meets with hospitality, kindness, and plenty everywhere; he beholds hardly any poor, he seldom hears of punishments and executions; and he wonders at the elegance of our towns, those miracles of industry and freedom. He cannot admire enough our rural districts, our convenient roads, good taverns, and our many accommodations; he involuntarily loves a country where everything is so lovely. . . .

Room for Everybody

There is room for everybody in America; has he any particular talent, or industry? he exerts it in order to procure a livelihood, and it succeeds. Is he a merchant? the avenues of trade are infinite; is he eminent in any respect? he will be employed and respected. Does he love a country life? pleasant farms present themselves; he may purchase what he wants, and thereby become an American farmer. Is he a labourer, sober and industrious? he need not go many miles, nor receive many informations before he will be hired, well fed at the table of his employer, and paid four or five times more than he can get in Europe. Does he want uncultivated lands? thousands of acres present themselves, which he may purchase cheap. Whatever be his talents or inclinations, if they are moderate, he may satisfy them. I do not mean that every one who comes will grow rich in a little time; no, but he may procure an easy, decent maintenance, by his industry. Instead of starving he will be fed, instead of being idle he will have employment; and these are riches enough for such men as come over here. The rich stay in Europe, it is only the middling and the poor that emigrate. Would you wish to travel in independent idleness, from north to south, you will find easy access, and the most cheerful reception at every house; society without ostentation, good cheer without pride, and every decent diversion which the country affords, with little expense. It is no wonder that the Euro-

Americans Are Alike

Novelist John Steinbeck traveled with his dog around the United States at mid-century. His book about his experiences, Travels with Charley *(1962), was a best-seller for many months. During the course of his journey, Steinbeck claimed to discover that despite numerous apparent differences, Americans do have a unique, identifiable character.*

If I were to prepare one immaculately inspected generality it would be this: *For all of our enormous geographic range, for all of our sectionalism, for all of our interwoven breeds drawn from every part of the ethnic world, we are a nation, a new breed.* Americans are much more American than they are Northerners, Southerners, Westerners, or Easterners. And descendants of English, Irish, Italian, Jewish, German, Polish are essentially American. This is not patriotic whoop-de-do; it is carefully observed fact. California Chinese, Boston Irish, Wisconsin Germans, yes, and Alabama Negroes, *have more in common than they have apart.* And this is the more remarkable because it has happened so quickly. It is a fact that Americans from all sections and of all racial extractions are more alike than the Welsh are like the English, the Lancashireman like the Cockney, or for that matter the Lowland Scot like the Highlander. It is astonishing that this has happened in less than two hundred years and most of it in the last fifty. The American identity is an *exact and provable thing.*

pean who has lived here a few years, is desirous to remain; Europe with all its pomp, is not to be compared to this continent, for men of middle stations, or labourers. . . .

But how is this accomplished in that crowd of low, indigent people, who flock here every year from all parts of Europe? I will tell you; they no sooner arrive than they immediately feel the good effects of that plenty of provisions we possess: they fare on our best food, and they are kindly entertained; their talents, character, and peculiar industry are immediately inquired into; they find countrymen everywhere disseminated, let them come from whatever part of Europe. Let me select one as an epitome of the rest; he is hired, he goes to work, and works moderately; instead of being employed by a haughty person, he finds himself with his equal, placed at the substantial table of the farmer, or else at an inferior one as good; his wages are high, his bed is not like that bed of sorrow on which he used to lie: if he behaves with propriety, and is faithful, he is caressed, and becomes as it were a member of the family. He begins to feel the effects of a sort of resurrection; hitherto he had not lived, but simply vegetated; he now feels himself a man, because he is treated as such; the laws of his own country had overlooked him in his insignificancy; the laws of this cover him with their mantle. Judge what an alteration there must arise in the mind and thoughts of this man; he begins to forget his former servitude and dependence, his heart involuntarily swells and glows; this first swell inspires him with those new thoughts which constitute an American. What love can he entertain for a country where his existence was a burthen to him; if he is a generous good man, the love of this new adoptive parent will sink deep into his heart. He looks around, and sees many a prosperous person, who but a few years before was as poor as himself. This encourages him much, he begins to form some little scheme, the first, alas, he ever formed in his life. If he is wise he thus spends two or three years, in which time he acquires knowledge, the use of tools, the modes of working the lands, felling trees, etc. This prepares the foundation of a good name, the most useful acquisition he can make. He is encouraged, he has gained friends; he is advised and directed, he feels bold, he purchases some land; he gives all the money he has brought over, as well as what he has earned, and trusts to the God of harvests for the discharge of the rest. His good name procures him credit. He is now possessed of the deed, conveying to him and his posterity the fee simple and absolute property of two hundred acres of land, situated on such a river. What an epocha in this man's life! He is become a freeholder, from perhaps a German boor—he is now an American, a Pennsylvanian, an English subject. He is naturalised, his name is enrolled with those of the other citizens of the province. Instead of being a vagrant, he has a place of residence; he is called the inhabitant of such a county, or of such a district, and for the first time in his life counts for something; for hitherto he has been a cypher. I only repeat what I have heard many say, and no wonder their hearts should glow, and be agitated with a multitude of feelings, not easy to describe. From nothing to start into being; from a servant to the rank of a master; from being the slave of some despotic prince, to become a free man, invested with lands, to which every municipal blessing is annexed! What a change indeed! It is in consequence of that change that he becomes an American. This great metamorphosis has a double effect, it extinguishes all his European prejudices, he forgets that mechanism of subordination, that servility of disposition which poverty had taught him; and sometimes he is apt to forget too much, often passing from one extreme to the other. If he is a good man, he forms schemes of future prosperity, he proposes to educate his children better than he has been educated himself; he thinks of future modes of conduct, feels an ardour to labour he never felt before. Pride steps in and leads him to everything that the laws do not forbid: he respects them; with a heart-felt gratitude he looks toward the east, toward that insular government from whose wisdom all his new felicity is derived, and under whose wings and protection he now lives. These reflections constitute him the good man and the good subject. Ye poor Europeans, ye, who sweat, and work for the great—ye, who are obliged to give so many sheaves to the church, so many to your lords, so many to your government, and have hardly any left for yourselves—ye, who are held in less estimation than favourite hunters or useless lap-dogs—ye, who only breathe the air of nature, because it cannot be withheld from you; it is here that ye can conceive the possibility of those feelings I have been describing; it is here the laws of naturalisation invite every one to partake of our great labours and felicity, to till unrented, untaxed lands! . . .

"Welcome to my Shores"

After a foreigner from any part of Europe is arrived, and become a citizen; let him devoutly listen to the voice of our great parent, which says to him, "Welcome to my shores, distressed European; bless the hour in which thou didst see my verdant fields, my fair navigable rivers, and my green mountains!—If thou wilt work, I have bread for thee; if thou wilt be honest, sober, and industrious, I have greater rewards to confer on thee—ease and independence. I will give thee fields to feed and clothe thee; a comfortable fireside to sit by, and tell thy children by what means thou hast prospered; and a decent bed to repose on. I shall endow thee beside with the immunities of a freeman. If thou wilt carefully educate thy children, teach them gratitude to God, and reverence to that government, that philanthropic government, which has collected here so many men and made them happy. I will also provide for thy progeny; and to every good man this ought to be the most holy, the most powerful, the most earnest wish he can possibly form, as well as the most consolatory prospect when he dies. Go thou and work and till; thou shalt prosper, provided thou be just, grateful, and industrious."

VIEWPOINT 2

"Try to think of the deep upheaval of the human soul, pulled up by the roots from its ancient, precious soil, cast abroad among you here, withering for a space."

Immigrants Cannot Easily Become Part of the American Culture

Marcus Eli Ravage (1884-1965)

Marcus Eli Ravage was a journalist, foreign correspondent, and author of several books of history and biography. A native of Rumania, he was introduced to the wonders of America when a former resident of his town, prosperous beyond belief, returned from New York for a visit. Ravage and many of his fellow townspeople determined that they too would travel to America to make their fortunes. Thus, in 1900, at age 16, Ravage began his journey.

His arrival in New York was unlike anything he had expected. Instead of a rich, egalitarian country, New York's dirty, noisy streets crowded with impoverished immigrants confronted him. Instead of becoming rich overnight, he found himself peddling chocolates on street corners for pennies and living in a relative's home, a five-room flat that by night became the bedroom of two dozen or more people.

While the people in his Rumanian-Jewish New York ghetto had more money than they had had in Rumania, the conditions under which they lived were degrading, young Ravage felt. People worked long, enervating hours in sweatshops or peddling on the street. Their earnings paid for exorbitant rents and fancy but cheaply made clothing and jewelry. And, Ravage saw, they were not truly Americans, for they were trapped in this East Side Jewish ghetto which they could not escape because of their foreignness. They would never, Ravage thought, be accepted by mainstream society unless they broke out of this secure but stultifying environment.

Like many immigrants, Ravage began a program of self-education, attending lectures of all sorts and becoming a member of a young socialists group. But finally he decided the only thing that would change his life was to learn English well and to gain a formal education.

After much study and hard work, he traveled to Missouri where, at the state university, his American transformation truly began. There Ravage found himself an outsider in a culture completely unlike the ethnic enclave he had come from. Instead of the ghetto's constant voluble and passionate arguments on every conceivable topic, he found in Missouri a soft-spoken, polite people who liked jokes and sports but found argument impolite and even threatening. Despite what had been considered his excellent English skills in New York, in Missouri he found himself continually misunderstood and looked upon as strange. With painstaking effort, he studied the language of his fellows, tried to learn football, and tried to become more like the Missouri students. But he was an outsider, shunned as different and strange.

By the end of his first year at Missouri, he felt as though he was beginning to understand the American character, but he still longed for the familiarity and comfort of New York's East Side. He traveled home for the summer, only to discover that he had changed too much. He no longer had anything in common with his relatives and friends. Now he had truly become an outsider—neither a "real" American nor any longer a member of the immigrant community.

Ravage's experiences are similar to those of many who emigrate to this country. His engaging autobiographical account of his first years in America, *An American in the Making* (New York: Harper and Brothers, 1917), is excerpted here. Despite its upbeat ending, Ravage may never have felt truly at home in America. He spent many years in Europe as a foreign correspondent for American periodicals, and he published several books in German and French.

―――――――

When I hear all around me the foolish prattle about the new immigration—"the scum of Europe," as it is called—that is invading and making itself master of this country, I cannot help saying to myself that Americans have forgotten America. The native, I must conclude, has, by long familiarity with the rich blessings of his own land, grown forgetful of his high privileges and ceased to grasp the lofty message which America wafts across the seas to all the oppressed of mankind. What, I wonder, do they know of America, who know only America? . . .

How Americans View Immigrants

The average American, when he thinks of immigrants at all, thinks, I am afraid, of something rather comical. He thinks of bundles—funny, picturesque bundles of every shape and size and color. The alien himself, in his incredible garb, as he walks off the gang-plank, appears like some sort of an odd, moving bundle. And always he carries more bundles. Later on, in his peculiar, transplanted life, he sells nondescript merchandise in fantastic vehicles, does violence to the American's language, and sits down on the curb to eat fragrant cheese and unimaginable sausages. He is, for certain, a character fit for a farce.

So, I think, you see him, you fortunate ones who have never had to come to America. I am afraid that the pathos and the romance of the story are quite lost on you. Yet both are there as surely as the comedy. No doubt, when you go slumming, you reflect sympathetically on the drudgery and the misery of the immigrant's life. But poverty and hard toil are not tragic things. They indeed are part of the comedy. Tragedy lies seldom on the surface. If you would get a glimpse of the pathos and the romance of readjustment you must try to put yourself in the alien's place. And that you may find hard to do. Well, try to think of leave-taking—of farewells to home and kindred, in all likelihood never to be seen again; of last looks lingering affectionately on things and places; of ties broken and grown stronger in the breaking. Try to think of the deep upheaval of the human soul, pulled up by the roots from its ancient, precious soil, cast abroad among you here, withering for a space, then slowly finding nourishment in the new soil, and once more thriving—not, indeed, as before—a novel, composite growth. If you can see this you may form some idea of the sadness and the glory of his adventure.

Oh, if I could show you America as we of the oppressed peoples see it! If I could bring home to you even the smallest fraction of this sacrifice and this upheaval, the dreaming and the strife, the agony and the heartache, the endless disappointments, the yearning and the despair—all of which must be ours before we can make a home for our battered spirits in this land of yours. Perhaps, if we be young, we dream of riches and adventure, and if we be grown men we may merely seek a haven for our outraged human souls and a safe retreat for our hungry wives and children. Yet, however aggrieved we may feel toward our native home, we cannot but regard our leaving it as a violent severing of the ties of our life, and look beyond toward our new home as a sort of glorified exile. So, whether we be young or old, something of ourselves we always leave behind in our hapless, cherished birthplaces. And the heaviest share of our burden inevitably falls on the loved ones that remain when we are gone. We make no illusions for ourselves. Though we may expect wealth, we have no thought of returning. It is farewell forever. We are not setting out on a trip; we are emigrating. Yes, we are emigrating, and there is our experience, our ordeal, in a nutshell. It is the one-way passport for us every time. . . .

Going to College

I got to Columbia, Missouri, in the evening. . . . I had written to the president of the university to tell him by what train I would arrive, and I was a little taken aback to find that he had not even sent any one to meet me. There were a lot of students at the station, but they paid no attention to me. They were making a great deal of noise and shaking hands in a boisterous sort of way with one or two decidedly rural-looking boys who had come in on the train with me. I began to feel very lonely. Yes, began was the word. It was to be continued. . . .

During . . . that first week in Missouri I found out what it was to be a stranger in a foreign land; and as the year wore on I found out more and more. Columbia seemed a thousand times farther removed from New York than New York had been from Vaslui [Ravage's home town]. Back there in the Ghetto everybody had thought me quite Americanized. Now I could not help seeing that Missouri was more genuinely American than the New York I had known; and against this native background I appeared greener than when I had landed. This new world I had suddenly dropped into was utterly without my experience and beyond my understanding, so that I could not even make up my mind whether I liked or hated it. I had to admire the heartiness, the genuineness, and the clean-cut manliness of it. But, on the other hand, it prided itself on a peculiar common sense, a cool-headedness, a practical indifference to things of the spirit, which the "intelligent" of the East Side in me revolted against.

Nevertheless, I tried very hard to make myself agreeable to my fellow-students. But I failed miserably. In the first two months I had, and lost, a half-dozen room-mates. Do what I might, I could not make them stay with me. There were never any hard words; we always parted as "good friends." But almost from the first day they would hardly talk to me, and before the week was out they would find some excuse for moving or asking me to move. I spent many sleepless nights trying to figure out the thing. It wounded my self-esteem to find my society so offensive to everybody. Besides, it touched my poor purse. Every time I was left alone in a room I had to pay the full rent. But my predicament had its comic side, too. It got so that when I found a new roommate I would take a perverse sort of pleasure in watching to see how soon he would begin to look the other way when I spoke to him. I never had to wait very long.

These broad intimations, so often repeated, should, I suppose, have convinced me that I lacked the stuff of which Missourians were made, and should have served to drive me back into my shell. Whatever their reasons and motives might be, it was quite clear that these fellows had no love for my presence; and common sense as well as a natural regard for my own sensibilities ought to have told me that the simplest way out of my scrape was to leave them alone. Besides, I may as well confess that this subtle distaste—this deep-lying repulsion of contrary temperaments—was by no means one-sided. Perhaps I liked my elusive roommates a little better than they liked me. But I possessed enough of self-esteem to tell myself that this was but a proof of my own superiority. If Missouri did not take to me, I argued, so much the worse for Missouri's powers of penetration and appreciation. It betrayed, at least, an extremely provincial state of mind. No doubt I had my share of damning imperfections, but even a college freshman, if he had eyes, could see that I was not altogether wanting in the virtues that make for grace. And if they should care to ask me, I could give these gentlemen a bill of particulars relative to their own shortcomings that would take as much of their conceit out of them as they avowedly persisted in trying to knock out of me.

All the same I did not leave them alone. I did the very opposite. How, in the first place, *was* I to avoid them? I was a lonely, deserted rock surrounded and buffeted by a vast ocean. Wherever I turned I must face them. If I wanted a job, I must work for and with them. The class-rooms, the library, the boarding-houses, the very streets swarmed and echoed with them. I had no choice but to walk with them, talk with them, and trade with them. Nay, my case was far worse than poor Shylock's: I must even eat with them and—at brief intervals—sleep with them. Think of it, an entire university, yes, a whole State, stretching over a hundred thousand square miles, filled with nothing but Missourians! Of course, there was one avenue of escape—I might go back to the Ghetto in New York; but I was not fool enough for that. Alive as I was from the very start to his deficiencies and his foibles, I could see that the Missourian had something to teach me that I needed very badly to learn. . . .

And so I flung myself into the battle with an intense fury. I deliberately went out of my way to get stepped on. I attended chapel religiously, in spite of the fact that the speeches bored me and the prayers jarred on me. I was punctual at meal-time so as not to miss my usual portion of sidelong glances and grins and open ho-hos. Timid as I was, I let no opportunity slip to get into an argument at the cost of getting myself thoroughly disliked. I even went so far as to join the cadet corps, and was bawled at by the commandant . . . and was laughed at by the members of my platoon for my unsoldierly bearing, and was eternally posted for soiled gloves or unpolished shoes or errors in executing commands, and was made to write excuses (when I would rather have read Heine or Huxley) for these delinquencies and to rewrite them over and over again until they conformed precisely to military etiquette, and was haled before the adjutant and bawled at some more when I revolted at the stupidity of it all, and was punished with extra drilling in the awkward squad—every bit of which was just what I deserved for betraying my radical faith by getting into the silly business at all. More than half the time—if you will pardon the unmasculine confession—I was in the depths of the blues, and during at least half of that I was contemplating suicide, which, however, I took no steps to commit, beyond the penning of an exceedingly vivid portrayal of the act, which was perpetrated with a vial of deadly substances filched from the chemistry laboratory, and the subsequent regrets of my fellow-students as they reviewed the history of their uncharitable dealings with me.

The worst of it was that all my heroic suffering seemed to be

---

The Immigrant's Challenge

Like Marcus Eli Ravage, Pascal D'Angelo, an Italian who emigrated to the United States in 1910, found life in America very difficult. D'Angelo also believed that if he could only find the key, he would achieve success as an American. This brief excerpt is from D'Angelo's autobiography, Son of Italy, *published in 1924.*

Something had grown in me during my stay in America. Something was keeping me in this wonderful perilous land where I had suffered so much and where I had so much more to suffer. Should I quit this great America without a chance to really know it? Again I shook my head. There was a lingering suspicion that somewhere in this vast country an opening existed, that somewhere I would strike the light. I could not remain in the darkness perpetually.

going for naught, at least for a long time. For the principal problem that I had set out to solve remained as obstinate as ever. Why would not those boys room with me? To this puzzling question none of my disagreeable adventures would furnish an answer. Of course, it was quite clear they found me a queer, unlikable animal. But I had known that all along. *Why* did they not like me? None of my guesses satisfied me. At the boarding-house where I stayed while waiting for money from New York I heard a great many stories in an impossible dialect about Jews, and judging from the satisfaction with which they were received I thought at first that I was a victim of ancient prejudice. But I could not long hold on to that theory. There was not a trace of venom in the yarns. Why, these chaps had not the remotest idea what a Jew was like! Their picture of him was the stage caricature of a rather mild individual with mobile hands who sold clothing and spoke broken English. No one in Missouri knew that I had had Jewish parents until three years later, when, on the occasion of my graduation, the newspapers of St. Louis and Kansas City thought my career of sufficient interest to have me interviewed and I made some passing allusion to my origin. No more tenable was my surmise about class antagonism. Indeed, I was not long in Missouri before I was struck with the absence of every real class feeling, and I said to myself, exultingly, that however America might have broken faith with me in other ways, her promise of democratic equality she had scrupulously fulfilled. . . . If, then, my isolation rested neither on race prejudice nor on class exclusiveness, what did it rest on? My poor, bewildered brain was unable to answer. . . .

A Foreign Tongue

Then it dawned upon me that one reason why I could not get on with these fellows was that I did not speak their language. Why, I had thought that I was a wonder at English. Hadn't I got the highest mark in freshman composition? Hadn't Doctor Wilbur, of the English division, encouraged me to drop medicine on the ground that I was cut out for a professorship in that subject? Yes; but while I pronounced like a native and otherwise spoke and wrote with considerable freedom, my English was still the very grammatical and very clumsy book-English of the foreigner. I was weak in the colloquial idiom, and always had to resort to roundabout locutions to express the simplest idea. I had mastered the science of English speech; I had yet to acquire the art of it. My vocabulary ran to the Latin elements of the hybrid tongue, while what I needed worst were the common, every-day words. Of course, the professors understood me, and having somehow got hold of the outlines of my history, they even commended me. But the rank and file of the student body pricked up their ears when I talked and simply stared. Every time I tried to tell a story it fell flat because of some subtle shade of meaning that escaped me. My stock of words and phrases was not varied enough. I might know one word like "earth," whereas the Missourian had his choice of "ground" and "soil" and "sod" and half a dozen others which he could draw on with a sure hand.

These little difficulties in making myself perfectly understood had an evil tendency toward making me self-conscious and aggravating my timidity. I fell into the habit of studying out my sentences before intrusting them to the ears of my critical friends, with the consequence that they turned out more stilted than ever. As soon as I opened my mouth I would realize, of course, what a bad job I had made of them, and then my confidence would fail me, my throat would get parched and lumpy, and my interlocutor would cry, "What is it?" in such a way as to knock the bottom out of me altogether. After a number of experiences of this harrowing kind I determined that my voice was in need of cultivation and I joined the class in elocution, where the instructor did most of the reading himself—he had once been an actor—and lectured interminably on deep breathing, and declared with much emphasis that a good delivery was essential to vivacious conversation, which was what I knew myself, and that it was largely a matter of intelligence, which was not true. So that I dropped elocution and borrowed a volume of Mark Twain from the library and read pages and pages of it aloud to myself, as every one at M.S.U. who happened to be walking in the neighborhood of Hinkson Creek before breakfast can testify. What is more, I bought a penny scrap-book and jotted down every word I overheard in my table-mates' conversation that was new to my foreign ear, and subsequently consulted the dictionaries to find out what it meant.

Unfortunately for me, the men of Missouri had command of a whole vast and varied vocabulary of which not a trace could be found in any dictionary, no matter how diligently I searched. It did not take me long to lay hold of their peculiar trick of cutting words off at the end, and after a month or so I could myself refer to professors as "profs," to a course in literature as "lit," and to the quadrangle as the "quad." I found that highly practical, like everything else in Missouri, and convenient. But when a chap asked me to pass him "that stuff," and pointed one day to the potatoes and another day to a pile of typewritten notes I was mystified. I could not easily perceive what quality it was the two commodities had in common that made the same name applicable to both. Moreover, I observed that my friends expressed every variety of emotion—disappointment, enthusiasm, anger, elation—by the one word (or was it two?) "doggone." Food in general was called "grub," although gravies and sauces were sometimes distinguished as "goo"; while, on the other hand, money had a whole chain of names to itself; "rocks" and "mazuma" and "wheels" and, of course, "stuff." It was all very bewildering.

Difficulties of Americanization

Henry P. Fairchild wrote The Melting-Pot Mistake *in 1926. In it, he argues that despite the common belief that America is a melting pot, immigrants do not easily become "Americans." He stated, "The typical immigrant of the present does not really live in America at all, but, from the point of view of nationality, in Italy, Poland. . . . or some other foreign country."*

The process of Americanization, then, for the immigrant is infinitely . . . difficult . . . because [he], during the years before his arrival in the United States, has already acquired more or less completely a foreign nationality. This nationality is dissimilar in most respects, and absolutely contradictory and inconsistent in many respects, to the American nationality. Yet to the foreigner it is his natural and authoritative spiritual tradition and social environment. He may hold a critical attitude toward certain aspects of it, just as most Americans are dissatisfied with some phases of the American nationality, but taken as a whole it represents to him truth, beauty, goodness, morality, justice, propriety, efficiency, custom, order, and—home. Let the critical and self-satisfied American of native birth reflect that in the process of Americanization this whole spiritual endowment must be abandoned, and another taken in its place, and it may help him dimly to perceive how tragic, how soul-wracking must be the experience of assimilation, though probably no one who has not actually gone through it can appreciate the stress and tragedy involved.

Perhaps the greatest stumbling-block in the way of my readjustment was the emphasis that my Missourian placed on what he called good manners. . . . Once or twice I succeeded in drawing an unwary freshman into an argument about religion or economics, and then I wished I had not. His good manners rendered him quite sterile as a debater. I could on no account get him to make a straightforward, flat-footed statement; and he exasperated me by a way he had of emasculating my own emphatic assertions with his eternal colorless conformity. He invariably introduced a remark with an "It seems to me," or an "It looks as if," or a "Don't you think?" And if I, with my ill-breeding, shot back at him, as I usually did, "No, I *don't* think so at all; I disagree with you entirely," he looked grieved and surprised and visibly chilled, and crawfished out of the embarrassing situation by admitting that there were two sides to every question, and that no doubt I was right, too. And the next time he spied me on the street he suddenly developed a preference for the opposite side. . . .

Going Home

As the summer drew near . . . I was longing for a sight of New York. It would cost fifty dollars to go there and back, but I tried to persuade myself that I would earn enough more in the city to make it worth while. . . .

So to New York I went, and lived through the last and the bitterest episode in the romance of readjustment. During that whole strenuous year, while I was fighting my battle for America, I had never for a moment stopped to figure the price it was costing me. I had not dreamed that my mere going to Missouri had opened up a gulf between me and the world I had come from, and that every step I was taking toward my ultimate goal was a stride away from everything that had once been mine, that had once been myself. Now, no sooner had I alighted from the train than it came upon me with a pang that that one year out there had loosened ties that I had imagined were eternal.

There was [my brother] Paul faithfully at the ferry, and as I came off he rushed up to me and threw his arms around me and kissed me affectionately. Did I kiss him back? I am afraid not. He took the grip out of my hand and carried it to the Brooklyn Bridge. Then we boarded a car. I asked him where we were going, and he said, mysteriously, "To Harry's." A surprise was awaiting me, apparently. As we entered the little alley of a store in the Italian quarter I looked about me and saw no one. But suddenly there was a burst of laughter from a dozen voices, a door or two opened violently, and my whole family was upon me—brothers, a new sister-in-law, cousins of various degrees, some old people, a few children. They rushed me into the apartment behind the store, pelting me with endearments and with questions. The table was set as for a Purim feast. There was an odor of pot-roasted chicken, and my eye caught a glimpse of chopped eggplant. As the meal progressed my heart was touched by their loving thoughtfulness. Nothing had been omitted—not even the red wine and the Turkish peas and rice. Harry and every one else kept on urging me to eat. "It's a long time since you have had a real meal," said my sister-in-law. How true it was! But I felt constrained, and ate very little. Here were the people and the things I had so longed to be with; but I caught myself regarding them with the eyes of a Western American. Suddenly—at one glance, as it were—I grasped the answer to the problem that had puzzled me so long; for here in the persons of those dear to me I was seeing myself as those others had seen me.

I went about revisiting old scenes and found that everything had changed in my brief absence. My friends were not the same; the East Side was not the same. They never would be the same. What had come over them? My kinsfolk and my old companions looked me over and declared that it was I who had become transformed. I had become soberer. I carried myself differently. There was an unfamiliar reserve, something mingled of coldness and melancholy, in my eye. My very speech had a new intonation. It was more incisive, but less fluent, less cordial, they thought. Perhaps so. At any rate, while my people were still dear to me, and always would be dear to me, the atmosphere about them repelled me. If it *was* I who had changed, then, as I took in the little world I had emerged from, I could not help telling myself that the change was a salutary one.

While calling at the old basement bookshop on East Broadway I suddenly heard a horrible wailing and lamenting on the street. A funeral procession was hurrying by, followed by several women in an open carriage. Their hair was flying, their faces were red with weeping, their bodies were swaying grotesquely to the rhythm of their violent cries. The oldest in the group continued mechanically to address the body in the hearse: "Husband dear, upon whom have you left us? Upon whom, husband dear?" A young girl facing her in the vehicle looked about in a terrified manner, seized every now and then the hand of her afflicted mother, and tried to quiet her. The frightful scene, with its tragic display, its abysmal ludicrousness, its barbarous noise, revolted me. I had seen the like of it before, but that was in another life. I had once been part of such a performance myself, and the grief of it still lingered somewhere in my motley soul. But now I could only think of the affecting simplicity, the quiet, unobtrusive solemnity of a burial I had witnessed the previous spring in the West. . . .

No Longer Home

There was no sense in deceiving myself, the East Side had somehow ceased to be my world. I had thought a few days ago that I was going home. I had yelled to [my college room-mate] Harvey from the train as it was pulling out of the station at Columbia, "I am going home, old man!" But I had merely come to another strange land. In the fall I would return to that other exile. I was, indeed, a man without a country. . . .

As long as I remained in New York I kept up the tragic farce of making Sunday calls on brother Harry and pretending that all was as before, that America and education had changed nothing, that I was still one of them. I had taken a room in a remote quarter of

Brooklyn, where there were few immigrants, under the pretense that it was nearer to the railway barns. But I was deceiving no one but myself. Most of my relatives, who had received me so heartily when I arrived, seemed to be avoiding Harry's house on Sundays, and on those rare occasions when I ran into one of them he seemed frigid and ill-at-ease. Once Paul said to me: "You are very funny. It looks as if you were ashamed of the family. You aren't really, are you? You know they said you would be when you went away. There is a lot of foolish talk about it. Everybody speaks of Harry and me as the doctor's brothers. Can't you warm up?"

I poured out my heart in a letter to Harvey. If a year ago I had been told that I would be laying my sorrows and my disappointments in my own kindred before any one out there, I would have laughed at the idea. But that barbarian in Missouri was the only human being, strangely enough, in whom I could now confide with any hope of being understood. I tried to convey to him some idea of the agonizing moral experience I was going through. I told him that I was aching to get back to Columbia (how apt the name was!) to take up again where I had left off the process of my transformation, and to get through with it as soon as might be.

And in the fall I went back—this time a week *before* college opened—and was met by Harvey at the station, just as those rural-looking boys had been met by their friends the year before. When I reached the campus I was surprised to see how many people knew me. Scores of them came up and slapped me on the back and shook hands in their hearty, boisterous fashion, and hoped that I had had a jolly summer. I was asked to join boarding-clubs, to become a member in debating societies, to come and see this fellow or that in his room. It took me off my feet, this sudden geniality of my fellows toward me. I had not been aware how, throughout the previous year, the barriers between us had been gradually and steadily breaking down. It came upon me all at once. I felt my heart going out to my new friends. I had become one of them. I was not a man without a country. I was an American.

VIEWPOINT 3

*"America is God's Crucible, the great
Melting-Pot where all the races of Europe
are melting and re-forming!"*

America Is a
Great Melting Pot

Israel Zangwill (1864-1926)

Israel Zangwill was born in London's East End Jewish ghetto
and lived there for much of his life. His entertaining short stories
first brought him recognition as a humorist. His fame increased
with the publication of a novel about ghetto life and the production of several of his plays. Although he achieved enough promi-
nence to allow him to escape the ghetto, he remained concerned
by the plight of many immigrants, especially those from Eastern
Europe, who were trapped there and who were caught up in the
constant conflict between the culture they had left behind and the
new one they now lived in. One of Zangwill's visions of hope was
that America would become a place where Christians and Jews of
all backgrounds could live together in peaceful brotherhood.

His play *The Melting-Pot* was produced in New York in 1908. The
excerpt published here is taken from an edition published in New
York by The Macmillan Company in 1913. It is an homage to the
idea that people of many backgrounds can come to America and
merge into one of the most opportunity-filled societies of all time.

The Melting-Pot tells the story of David Quixano, a young Jewish musician who has emigrated to New York from Russia, and
his romance with Vera Revendal, also an immigrant, the daughter
of a Russian aristocrat who was responsible for the bloody
pogrom that murdered David's family. After many crises, David
and Vera's love overcomes their own prejudices and the prejudices of their families, showing that, indeed, America is a place

where all races—or at least Christian and Jew—can blend together to create a new, happy race.

Today, Zangwill's play is remembered primarily for the phrase it coined for America: *the melting pot.*

[Vera *has come to the apartment of* David *and his uncle,* Mendel, *also a musician, to ask* David *to perform for the settlement house in which she works.*]

DAVID

Oh, I love going to Ellis Island to watch the ships coming in from Europe, and to think that all those weary, sea-tossed wanderers are feeling what *I* felt when America first stretched out her great mother-hand to *me!*

VERA
[*Softly.*]

Were you very happy?

DAVID

It was heaven. You must remember that all my life I had heard of America—everybody in our town had friends there or was going there or got money orders from there. The earliest game I played at was selling off my toy furniture and setting up in America. All my life America was waiting, beckoning, shining—the place where God would wipe away tears from off all faces.

[*He ends in a half-sob.*]
MENDEL
[*Rises, as in terror.*]

Now, now, David, don't get excited.

[*He approaches him.*]
DAVID

To think that the same great torch of liberty which threw its light across all the broad seas and lands into my little garret in Russia, is shining also for all those other weeping millions of Europe, shining wherever men hunger and are oppressed—

MENDEL
[*Soothingly.*]

Yes, yes, David.

[*Laying hand on his shoulder.*]
Now sit down and—

DAVID
[*Unheeding.*]

Shining over the starving villages of Italy and Ireland, over the swarming stony cities of Poland and Galicia, over the ruined

farms of Roumania, over the shambles of Russia—
MENDEL

[*Pleadingly.*]

David!
DAVID

Oh, Miss Revendal, when I look at our Statue of Liberty, I just seem to hear the voice of America crying: "Come unto me all ye that labour and are heavy laden and I will give you rest—rest—"

[*He is now almost sobbing.*]
MENDEL

Don't talk any more—you know it is bad for you.
DAVID

But Miss Revendal asked—and I want to explain to her what America means to me.
MENDEL

You can explain it in your American symphony.
VERA

[*Eagerly. To David.*]

You compose?
DAVID

[*Embarrassed.*]

Oh, uncle, why did you talk of—? uncle always—my music is so thin and tinkling. When I am *writing* my American symphony, it seems like thunder crashing through a forest full of bird songs. But next day—oh, next day!

[*He laughs dolefully and turns away.*]
VERA

So your music finds inspiration in America?
DAVID

Yes—in the seething of the Crucible.
VERA

The Crucible? I don't understand!
DAVID

Not understand! You, the Spirit of the Settlement!

[*He rises and crosses to her and leans over the table, facing her.*]

Not understand that America is God's Crucible, the great Melting-Pot where all the races of Europe are melting and re-forming! Here you stand, good folk, think I, when I see them at Ellis Island, here you stand

[*Graphically illustrating it on the table.*]

in your fifty groups, with your fifty languages and histories, and your fifty blood hatreds and rivalries. But you won't be long like that, brothers, for these are the fires of God you've come to—these are the fires of God. A fig for your feuds and vendettas! Germans and Frenchmen, Irishmen and Englishmen, Jews and Russians—into the Crucible with you all! God is making the American.

A few of the sixteen million immigrants who passed through Ellis Island between 1892 and 1924. Most wanted to become part of the melting pot.

MENDEL

I should have thought the American was made already—eighty millions of him.

DAVID

Eighty millions!

[*He smiles toward* Vera *in good-humoured derision.*]

Eighty millions! Over a continent! Why, that cockleshell of a Britain has forty millions! No, uncle, the real American has not yet arrived. He is only in the Crucible, I tell you—he will be the fusion of all races, the coming superman. . . .

[*The end of the play:* David *and* Vera *stand on the roof of the settlement house after the successful performance of* David's *symphony.*]

VERA

Look! How beautiful the sunset is after the storm!

[David *turns. The sunset, which has begun to grow beautiful just after* Vera's *entrance, has now reached its most magnificent moment; below there are narrow lines of saffron and pale gold, but above the whole sky is one glory of burning flame.*]

DAVID

[*Prophetically exalted by the spectacle.*]

It is the fires of God round His Crucible.

[*He drops her hand and points downward.*]

There she lies, the great Melting-Pot—listen! Can't you hear the roaring and the bubbling? There gapes her mouth

[*He points east.*]

—the harbour where a thousand mammoth feeders come from the ends of the world to pour in their human freight. Ah, what a stirring and a seething! Celt and Latin, Slav and Teuton, Greek and Syrian,—black and yellow—

VERA

[*Softy, nestling to him.*]

Jew and Gentile—

DAVID

Yes, East and West, and North and South, the palm and the pine, the pole and the equator, the crescent and the cross—how the great Alchemist melts and fuses them with his purging flame! Here shall they all unite to build the Republic of Man and the Kingdom of God. Ah, Vera, what is the glory of Rome and Jerusalem where all nations and races come to worship and look back, compared with the glory of America, where all races and nations come to labour and look forward!

[*He raises his hands in benediction over the shining city.*]

Peace, peace, to all ye unborn millions, fated to fill this giant continent—the God of our *children* give you Peace.

[*An instant's solemn pause. The sunset is swiftly fading, and the vast panorama is suffused with a more restful twilight, to which the many-gleaming lights of the town add the tender poetry of the night. Far back, like a lonely, guiding star, twinkles over the darkening water the torch of the Statue of Liberty. From below comes up the softened sound of voices and instruments joining in "My Country, 'tis of Thee." The curtain falls slowly.*]

VIEWPOINT 4

"We did not feel this country belonged to us. We felt fierce pride in it, more loyalty than anyone could know. But we felt blocked at every turn."

Ethnic Groups Never Truly "Melt" into American Culture

Michael Novak (1933-)

The 1990 U.S. census showed that the foreign-born population of the United States rose dramatically during the previous decade. In 1980, approximately 6.2 percent of the population was foreign-born; in 1990, the number was 7.9 percent. Even during America's gigantic immigration waves of the late nineteenth and early twentieth centuries, the number stayed at a fairly stable 7.3 percent. In addition to the foreign-born, U.S. society is increasingly made up of unassimilated ethnic groups of all types, including second, third, and fourth generations that have never become fully Americanized. The tendency is to think that all of these people are easily identifiable people of color—Haitians, Hispanics, and Asians, for example. But in truth sizable numbers of "white ethnics" also remain unassimilated. What is the consequence to American society of such large numbers of people who are different from the mainstream?

In the 1970s, a time of great social and political turmoil inspired by the Vietnam War, the Civil Rights Movement of the 1960s, and the Women's Movement, people of many different national backgrounds began to recognize and assert their ethnic identities. They objected to ethnic stereotypes and promoted the benefits of their individual cultures. They took the view that rather than a "melting pot," America was more like a "tossed salad," in which each ingredient is distinct and adds its own flavor to the whole.

It was during this time that Michael Novak, a prolific journalist and author, took the time to explore his own Slovakian immigrant heritage. His reflections led him to conclude that American society, by history and tradition, is a WASP (White Anglo-Saxon Protestant) society. Novak believes that the people in power—WASPs—expect all who are not WASPs to give up their differences or to submit to the will and ways of the dominant WASP culture. Until recent times, Novak said, ethnic groups were more than willing to try to follow this tradition. It was only people of color—those who looked very unlike WASPs—who could not assimilate and who thus could not fully reap the benefits of membership in American society.

In 1971, Novak's book *The Rise of the Unmeltable Ethnics*, excerpted here, explored the difficulties encountered by white ethnics in American society and the benefits for society of their not assimilating.

———————

Growing up in America has been an assault upon my sense of worthiness. It has also been a kind of liberation and delight. . . .

I am born of PIGS—those Poles, Italians, Greeks, and Slavs, those non-English-speaking immigrants numbered so heavily among the workingmen of this nation. Not particularly liberal or radical; born into a history not white Anglo-Saxon and not Jewish; born outside what, in America, is considered the intellectual mainstream—and thus privy to neither power nor status nor intellectual voice.

Those Poles of Buffalo and Milwaukee—so notoriously taciturn, sullen, nearly speechless. Who has ever understood them? It is not that Poles do not feel emotion—what is their history if not dark passion, romanticism, betrayal, courage, blood? But where in America is there anywhere a language for voicing what a Christian Pole in this nation feels? He has no Polish culture left him, no Polish tongue. Yet Polish feelings do not go easily into the idiom of happy America, the America of the Anglo-Saxons and yes, in the arts, the Jews. (The Jews have long been a culture of the word, accustomed to exile, skilled in scholarship and in reflection. The Christian Poles are largely of peasant origin, free men for hardly more than a hundred years.) Of what shall the young man of Lackawanna think on his way to work in the mills, departing his relatively dreary home and street? What roots does he have? What language of the heart is available to him?

The PIGS are not silent willingly. The silence burns like hidden coals in the chest.

All four of my grandparents, unknown to one another, arrived in America from the same county in Slovakia. My grandfather had a small farm in Pennsylvania; his wife died in a wagon accident. Meanwhile, Johanna, fifteen, arrived on Ellis Island, dizzy from witnessing births and deaths and illnesses aboard the crowded ship. She had a sign around her neck lettered PASSAIC. There an aunt told her of a man who had lost his wife in Pennsylvania. She went. They were married. She inherited his three children.

Each year for five years Grandma had a child of her own. She was among the lucky; only one died. When she was twenty-two and the mother of seven (my father was the last), her husband died. "Grandma Novak," as I came to know her many years later, resumed the work she had begun in Slovakia at the town home of a man known to my father only as "the Professor"; she house-cleaned and she laundered.

I heard this story only weeks ago. Strange that I had not asked insistently before. Odd that I should have such shallow knowledge of my roots. Amazing to me that I do not know what my family suffered, endured, learned, and hoped these last six or seven generations. It is as if there were no project in which we all have been involved, as if history in some way began with my father and with me.

Uneasy Estrangement

The estrangement I have come to feel derives not only from lack of family history. Early in life, I was made to feel a slight uneasiness when I said my name.

Later "Kim" helped. So did Robert. And "Mister Novak" on TV. The name must be one of the most Anglo-Saxon of the Slavic names. Nevertheless, when I was very young, the "American" kids still made something out of names unlike their own, and their earnest, ambitious mothers thought long thoughts when I introduced myself.

Under challenge in grammar school concerning my nationality, I had been instructed by my father to announce proudly: "American." When my family moved from the Slovak ghetto of Johnstown to the WASP suburb on the hill, my mother impressed upon us how well we must be dressed, and show good manners, and behave—people think of us as "different" and we mustn't give them any cause. "Whatever you do, marry a Slovak girl," was other advice to a similar end: "They cook. They clean. They take good care of you. For your own good." I was taught to be proud of being Slovak, but to recognize that others wouldn't know what it meant, or care.

When I had at last pierced the deception—that most movie stars and many other professionals had abandoned their European names in order to feed American fantasies—I felt only a little sadness. . . .

A Sizzling Cauldron

Barbara Mikulski, a Polish-American, wrote an article called "The Myth of the Melting Pot" in 1970. Like Michael Novak, she believes that white ethnics are as much victims of prejudice in America's WASP society as are people of color.

America is not a melting pot. It is a sizzling cauldron for the ethnic American who feels that he has been politically extorted by both government and private enterprise. The ethnic American is sick of being stereotyped as a fascist and dullard by phoney white liberals, pseudo black militants and patronizing bureaucrats. He pays the bill for every major government program and gets nothing or little in the way of return. Tricked by the political rhetoric of the illusionary funding for black-oriented social programs, he turns his anger to race—when he himself is the victim of class prejudice. He has worked hard all of his life to become a "good American." He and his sons have fought on every battlefield—then he is made fun of because he likes the flag. . . .

The ethnic American also feels unappreciated for the contribution he makes to society. He resents the way the working-class is looked down upon. In many instances he is treated like the machine he operates or the pencil he pushes. He is tired of being treated like an object of production. The public and private institutions have made him frustrated by their lack of response to his needs. At present he feels powerless in his daily dealings with and efforts to change them.

Unfortunately, because of old prejudices and new fears, anger is generated against other minority groups rather than those who have power. What is needed is an alliance of white and black; white collar, blue collar, and no collar based on mutual need, interdependence and respect . . . an alliance to develop the strategy for a new kind of community organization and political participation.

Nowhere in my schooling do I recall any attempt to put me in touch with my own history. The strategy was clearly to make an American of me. English literature, American literature, and even the history books, as I recall them, were peopled mainly by Anglo-Saxons from Boston (where most historians seemed to live). . . .

The fact that I was born a Catholic also complicated life. What is a Catholic but what everybody else is in reaction against? Protestants reformed "the whore of Babylon." Others were "enlightened" from it, and Jews had reason to help Catholicism and the social structure it was rooted in fall apart. The history books and the whole of education hummed in upon that point (for during crucial years I attended a public school): to be modern is decidedly not to be medieval; to be reasonable is not to be dogmatic; to be free is clearly not to live under ecclesiastical authority; to be scientific is not to attend ancient rituals, cherish irrational symbols, indulge in mythic practices. It is hard to grow up Catholic in America without becoming defensive, perhaps a little paranoid, feeling forced to divide the world between "us" and "them." . . .

We did not feel this country belonged to us. We felt fierce pride in it, more loyalty than anyone could know. But we felt blocked at every turn. There were not many intellectuals among us, not even very many professional men. Laborers mostly. Small businessmen, agents for corporations perhaps. Content with a little, yes, modest in expectation, and content. But somehow feeling cheated. For a thousand years the Slovaks survived Hungarian hegemony and our strategy here remained the same: endurance and steady work. Slowly, one day, we would overcome. . . .

Distrust of Intellectuals

The ethnics do not like, or trust, or even understand the intellectuals. It is not easy to feel uncomplicated affection for those who call you "pig," "fascist," "racist." One had not yet grown accustomed to not hearing "hunkie," "Polack," "spic," "mick," "dago," and the rest. A worker in Chicago told reporter Lois Wille in a vividly home-centered outburst:

> The liberals always have despised us. We've got these mostly little jobs, and we drink beer and, my God, we bowl and watch television and we don't read. It's goddamn vicious snobbery. We're sick of all these phoney integrated TV commercials with these upper-class Negroes. We know they're phoney.
>
> The only time a Pole is mentioned it's to make fun of him. He's Ignatz Dumbrowski, 274 pounds and 5-foot-4, and he got his education by writing into a firm on a matchbook cover. But what will we do about it? Nothing, because we're the new invisible man, the new whipping boy, and we still think the measure of a man's what he does and how he takes care of his children and what he's doing in his own home, not what he thinks about Vietnam.

At no little sacrifice, one had apologized for foods that smelled too strong for Anglo-Saxon noses; moderated the wide swings of Slavic and Italian emotion; learned decorum; given oneself to education, American style; tried to learn tolerance and assimilation. Each generation criticized the earlier for its authoritarian and European and old-fashioned ways. "Up-to-date" was a moral lever. And now when the process nears completion, when a generation appears that speaks without accent and goes to college, still you are considered "pigs," "fascists," and "racists."

Racists? Our ancestors owned no slaves. Most of us ceased being serfs only in the last two hundred years—the Russians in 1861....

It is impossible to define people out of existence, or to define their existence for them. Sooner or later, being free, they will explode in rage.

If you are a descendant of southern and eastern Europeans, everyone else *has* defined your existence. A pattern of "Americanization" is laid out. You are catechized, cajoled, and condescended to by guardians of good Anglo-Protestant attitudes. You are chided by Jewish libertarians. Has ever a culture been so moralistic?

The entire experience of becoming American is summarized in the experience of being made to feel guilty....

Our parents "began to go out of their way in order to act American. You see, they could not stand shame, and shame was one of the means used to get them to come over and change their habits."...

The Myth of Assimilation

Many sociologists have begun to doubt the conventional wisdom about American society. That wisdom was a rationalization of the WASP conception of America. As a Jew, [Ben] Halpern [in his book *Jews and Blacks*] understands the rules limpidly:

> In those not so old but nearly forgotten days, a simple conception of the way newcomers could be "Americanized" was generally accepted. The public view was that the old settlers, the real Americans, had established an open society based on the American Way of Life: on freedom of belief and opinion and free enterprise. Participation in it was open, in principle, to anyone according to his individual merit. There was no discrimination—but admission to the real America was subject to a test of individual performance.
>
> America was the New World, come to redress the balance of the Old, to replace it by something bigger and better. Everyone in it, in principle, had turned his back on the corrupt Old World; and, in order to enter, newcomers had to be willing to do the same. This was *the price* of assimilation into the real America, the preliminary test and condition that must be met.
>
> The American idea of proper social organization was not that of a totally unstratified, unsegregated, undifferentiated society, but of

a society with class differences and loose, permeable segregations, open to the passage of individuals who proved their worth.

In a word, America will assimilate *individuals*. It will not assimilate groups.

The new ethnic politics is a direct challenge to the WASP conception of America. It asserts that *groups* can structure the rules and goals and procedures of American life. It asserts that individuals, if they do not wish to, do not have to "melt." They do not have to submit themselves to atomization. "Subcultures" are refusing to concede the legitimacy of one (modernized WASP) "Superculture." A black sociologist, L. Paul Metzger, puts it best:

> To abandon the idea that ethnicity is a dysfunctional survival from a prior stage of social development will make it possible for sociologists to reaffirm that minority-majority relations are in fact group relations and not merely relations between prejudiced and victimized individuals. As such, they are implicated in the struggle for power and privilege in the society, and the theory of collective behavior and political sociology may be more pertinent to understanding them than the theory of social mobility and assimilation. . . .

Can ethnic consciousness be restored? Each person has an answer in his own autobiography. No one is so godlike that he perceives like all other Americans combined. Very well, then, what are the edges of the particularity of each of us? Inescapably, there is in all but the most mongrel, orphaned, and rootless of us a considerable inheritance from grandparents. That inheritance colors the eyes through which we discern what is reasonable, fair, cause for joy, or for alarm. Each of us is different from any other, and yet our similarities with some others tend to cluster around shared ethnicities. It is more comfortable for us to be with people whose range of feeling, irony, instinct, and word is like our own. Each of us finds certain other groups offensive, puzzling, menacing, taxing. Such findings are marks, not of our malice, but of our finitude. No ethnic group (dearly as we each believe it) is God's people. No individual (dearly as we each would love to be) is universalist. It's all right to have limited perceptions. It's really all right. Self-hatred isn't necessary.

Diversity of ethnic consciousness is exciting and valuable. It is so utterly refreshing to meet people in touch with their roots, secure in them even if long ago having transcended them. . . .

Diversity of ethnic consciousness is becoming more rare, as people uproot convictions in order to plant opinions, uproot values of substance in order to plant values of process, uproot personal angularities in order to plant professional sentiments. The human question is *Who?* It is not *How?* It is a social question. Perish diversity of groups, perish humanity.

CHAPTER 2

The Nineteenth Century: The Northern and Western Europeans

Chapter Preface

Between 1820 and 1890, fifteen million people emigrated to the United States, two-thirds of them from Germany, Ireland, and Great Britain (including English, Welsh, and Scots). These newcomers made up nearly 10 percent of the total population by 1860 and nearly 15 percent by 1890. Many of the British immigrants were paupers who improved their economic status in the United States and returned to their homeland; those who stayed were assimilated into American culture fairly readily. But the Germans and Irish, because of their cultural differences, had more difficulty.

Often the focus of a vocal nativist movement to keep them out (the nativists' favorite slogan was "America for Americans!"), the

Irish, German, and Scandinavian Immigration, 1840-1890

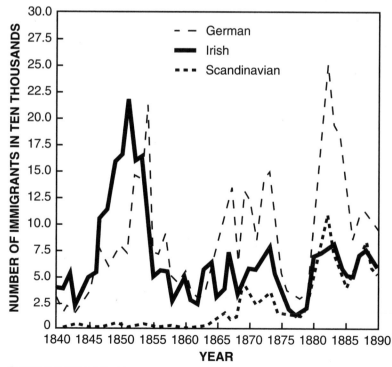

Source: U.S. Census Bureau.

immigrants' difficulties in melting into American society added to their often already difficult adjustment to life away from the family, friends, language, and professions they had left behind.

Although these immigrants undeniably contributed to the nation's growth and productivity, many established Americans still feared their ultimate impact on American society. Nativists, both those who were members of formal groups such as the small but powerful Know-Nothing political party of the 1850s and those informal nativists—individuals who were suspicious of foreigners —were particularly concerned about the influence of the Catholic religion practiced by most of the Irish and many of the German immigrants. Catholics' loyalties, nativists felt, were to church first and to country a distant second. Nativists could envision the prolific Catholics gaining enough numbers and political strength to create a future America having a monarchical pope as its head instead of a popularly elected president.

Nativists also pointed to the active immigrant societies, both German and Irish, that they believed showed the immigrants were more loyal to their native countries than to their adopted home. Nativists feared these foreigners would undermine the stability and democracy of the formerly homogeneous United States.

A second major concern was the impact of the immigrants on America's economy. Nativists and other Americans had deep-seated fears that the foreigners, who were willing to work for less money, would steal jobs from needy Americans, or, conversely, would not work at all and be a drain on America's resources.

Immigrants, often leaving behind untenable economic and political situations, viewed America as their hope for the future. Upon their arrival, however, they were faced not only with the struggle to make their way economically but with the need to combat such attitudes as those the nativists exhibited. In addition, they found dissension within their own ranks. They faced conflict among themselves over maintaining or letting go of their religion, language, and family and cultural values. Torn between maintaining ties with the old and starting anew, many immigrants lived in a constant turmoil of conflicting emotions as they confronted their own fears and those of their new neighbors.

VIEWPOINT 1

"The danger of foreign influence, threatening the gradual destruction of our national institutions . . . has awakened deep alarm in the mind of every intelligent patriot, from the days of Washington to the present time."

Immigrants Endanger America

Native American Party

Nativism, a movement devoted to the idea that immigrants threatened the economic and political security of "native" Americans—white, Protestant, established citizens—became entrenched in the American political scene during the early decades of the nineteenth century.

In 1836, the inventor Samuel F. B. Morse helped found one of the first nativist political organizations, the New York Native American Democratic Association. Although this political party did not do particularly well in New York's elections that year, the party's motivating spirit—anti-immigrantism—remained a strong undercurrent in the politics of New York and other states, ready to be sparked by the anti-Irish, anti-Catholic sentiments that roared through the country in the 1840s. (Nearly 2 million Irish immigrants, most of them destitute, most of them Catholic, and most of them still deeply attached to their native country, entered the United States in the 1840s and 1850s.)

In 1844, a new nativist organization, the American Republican Party, managed to elect dozens of officials in the states of New York, Pennsylvania, and Massachusetts. These officials and their followers were dedicated to suppressing the immigrant menace. In 1845, they held their first national convention in Philadelphia, where they changed their name to the Native American Party and adopted a platform which delineated the threats they felt from immigrants. The following viewpoint is excerpted from that platform.

We, the delegates elect to the first National Convention of the Native American body of the United States of America, assembled at Philadelphia, on the 4th of July, A.D. 1845, for the purpose of devising a plan of concerted political action in defence of American institutions against the encroachments of foreign influence, open or concealed, hereby solemnly, and before Almighty God, make known to our fellow citizens, our country, and the world, the following incontrovertible facts, and the course of conduct consequent thereon, to which, in duty to the cause of human rights and the claims of our beloved country, we mutually pledge our lives, our fortunes, and our sacred honour.

The danger of foreign influence, threatening the gradual destruction of our national institutions, failed not to arrest the attention of the Father of his Country, in the very dawn of American Liberty. Not only its direct agency in rendering the American system liable to the poisonous influence of European policy—a policy at war with the fundamental principles of the American Constitution—but also its still more fatal operation in aggravating the virulence of partisan warfare—has awakened deep alarm in the mind of every intelligent patriot, from the days of Washington to the present time.

The influx of a foreign population, permitted after little more than a nominal residence, to participate in the legislation of the country and the sacred right of suffrage, produced comparatively little evil during the earlier years of the Republic; for that influx was then limited by the considerable expenses of a transatlantic voyage, by the existence of many wholesome restraints upon the acquisition of political prerogatives, by the constant exhaustion of the European population in long and bloody continental wars, and by the slender inducements offered for emigration to a young and sparsely peopled country, contending for existence with a boundless wilderness, inhabited by savage men. Evils which are only prospective rarely attract the notice of the masses, and until peculiar changes in the political condition of Europe, the increased facilities for transportation, and the madness of partisan legislation in removing all effective guards against the open prostitution of the right of citizenship had converted the slender current of naturalization into a torrent threatening to overwhelm the influence of the natives of the land, the far-seeing vision of the statesman, only, being fixed upon the distant, but steadily approaching, cloud.

But, since the barriers against the improper extension of the right of suffrage were bodily broken down, for a partisan purpose, by the Congress of 1825, the rapidly increasing numbers and unblushing insolence of the foreign population of the worst classes have caused the general agitation of the question, "How shall the institutions of the country be preserved from the blight of foreign influence, insanely legalized through the conflicts of domestic parties?" Associations under different names have been formed by our fellow citizens, in many States of this confederation, from Louisiana to Maine, all designed to check this imminent danger before it becomes irremediable, and, at length, a National Convention of the great American people, born upon the soil of Washington, has assembled to digest and announce a plan of operation, by which the grievances of an abused hospitality, and the consequent degradation of political morals, may be redressed, and the tottering columns of the temple of Republican Liberty secured upon the sure foundation of an enlightened nationality.

In calling for support upon every American who loves his country pre-eminently, and every adopted citizen of moral and intellectual worth who would secure, to his compatriots yet to come amongst us, the blessings of political protection, the safety of person and property, it is right that we should make known the grievances which we propose to redress, and the manner in which we shall endeavour to effect our object.

Imminent Peril

It is an incontrovertible truth that the civil institutions of the United States of America have been seriously affected, and that they now stand in imminent peril from the rapid and enormous increase of the body of residents of foreign birth, imbued with foreign feelings, and of an ignorant and immoral character, who receive, under the present lax and unreasonable laws of naturalization, the elective franchise and the right of eligibility to political office.

The whole body of foreign citizens, invited to our shores under a constitutional provision adapted to other times and other political conditions of the world, and of our country especially, has been endowed by American hospitality with gratuitous privileges unnecessary to the enjoyment of those inalienable rights of man—life, liberty, and the pursuit of happiness—privileges wisely reserved to the Natives of the soil by the governments of all other civilized nations. But, familiarized by habit with the exercise of these indulgences, and emboldened by increasing numbers, a vast majority of those who constitute this foreign body, now claim as an original right that which has been so incautiously granted as a favour—thus attempting to render inevitable the prospective action of laws adopted upon a principle of mere expediency, made variable at the will of Congress by the express terms of the Constitution, and heretofore repeatedly revised to meet the exigencies of the times.

In former years, this body was recruited chiefly from the victims of political oppression, or the active and intelligent mercantile adventurers of other lands; and it then constituted a slender representation of the best classes of the foreign population well fitted to add strength to the state, and capable of being readily educated in the peculiarly American science of political self-government. Moreover, while welcoming the stranger of every condition, laws then wisely demanded of every foreign aspirant for political rights a certificate of practical good citizenship. Such a class of aliens were followed by no foreign demagogues—they were courted by no domestic demagogues; they were purchased by no parties—they were debauched by no emissaries of kings. A wall of fire separated them from such a baneful influence, erected by their intelligence, their knowledge, their virtue and love of freedom. But for the last twenty years the road to civil preferment and participation in the legislative and executive government of the land has been laid broadly open, alike to the ignorant, the vicious and the criminal; and a large proportion of the foreign body of citizens and voters now constitutes a representation of the worst and most degraded of the European population—victims of social oppression or personal vices, utterly divested, by ignorance or crime, of the moral and intellectual requisites for political self-government.

Thus tempted by the suicidal policy of these United States, and favoured by the facilities resulting from the modern improvements of navigation, numerous societies and corporate bodies in foreign countries have found it economical to transport to our shores, at public and private expense, the feeble, the imbecile, the idle, and intractable, thus relieving themselves of the burdens resulting from the vices of the European social systems by availing themselves of the generous errors of our own.

The almshouses of Europe are emptied upon our coast, and this by our own invitation—not casually, or to a trivial extent, but systematically, and upon a constantly increasing scale. The Bedlams of the old world have contributed their share to the torrent of immigration, and the lives of our citizens have been attempted in the streets of our capital cities by mad-men, just liberated from European hospitals upon the express condition that they should be transported to America. By the orders of European governments, the punishment of crimes has been commuted for banishment to the land of the free; and criminals in iron have crossed the ocean to be cast loose upon society on their arrival upon our shores. The United States are rapidly becoming the lazar house and penal colony of Europe; nor can we reasonably censure such proceedings. They are legitimate consequences of our own unlimited benevolence; and it is of such material that we profess to manufacture free and enlightened citizens, by a process occupying five short years at most, but practically oftentimes embraced in a much shorter period of time.

Benefits Not Worth the Drawbacks

Author Jesse Chickering published Immigration into the United States *in 1848. Much of the book reflects his concerns about the negative impact of immigrants on the country.*

But is the country truly benefited by this great foreign immigration? Have the people been made wiser or better or happier? It has been said that without these foreigners our railroads and canals could not have been constructed. These improvements, it is true, may have been made a year or two earlier (and in many of the states it would have been better if we had hurried less) in consequence of so many foreigners being in the country, whom we were obliged to employ in some way or other, or support them without labor. The progress of the internal improvements, a year or two in advance of what they would have been without this foreign labor, will be a very poor compensation, if offset by the corruption of manners, the forfeiture of freedom, and the transfer of power to those who know not how to use it wisely. There are other things of value in this world besides merely physical aggrandizement.

These foreigners come here to benefit themselves, not from any love of us or of our country.

The mass of foreign voters, formerly lost among the Natives of the soil, has increased from the ratio of 1 in 40 to that of 1 in 7! A like advance in fifteen years will leave the Native citizens a minority in their own land! Thirty years ago these strangers came by units and tens—now they swarm by thousands. Formerly, most of them sought only for an honest livelihood and a provision for their families, and rarely meddled with the institutions, of which it was impossible they could comprehend the nature; now each newcomer seeks political preferment, and struggles to fasten on the public purse with an avidity, in strict proportion to his ignorance and unworthiness of public trust—having been sent for the purpose of obtaining political ascendancy in the government of the nation; having been sent to exalt their allies to power; having been sent to work a revolution from republican freedom to the divine rights of monarchs.

From these unhappy circumstances has arisen an *Imperium in Imperio*—a body uninformed and vicious—foreign in feeling, prejudice, and manner, yet armed with a vast and often a controlling influence over the policy of a nation, whose benevolence it abuses, and whose kindness it habitually insults; a body as dangerous to the rights of the intelligent foreigner as to the prospect of its own immediate progeny, as it is threatening to the liberties of the country, and the hopes of rational freedom throughout the world; a body ever ready to complicate our foreign relations by embroiling us with the hereditary hates and feuds of other lands, and to disturb our domestic peace by its crude ideas, mistaking license for liberty, and the overthrow of individual rights for republican political equality; a body ever the ready tool of foreign and domestic demagogues, and steadily endeavouring by misrule to establish popular tyranny under a cloak of false democracy. Americans, false to their country, and led on to moral crime by the desire of dishonest gain, have scattered their agents over Europe, inducing the malcontent and the unthrifty to exchange a life of compulsory labour in foreign lands for relative comfort, to be maintained by the tax-paying industry of our overburdened and deeply indebted community. Not content with the usual and less objectionable licenses of trade, these fraudulent dealers habitually deceive a worthier class of victims, by false promises of employment, and assist in thronging the already crowded avenues of simple labour with a host of competitors, whose first acquaintance with American faith springs from a gross imposture, and whose first feeling on discovering the cheat is reasonable mistrust, if not implacable revenge. The importation of the physical necessities of life is burdened with imposts which many deem extravagant; but the importation of vice and idleness—of seditious citizens and factious rulers—is not only unrestricted by anything beyond a nominal tax, but is actually encouraged by a system which transforms the great patrimony of the nation, purchased by the blood of our fathers, into a source of bounty for the promotion of immigration.

Fatal Evil

Whenever an attempt is made to restrain this fatal evil, the native and adopted demagogues protest against an effort which threatens to deprive them of their most important tools; and such is the existing organization of our established political parties, that should either of them essay the reform of an abuse which both acknowledge to be fraught with ruin, that party sinks upon the instant into a minority, divested of control, and incapable of result.

From such causes has been derived a body, armed with political power, in a country of whose system it is ignorant, and for whose institutions it feels little interest, except for the purpose of personal advancement. . . .

The body of adopted citizens, with foreign interests and prejudices, is annually advancing with rapid strides, in geometrical progression. Already it has acquired a control over our elections which cannot be entirely corrected, even by the wisest legislation, until the present generation shall be numbered with the past. Already it has notoriously swayed the course of national legislation, and invaded the purity of local justice. In a few years its unchecked progress would cause it to outnumber the native defenders of our rights, and would then inevitably dispossess our offspring, and its own, of the inheritance for which our fathers bled, or plunge this land of happiness and peace into the horrors of civil war.

The correction of these evils can never be effected by any combination governed by the tactics of other existing parties. If either of the old parties, as such, were to attempt an extension of the term of naturalization, it would be impossible for it to carry out the measure, because they would immediately be abandoned by the foreign voters. This great measure can be carried out only by an organization like our own, made up of those who have given up their former political preferences.

For these reasons, we recommend the immediate organization of the truly patriotic native citizens throughout the United States, for the purpose of resisting the progress of foreign influence in the conduct of American affairs, and the correction of such political abuses as have resulted from unguarded or partisan legislation on the subject of naturalization, so far as these abuses admit of remedy without encroachment upon the vested rights of foreigners who have been already legally adopted into the bosom of the nation.

VIEWPOINT 2

"The emigration of foreigners to this country is not only defensible on grounds of abstract justice . . . but . . . it has been in various ways highly beneficial to this country."

Immigrants Do Not Endanger America

Thomas L. Nichols (1815-1901)

Although the nativist movement was strong in the middle of the nineteenth century, there were those who enthusiastically defended immigrants as well. One such person was Thomas L. Nichols, author of several books, including *Esoteric Anthropology: A . . . Treatise on the . . . Intimate Relations of Men and Women.* In the following viewpoint, excerpted from a speech Nichols made in New York in 1845, he defends the innate right of people to emigrate from one place to another. He also details many contributions immigrants have made to the United States, and he answers the fears expressed by many nativists.

The questions connected with emigration from Europe to America are interesting to both the old world and the new—are of importance to the present and future generations. They have more consequence than a charter or a state election; they involve the destinies of millions; they are connected with the progress of civilization, the rights of man, and providence of God!

I have examined this subject the more carefully, and speak upon it the more earnestly, because I have been to some extent, in former years, a partaker of the prejudices I have since learned to pity. A native of New England and a descendant of the puritans, I early imbibed, and to some extent promulgated, opinions of which reflection and experience have made me ashamed. . . .

But while I would speak of the motives of men with charity, I claim the right to combat their opinions with earnestness. Believing that the principles and practices of Native Americanism are wrong in themselves, and are doing wrong to those who are the objects of their persecution, justice and humanity require that their fallacy should be exposed, and their iniquity condemned. It may be unfortunate that the cause of the oppressed and persecuted, in opinion if not in action, has not fallen into other hands; yet, let me trust that the truth, even in mine, will prove mighty, prevailing from its own inherent power!

The Right to Emigrate

The right of man to emigrate from one country to another, is one which belongs to him by his own constitution and by every principle of justice. It is one which no law can alter, and no authority destroy. "Life, liberty, and the pursuit of happiness" are set down, in our Declaration of Independence, as among the self-evident, unalienable rights of man. If I have a right to live, I have also a right to what will support existence—food, clothing, and shelter. If then the country in which I reside, from a superabundant population, or any other cause, does not afford me these, my right to go from it to some other is self-evident and unquestionable. The *right to live*, then, supposes the right of emigration. . . .

I proceed, therefore, to show that the emigration of foreigners to this country is not only defensible on grounds of abstract justice—what we have no possible right to prevent, but that it has been in various ways highly beneficial to this country.

Emigration first peopled this hemisphere with civilized men. The first settlers of this continent had the same right to come here that belongs to the emigrant of yesterday—no better and no other. They came to improve their condition, to escape from oppression, to enjoy freedom—for the same, or similar, reasons as now prevail. And so far as they violated no private rights, so long as they obtained their lands by fair purchase, or took possession of those which were unclaimed and uncultivated, the highly respectable natives whom the first settlers found here had no right to make any objections. The peopling of this continent with civilized men, the cultivation of the earth, the various processes of productive labor, for the happiness of man, all tend to "the greatest good of the greatest number," and carry out the evident design of Nature or Providence in the formation of the earth and its inhabitants.

Emigration from various countries in Europe to America, producing a mixture of races, has had, and is still having, the most important influence upon the destinies of the human race. It is a principle, laid down by every physiologist, and proved by abundant observation, that man, like other animals, is improved and brought to its highest perfection by an intermingling of the blood and qualities of various races. That nations and families deteriorate from an opposite course has been observed in all ages. The great physiological reason why Americans are superior to other nations in freedom, intelligence, and enterprize, is because that they are the offspring of the greatest intermingling of races. The mingled blood of England has given her predominance over several nations of Europe in these very qualities, and a newer infusion, with favorable circumstances of climate, position, and institutions, has rendered Americans still superior. The Yankees of New England would never have shown those qualities for which they have been distinguished in war and peace throughout the world had there not been mingled with the puritan English, the calculating Scotch, the warm hearted Irish, the gay and chivalric French, the steady persevering Dutch, and the transcendental Germans, for all these nations contributed to make up the New England character, before the Revolution, and ever since to influence that of the whole American people.

America's Destiny Is to Be Peopled with Immigrants

It is not too much to assert that in the order of Providence this vast and fertile continent was reserved for this great destiny; to be the scene of this mingling of the finest European races, and consequently of the highest condition of human intelligence, freedom, and happiness; for I look upon this mixture of the blood and qualities of various nations, and its continual infusion, as absolutely requisite to the perfection of humanity. . . . Continual emigration, and a constant mixing of the blood of different races, is highly conducive to physical and mental superiority.

This country has been continually benefited by the immense amount of capital brought hither by emigrants. There are very few who arrive upon our shores without some little store of wealth, the hoard of years of industry. Small as these means may be in each case, they amount to millions in the aggregate, and every dollar is so much added to the wealth of the country, to be reckoned at compound interest from the time of its arrival, nor are these sums like our European loans, which we must pay back, both principal and interest. Within a few years, especially, and more or less at all periods, men of great wealth have been among the emigrants driven from Europe, by religious oppression or political revolutions. Vast sums have also fallen to emigrants and their descendants by inheritance, for every few days we read in the papers of some poor foreigner, or descendant of foreigners, as are we all, becoming the heir of a princely fortune, which in most cases, is added to the wealth of his adopted country. Besides this, capital naturally follows labor, and it flows upon this country in a constant current, by the laws of trade.

But it is not money alone that adds to the wealth of a country, but every day's productive labor is to be added to its accumulating capital. Every house built, every canal dug, every railroad graded, has added so much to the actual wealth of society; and who have built more houses, dug more canals, or graded more railroads, than the hardy Irishmen? I hardly know how our great national works could have been carried on without them—then; while every pair of sturdy arms has added to our national wealth, every hungry mouth has been a home market for our agriculture, and every broad shoulder has been clothed with our manufactures.

Europe's Most Valuable Members

From the very nature of the case, America gets from Europe the most valuable of her population. Generally, those who come here are the very ones whom a sensible man would select. Those who are attached to monarchical and aristocratic institutions stay at home where they can enjoy them. Those who lack energy and enterprize can never make up their minds to leave their native land. It is the strong minded, the brave hearted, the free and self-respecting, the enterprizing and the intelligent, who break away from all the ties of country and of home, and brave the dangers of the ocean, in search of liberty and independence, for themselves and for their children, on a distant continent; and it is from this, among other causes, that the great mass of the people of this country are distinguished for the very qualities we should look for in emigrants. The same spirit which sent our fathers across the ocean impels us over the Alleghanies, to the valley of the Mississippi, and thence over the Rocky mountains into Oregon.

For what are we not indebted to foreign emigration, since we are all Europeans or their descendants? We cannot travel on one of our steamboats without remembering that Robert Fulton was the son of an Irishman. We cannot walk by St. Paul's churchyard without seeing the monuments which admiration and gratitude have erected to Emmet, and Montgomery. Who of the thousands who every summer pass up and down our great thoroughfare, the North River, fails to catch at least a passing glimpse of the column erected to the memory of Kosciusko? I cannot forget that only last night a portion of our citizens celebrated with joyous festivities the birthday of the son of Irish emigrants, I mean the

"Let Them Come"

The Western Journal, published in St. Louis, Missouri, in 1851 commented favorably on the impact of immigrants in the expanding United States.

The poor flock to our shores to escape from a state of penury, which cannot be relieved by toil in their own native land. The man of enterprise comes, to avail himself of the advantages afforded by a wider and more varied field for the exercise of his industry and talents; and the oppressed of every land, thirsting for deliverance from the paralyzing effects of unjust institutions, come to enjoy the blessings of a government which secures life, liberty, and the pursuit of happiness to all its constituents. Let them come. They will convert our waste lands into fruitful fields, vineyards, and gardens; construct works of public improvement; build up and establish manufactures; and open our rich mines of coal, of iron, of lead, and of copper. And more than all, they will be the means of augmenting our commerce, and aiding us in extending the influence of our political, social, and religious institutions throughout the earth. . . .

Thus united in the great cause of civilization, and acting in concert, the influence of our political and social institutions shall gain strength from increase of numbers, until the principles of despotism which have enthralled the masses of the old world, shall be eradicated, and the condition of all nations improved by our example.

Hero of New Orleans!

Who speaks contemptuously of Alexander Hamilton as a foreigner, because he was born in one of the West India Islands? Who at this day will question the worth or patriotism of Albert Gallatin, because he first opened his eyes among the Alps of Switzerland—though, in fact, this was brought up and urged against him, when he was appointed special minister to Russia by James Madison. What New Yorker applies the epithet of "degraded foreigner" to the German immigrant, John Jacob Astor, a man who has spread his canvas on every sea, drawn to his adopted land the wealth of every clime, and given us, it may be, our best claim to vast territories!

Who would have banished the Frenchman, Stephen Girard, who, after accumulating vast wealth from foreign commerce, endowed with it magnificent institutions for education in his adopted land? So might I go on for hours, citing individual examples of benefits derived by this country from foreign immigration. . . .

I have enumerated some of the advantages which such emigration has given to America. Let us now very carefully inquire, whether there is danger of any injury arising from these causes, at all proportionable to the palpable good.

"Our country is in danger," is the cry of Nativism. During my brief existence I have seen this country on the very verge of ruin a considerable number of times. It is always in the most imminent peril every four years; but, hitherto, the efforts of one party or the other have proved sufficient to rescue it, just in the latest gasp of its expiring agonies, and we have breathed more freely, when we have been assured that "the country's safe." Let us look steadily in the face of this new danger.

Are foreigners coming here to overturn our government? Those who came before the Revolution appear to have been generally favorable to Republican institutions. Those who have come here since have left friends, home, country, all that man naturally holds dearest, that they might live under a free government—they and their children. Is there common sense in the supposition that men would voluntarily set about destroying the very liberties they came so far to enjoy?

"But they lack intelligence," it is said. Are the immigrants of to-day less intelligent than those of fifty or a hundred years ago? Has Europe and the human race stood still all this time?. . . The facts of men preferring this country to any other, of their desire to live under its institutions, of their migration hither, indicate to my mind anything but a lack of proper intelligence and enterprize. It has been charged against foreigners, by a portion of the whig press, that they generally vote with the democratic party. Allowing this to be so, I think that those who reflect upon the policy of the two parties, from the time of John Adams down to that of Mayor Harper, will scarcely bring this up as the proof of a lack of intelligence!

Immigrant Patriots

The truth is, a foreigner who emigrates to this country comes here saying, "Where Liberty dwells, there is my country." He sees our free institutions in the strong light of contrast. The sun seems brighter, because he has come out of darkness. What we know by hearsay only of the superiority of our institutions, he knows by actual observation and experience. Hence it is that America has had no truer patriots—freedom no more enthusiastic admirers—the cause of Liberty no more heroic defenders, than have been found among our adopted citizens. . . .

But if naturalized citizens of foreign birth had the disposition, they have not the power, to endanger our liberties, on account of their comparatively small and decreasing numbers. There appears to be a most extraordinary misapprehension upon this subject. To read one of our "Native" papers one might suppose that our country was becoming overrun by foreigners, and that there was real danger of their having a majority of votes. . . .

There is a point beyond which immigration cannot be carried. It must be limited by the capacity of the vessels employed in bringing passengers, while our entire population goes on increasing in geometrical progression, so that in one century from now, we shall have a population of one hundred and sixty millions, but a few hundred thousands of whom at the utmost can be citizens of foreign birth. Thus it may be seen that foreign immigration is of very little account, beyond a certain period, in the population of a country, and at all times is an insignificant item. . . .

In the infancy of this country the firstborn native found himself among a whole colony of foreigners. Now, the foreigner finds himself surrounded by as great a disproportion of natives, and the native babe and newly landed foreigner have about the same amount, of either power or disposition, to endanger the country in which they have arrived; one, because he chose to come—the other because he could not help it.

I said the power or the disposition, for I have yet to learn that foreigners, whether German or Irish, English or French, are at all disposed to do an injury to the asylum which wisdom has prepared and valor won for the oppressed of all nations and religions. I appeal to the observation of every man in this community, whether the Germans and the Irish here, and throughout the country, are not as orderly, as industrious, as quiet, and in the habit of performing as well the common duties of citizens as the great mass of natives among us.

The worst thing that can be brought against any portion of our foreign population is that in many cases they are poor, and when they sink under labor and privation, they have no resources but the almshouse. Alas! shall the rich, for whom they have labored, the owners of the houses they have helped to build, refuse to treat them as kindly as they would their horses when incapable of further toil? Can they grudge them shelter from the storm, and a place where they may die in peace?

VIEWPOINT 3

"America for the Americans—to shape and to govern; to make great, and to keep great, strong and free, from home foes and foreign demagogues and hierarchs."

America Belongs to Americans

New York Mirror

In 1855, the largest nativist political party, the American party, attracted more than 1 million members. The American party was better known as the Know-Nothings, supposedly for the response members made when asked about the workings of their party. The Know-Nothings, deeply concerned about the negative influence foreigners might have on the United States, built their party's platform around anti-immigrant policy. They fielded a presidential candidate in 1855 but lost the election. The Civil War turned America's minds and hearts to other matters, and the Know-Nothing party died an early death.

The following viewpoint was originally published in the *New York Mirror*, an eight-page periodical founded by poets George Pope Morris and Samuel Wordsworth. The magazine contained articles on topics of all kinds and was particularly known for its commentary on issues of the day. The viewpoint reprinted here was later collected in a Know-Nothing commemorative book, *The Wide-Awake Gift: A Know-Nothing Token for 1855* (New York: 1855). It dramatically expresses the Know-Nothing's plea of "America for Americans!"

"America for Americans!"

Well, why not? Is there another country under the sun, that does not belong to its own native-born people? Is there another country where the alien by birth, and often by openly boasted sympathy, is permitted to fill the most responsible offices, and preside over the most sacred trusts of the land? Is there another country that would place its secret archives and its diplomacy with foreign states, in other than native hands—with tried and trusty native hearts to back them? Is there another country that would even permit the foreigner to become a citizen, shielded by its laws and its flag, on terms such as we exact, leaving the political franchise out of sight? More than all else, is there a country, other than ours, that would acknowledge as a citizen, a patriot, a republican, or a safe man, one who stood bound by a religious oath or obligation, in political conflict with, and which he deemed temporarily higher than, the Constitution and Civil Government of that country—to which he also professes to swear fealty?

America for the Americans, we say. And why not? Didn't they plant it, and battle for it through bloody revolution—and haven't they developed it, as only Americans could, into a nation of a century and yet mightier than the oldest empire on earth? Why shouldn't they shape and rule the destinies of their own land—the land of their birth, their love, their altars, and their graves; the land red and rich with the blood and ashes, and hallowed by the memories of their fathers? Why not rule their own, particularly when the alien betrays the trust that should never have been given him, and the liberties of the land are thereby imperilled?

Majority Right

Lacks the American numbers, that he may not rule by the right of majority, to which is constitutionally given the political sovereignty of this land? Did he not, at the last numbering of the people, count seventeen and a half millions, native to the soil, against less than two and a half millions of actually foreign-born, and those born of foreigners coming among us for the last three-quarters of a century? Has he not tried the mixed rule, with a tolerance unexampled, until it has plagued him worse than the lice and locust plagued the Egyptian? Has he not shared the trust of office and council, until foreign-born pauperism, vice and crime, stain the whole land—until a sheltered alien fraction have become rampant in their ingratitude and insolence? Has he not suffered burdens of tax, and reproach, and shame, by his ill-bestowed division of political power?

America for the Americans! That is the watchword that should ring through the length and breadth of the land, from the lips of the whole people. America for the Americans—to shape and to govern; to make great, and to keep great, strong and free, from home foes and foreign demagogues and hierarchs. In the hour of Revolutionary peril, Washington said, "Put none but Americans on guard to-night." At a later time, Jefferson wished "an ocean of fire rolled between the Old World and the New." To their children, the American people, the fathers and builders of the Republic, bequeathed it. "Eternal vigilance is the price of liberty!"—let the American be vigilant that the alien seize not his birth-right.

The Destruction of Rome by Foreigners

In 1825, Samuel Whelpley published the eighth edition of his two-volume history A Compend of History from the Earliest Times; Comprehending a General View of the State of the World. *In this excerpt, he compares the fall of Rome to the potential fall of the United States if it continues to allow immigrants to enter the country.*

The history of Rome furnishes a striking instance of the deplorable effects of an influx of strangers into a country. After the Romans had conquered Carthage, Greece, Asia, and Gaul, Italy presently was filled with enterprising emigrants from all quarters. Though they came, as it were, singly, and as humble suppliants, yet they in effect conquered their conquerors. They inundated all Italy. The majesty of the ancient Romans was obscured, overwhelmed, and utterly lost in an innumerable swarm of foreigners. The evil came on by slow and imperceptible degrees; but was at last irresistible and fatal. These were the persons generally employed in the civil wars. A multitude made up of such people is always fickle, inflammatory, outrageous, vindicative, and burning with ambition to level all distinctions.

America for the Americans! Shelter and welcome let them give to the emigrant and the exile, and make them citizens in so far as civil privileges are concerned. But let it be looked to that paupers and criminals are no longer shipped on us by foreign states. Let it be looked to that foreign nationalities in our midst are rooted out; that foreign regiments and battalions are disarmed; that the public laws and schools of the country are printed and taught in the language of the land; that no more charters for foreign titled or foreign charactered associations—benevolent, social or other—are granted by our legislatures; that all National and State support given to Education, have not the shadow of sectarianism about it.

There is work for Americans to do. They have slept on guard—if, indeed, they have been on guard—and the enemy have grown strong and riotous in their midst.

America for the Americans! We have had enough of "Young Irelands," "Young Germanys," and "Young Italys." We have had enough of insolent alien threat to suppress our "Puritan Sabbath," and amend our Constitution. We have been a patient camel, and borne foreign burden even to the back-breaking pound. But the time is come to right the wrong; the occasion is ripe for reform in whatever we have failed. The politico-religious foe is fully discovered; he must be squarely met, and put down. We want in this free land none of this political dictation. . . . Our feeling is earnest, not bitter. The matters of which we have written are great and grave ones, and we shall not be silent until we have aided in wholly securing *America for the Americans!*

VIEWPOINT 4

"The real American, then, is he . . . who, abandoning every other country and forswearing every other allegiance, gives his mind and heart to the grand constituent ideas of the Republic."

America Has Room for All Loyal Citizens

Putnam's Monthly

Putnam's Monthly was founded by George Putnam in 1853 and was published until 1857. It was a lively periodical, filled with unsigned writings on politics and the arts by some of America's most famous writers and intellectuals. Contributors included Horace Greeley, James Fenimore Cooper, and Henry David Thoreau.

In May 1855, the height of the Know-Nothing party's visibility, *Putnam's* responded to the Know-Nothing's slogan of "America for Americans!" with an editorial called "Who Are Americans?" *Putnam's* pointed out that so-called native Americans really are immigrants who came to this land long after earlier natives, the American Indian tribes. *Putnam's* also defines America not merely as a country, but an ideal to which all people can aspire. It urges Americans to welcome any people who sincerely desire to be part of the great republican experiment.

What is America, and who are Americans? . . . Accordingly as you answer will the phrase appear very wise or very foolish. If you are determined to consider American as nothing more than the two or three million square miles of dirt included between the Granite Hills and the Pacific, and Americans as those men exclusively whose bodies happened to be fashioned from it, we fear that you have not penetrated to the real beauty and significance of the terms. The soul of a muckworm may very naturally be contented with identifying itself with the mould from which it is bred, and into which it will soon be resolved, but the soul of a man, unless we are hugely misinformed, claims a loftier origin and looks forward to a nobler destiny.

America Is More than a Place

America, in our sense of the word, embraces a complex idea. It means, not simply the soil with its coal, cotton, and corn, but the nationality by which that soil is occupied, and the political system in which such occupants are organized. . . .

America is the democratic republic—not the government of the people by a despot, nor by an oligarchy, nor by any class such as the red-haired part of the inhabitants, or the blue-eyed part; nor yet a government for any other end than the good of the entire nation—but the democratic republic, pure and simple. This is the political organism which individualizes us, or separates us as a living unity from all the rest of the world. All this, of course, would be too elementary to be recounted in any mature discussion, if recent events had not made it necessary to an adequate answer of our second question—who, then, are Americans? Who constitute the people in whose hands the destinies of America are to be deposited?

The fashionable answer in these times is "the natives of this continent, to be sure!" But let us ask again, in that case, whether our old friends Uncas and Chingachgook, and Kag-ne-ga-bow-wow, whether Walk-in-the-water, and Talking-snake, and Big-yellow-thunder, are to be considered Americans par excellence? Alas, no! for they, poor fellows! are all trudging towards the setting sun, and soon their red and dusky figures will have faded in the darker shadows of the night! Is it, then, the second generation of natives—they who are driving them away—who compose exclusively the American family? You say yes; but we say no! Because, if America be as we have shown, more than the soil of America, we do not see how a mere cloddy derivation from it entitles one to the name of American. . . .

The real American, then, is he . . . who, abandoning every other country and forswearing every other allegiance, gives his mind and heart to the grand constituent ideas of the Republic—to the impulses and ends in which and by which alone it subsists. If he have arrived at years of discretion—if he produces evidence of a capacity to understand the relations he undertakes—if he has resided in the atmosphere of freedom long enough to catch its genuine spirit—then is he an American, in the true and best sense of the term.

"America for Americans"

In a reversal of the nativist view, the American poet Parke Goodwin suggests that America is not simply a land but a spirit, and that America has been created by immigrants and should therefore continue to welcome these strangers. This excerpt is from an article Goodwin wrote for Putnam's Monthly *in 1855, called "Secret Societies—The Know-Nothings."*

We that have made it our song ever since we were born, that here humanity had at last found a home, that here all the antiquated distinctions of race, nationality, sect, and caste, were merged in the single distinction of manhood—that here man was to be finally recognized as man, and not as Jew or Gentile, as Christian or Mohammedan, as Protestant or Catholic—we, who have made the world ring with self-glorifications of the asylum of the oppressed of all creeds and nations, of the city of refuge to all the weary exiles of freedom, "whom earth's proud lords, in rage or fear, drive from their wasted homes," we are now asked to erect political barriers, to deal out political excommunication as narrow, as mean, as selfish, and as unwarrantable as ever debased the elder governments. . . .

The cry is, "America for Americans," and we agree to it heartily, but what is America, and who are Americans? . . . America is the cognomen of a nation of men, and not of a collection of arable acres; and Americans are not simply the individual Indians, negroes, and whites who first saw light between Passamaquoddy and Pensacola but all who are Americans inwardly—who are built up on the American idea, who live in the true sentiment of democracy, whose political "circumcision is of the heart, in the spirit and not in the letter, and whose praise is not of men but of God." These are the true Americans, wherever they chanced to be born—whether Turk, Russian, Milesian, or Choctaw.

Or, if not an American, pray what is he? An Englishman, a German, an Irishman he can no longer be; he has cast off the slough of his old political relations forever; he has asserted his sacred right of expatriation (which the United States was the first of nations to sanction) or been expatriated by his too ardent love of the cause which the United States represents; and he can never return to the ancient fold. It would spurn him more incontinently than powder spurns the fire. He must become, then, either a wanderer and a nondescript on the face of the earth, or be received into our generous republican arms. It is our habit to say that we know of no race or creed, but the race of man and the creed of democracy, and if he appeals to us, as a man and a democrat, there is no alternative in the premises. We must either deny his claims altogether—deny that he is a son of God and our brother—or else we must incorporate him, in due season, into the household. It is not enough that we offer him shelter from the rain—not enough that we mend his looped and windowed raggedness—not enough that we replenish his wasted midriff with bacon and hominy, and open to his palsied hands an opportunity to toil. These are commendable charities, but they are such charities as any one, not himself a brute, would willingly extend to a horse found astray on the common. Shall we do no more for our fellows? . . .

Sentiment Does Not Mean Disloyalty

The adoptive citizen, no doubt, preserves a keen remembrance of his native land; but "lives there on earth a soul so dead" as not to sympathize in that feeling? Let us ask you, oh patriotic Weissnicht, all fresh as you are from the vociferations of the lodge, whether you do at heart think the less of a man because he cannot wholly forget the play-place of his infancy, the friends and companions of his boyhood, the old cabin in which he was reared, and the grave in which the bones of his honored mother repose? Have you never seen two long-separated friends, from the old world, meet again in the new, and clasp each other in a warm embrace, while their conversation blossomed up from a vein of common memory, in "Sweet household talk, and phrases of the hearth," and did you not love them the more, in that their eyes grew liquid with the dear old themes? Or is there, in the whole circle of your large and respectable private acquaintance, a single Scotchman to whom you refuse your hand because his affections melt under the "Auld Lang Syne" of Burns, or because his sides shake like a falling house when "Halloween" or "Tam O'Shanter" is read? Can you blame even the poor Frenchman if his eyes light up into a kind of deathless glow when the "Marseillaise," twisted from some wandering hurdy-gurdy, has yet power to recall the glorious days in which his fathers and brothers danced for liberty's sake, and with gay audacity, towards the guillotine? We venture to say for you, No! and we believe, if the truth were told, that often, on the lonely western plains, you have dreamed over again with the German his sweet dream of the resurrection and unity of the Fatherland? We have ourselves seen you, at the St. George dinners, oh Weissnicht, swell with a very evident pride when some flagrant Englishman, recounting, not the battles which his ancestors for ten centuries had won on every field of Europe, but the better trophies gained by Shakespeare, Milton,

80

Bacon, or Cromwell, told you that a little of that same blood coursed in your veins! The blood itself, as it tingled through your body and suffused your cheeks, confessed the fact, if your words did not! How, then, can you, who gaze at Bunker Hill with tears in your eyes, and fling up your hat of a Fourth of July with a jerk that almost dislocates the shoulder, retire to your secret conclave, and chalk it up behind the door, against the foreigner, that he has a lingering love for his native country? Why, he ought to be despised if he had not, if he could forget his heritages of old renown, for it is this traditional tenderness, these genial memories of the immortal words and deeds and places, that constitute his patronymic glories, which show that he has a human heart still under his jacket, and is all the more likely, on account of it, to become a worthy American. . . .

Compare the farmers of our prairies to the boors of the Russian steppes, or to the peasants of the French valleys! Or compare the great body of the working men in England with those of the United States! Now, the American is not of a better nature than the European—for he is often of the same stock—nor is there any charm in our soil and climate unknown to the soil and climate of the other hemisphere; but there is a difference in institutions. Institutions, with us, are made for men, and not men for the institutions. It is the jury, the ballot-box, the free public assemblage, the local committee, the legislative assembly, the place of trust, and as a result of these, the school and the newspaper, which give such a spur to our activities, and endow us with such political competence. The actual responsibilities of civil life are our support and nutriment, and the wings wherewith we fly.

If, consequently, you desire the foreigner to grow into a good citizen, you must subject him to the influences by which good citizens are made. Train him as you are yourselves trained, under the effective tutelage of the regular routine and responsibility of politics. He will never learn to swim by being kept out of the water, anymore than a slave can become a freeman in slavery. He gets used to independence by the practice of it, as the child gets used to walking by walking. It is exercise alone which brings out and improves all sorts of fitnesses—social as well as physical—and the living of any life alone teaches us how it is to be best lived. Nor will any one work for an end in which he and his have no part. They only act for the community who are of the community. Outsiders are always riders. They stand or sit aloof. They have no special call to promote the internal thrift and order, which may get on as it can, for all them. But incorporate them into it, and it is as dear as the apple of their eye.

Viewpoint 5

"Those who are loudest in their denunciations of 'foreigners' seem to forget what 'foreigners' have done for the country."

Immigrants Should Be Allowed to Vote

Martin J. Spalding (1810-1872)

Most of the founders of the American nation were people of Protestant background. They and their descendants remained suspicious of Catholicism, the monolithic religious and political power from which their ancestors had rebelled. Their suspicion led them to fear the repercussions of political participation in American society by the Catholic immigrants who made up the largest number of immigrants during the nineteenth century. They feared Catholics would overturn American democracy in favor of a church-ruled society. Even though the number of Catholic immigrants comprised only a small percentage of voters, the specter of an organized Catholic vote sent some Americans into anti-Catholic and anti-immigrant hysteria. These nativists also feared that immigrants, particularly the Irish, held far more loyalty to their native land than to the United States. Consequently, there were many calls to restrict immigrants from voting.

Some people, however, believed this view was illogical. Martin J. Spalding, the author of the following viewpoint, was one such person. A prominent Catholic archbishop, founder of schools and churches, and outspoken against the bigotry of Know-Nothings and other nativists, he points out that immigrants contribute much to America, that Catholics are a small percentage of the total voting class, and that Catholicism promotes values that are beneficial rather than detrimental to America's democratic society. The viewpoint is excerpted from an anthology of lectures by

Spalding, originally published in Kentucky in 1855.

Much has been said and written of late years about the "foreign vote." Both parties, on the eve of elections, have been in the habit of courting "foreigners;" who have thus, against their own choice and will, been singled out from the rest of the community, and placed in a false and odious position, by political demagogues for their own vile purposes. That they have been thus severed from their fellow citizens, and insulted with the compliment of their influence as a separate body, has not been so much their fault, as it has been their misfortune. From the successful party they have generally received,—with a few honorable exceptions—little but coldness *after* the election; while from the party defeated, they have invariably received nothing but abuse and calumny. So they have been, without their own agency, placed between two fires, and have been caressed and outraged by turns. Any appeal made to them by politicians, in their character of religionists or foreigners, and not in that of American citizens, is manifestly an insult, whether so intended or not; and we trust that Catholics will always view such appeals in this light. Whenever it is question of state policy, they can have no interests different from those of their fellow citizens. The laws which will be good for the latter, will be good for them; at least they can live under any system of equal legislation which will suit the Protestant majority, with whom they cheerfully share all the burdens of the country.

Clergy Do Not Influence Vote

The Catholic bishops and clergy of the country have discreetly stood aloof, and wisely abstained from exercising any influence in the exciting political contests which have successively arisen. We ourselves, though to the manor born, have never even voted on a political question; and we believe that most of our brother prelates and clergy have adopted the same prudent precaution; not surely through any want of interest in the country, but chiefly with a view to remove from the enemies of our Church the slightest pretext for slandering our religious character. The only influence, we have sought to bring to bear on the members of our communion, has been invariably in the interests of peace, of order, and of charity for all men, even for our most bitter enemies. Whenever we have had occasion to address our people on the eve of elections, we have counseled them to avoid all violence, to be-

No Danger from Immigrant Vote

The New Englander *was published from 1834 to 1877 and then continued by the* Yale Review, *still published today. This extract was written by A. Woodbury in 1855. It points out the mathematical unlikelihood of immigrants gaining unwonted power through voting.*

Whatever danger there is to be apprehended from the mixture of foreigners with the native population, it certainly does not arise from the number of foreigners. For that is comparatively small. Does it come from the number of votes which they are able to throw, in a hotly contested election? By the tables presented in a speech delivered by Hon. N.P. Banks, of Massachusetts, during the late session of Congress, we find that, at the last presidential election, out of a canvass of 1,931,024 votes in fourteen states, giving a majority of the electoral vote, the foreign vote numbered just 258,548, or in a proportion of one to seven and a fraction. In these states there was then a foreign population of 1,763,497. The proportion of the number of voters to the population is nearly the same with the proportion of foreign voters to the whole number of votes cast. In these fourteen states it is found that of the whole foreign population 856,480 were Irish born, who were mostly Catholics. Of the remainder, nearly 1,000,000, a large proportion must be Protestants, or at least not Catholics. Assuming that seven is the ratio, we have for the sum total, in these states, of Irish voters, Catholic and Protestant, 122,354. We are very apt to hear of "millions of foreigners," and of "a half-million of Catholic voters, ignorant, superstitious, and semi-civilized, controlling our elections," and the like. We suggest that a little caution on this score, and a stricter adherence to facts, in such a discussion as the nation happens now to be engaged in, would by no means be amiss. We do not see a great deal of danger in the number of foreign voters. We apprehend that there is more to be feared from native demagogues.

ware of being carried away by passion, to be temperate, to respect the feelings and principles of their opponents; and, in the exercise of their franchise as citizens, to vote conscientiously for the men and measures they might think most likely to advance the real and permanent interests of the republic. We defy any one to prove, that we have ever attempted to exercise any other influence than this. The contrary has been occasionally asserted by unprincipled demagogues, for political effect; but the accusation, like many others made in the heat of political contests, has in every instance turned out to be a grievous slander; which was scarcely believed at the time, even by those who were most busy in giving it circulation. . . .

Catholics of foreign birth are charged, in the same breath, with voting the democratic ticket, and with being the secret or open enemies of republican government! Is it then true, that a man cannot be a democrat, without being a traitor to his country? If so, then have the destinies of this great republic been ruled, with very slight intermission, for nearly thirty years by an organized band of traitors, consisting of the vast majority of our population! Catholics can well afford to be traitors in such goodly company. We are no politicians ourselves, and, so far as we have had any political leanings, they have heretofore been to the policy of the whigs; but, in common with every man of sound judgment and liberal mind, we reprobate the spirit, which would thus inconsistently and absurdly brand the advocates of different principles as enemies of the country and of all liberty. The genius of our noble constitution is in favor of allowing to every man the largest liberty of opinion in matters of state policy, without his thereby incurring the risk of having his motives questioned or his loyalty impeached. If any charge could be consistently made or sustained against this large portion of our Catholic population, it would be, on the contrary, that they have been generally in favor of too enlarged a liberty, to tally with the views of those who profess to belong to the conservative school; but to charge them with an intention to undermine our republic, is simply an absurdity, as glaring as it is malicious.

Immigrants' Contributions

Those who are loudest in their denunciations of "foreigners" seem to forget what "foreigners" have done for the country. They have filled our army and navy; they have fought our battles; they have leveled our forests, peopled our vast unoccupied territory, and filled our cities with operatives and mechanics; they have dug our canals, built our turnpikes and railroads, and have thus promoted, more perhaps than any other class, the improvement of the country and the development of its vast resources; in a word, they have, in every way, largely contributed towards enhancing the wealth and increasing the prosperity of the republic. Do they deserve nothing but bitter denunciation and unsparing invective for all these services? Are they to be branded as aliens and traitors, for having thus effectually labored to serve their adopted country?

But they are foreigners in feeling and in interest, and they still prefer their own nationality to ours. We answer first, that if this their alleged feeling be excessive, and if it tend to diminish their love for the country of their adoption, it is certainly in so far reprehensible; but where is the evidence that this is the case? Has their lingering love for the country of their birth,—with its glowing memories of early childhood and ripening manhood, of a mother's care and a sister's love,—interfered in aught with their new class of duties as American citizens? Has it prevented their sharing cheerfully in the burdens, in the labors, and in the perils of the country? We believe not. Instead of their being unconcerned and indifferent, their chief fault, in the eyes of their enemies, lies precisely in the opposite,—in their taking *too much* interest in the affairs of the republic. We answer, in the second place, that this natural feeling of love for the country of their birth, growing as it does out of that cherished and honorable sentiment which we denominate patriotism, will, in the very nature of things, gradually diminish under the influence of new associations, until it will finally be absorbed into the one homogeneous nationality; and thus the evil—if it be an evil—will remedy itself. The only thing which can possibly keep it alive for any considerable time, would be precisely the narrow and proscriptive policy, adopted in regard to citizens of foreign birth by the Know Nothings and their sympathizers. The endeavor to stifle this feeling by clamor and violence will but increase its intensity.

Loyal Citizens

This extract from an 1848 document from the New York State Assembly, called Report of Select Committee on Allowing Resident Aliens to Hold Real Estate, *asserts that immigrants are just as likely to be loyal citizens as are "native" Americans.*

To all those foreigners, who in good faith desire to assume the political rights and duties of American citizens, we wisely offer a cordial welcome, and every facility for investing themselves with all the rights and privileges of our republican brotherhood. We act on the principle, that although they may not be as thoroughly American as those who are born on the soil, still they are sure to be much more so, with the rights, duties, and privileges of citizens voluntarily assumed, than they can be as the dissatisfied, partially proscribed, and merely tolerated inhabitants, whom we mark with disabilities, and look upon with suspicion. . . . All experience and observation has shown that there are no truer American citizens than the children of those who came among us as aliens.

We answer thirdly, that the influence of Catholicity tends strongly to break down all barriers of separate nationalities, and to bring about a brotherhood of citizens, in which the love of our common country and of one another would absorb every sectional feeling. Catholicity is of no nation, of no language, of no people; she knows no geographical bounds; she breaks down all the walls of separation between race and race, and she looks alike upon every people, and tribe, and caste. Her views are as enlarged as the territory which she inhabits; and this is as wide as the world. Jew and gentile, Greek and barbarian; Irish, German, French, English, and American, are all alike to her. In this country, to which people of so many nations have flocked for shelter against the evils they endured at home, we have a striking illustration of this truly Catholic spirit of the Church. Germans, Irish, French, Italians, Spaniards, Poles, Hungarians, Hollanders, Belgians, English, Scotch, and Welch; differing in language, in national customs, in prejudices,—in every thing human,—are here brought together in the same Church, professing the same faith, and worshiping like brothers at the same altars! The evident tendency of this principle is, to level all sectional feelings and local prejudices, by enlarging the views of mankind, and thus to bring about harmony in society, based upon mutual forbearance and charity. And in fact, so far as the influence of our Church could be brought to bear upon the anomalous condition of society in America, it has been exercised for securing the desirable result of causing all its heterogeneous elements to be merged in the one variegated, but homogeneous nationality. Protestantism isolates and divides; Catholicity brings together and unites. Such have been the results of the two systems in times past; such, from their very nature, must be their influence on society at all times and in all places.

"Satan Against Christ"

The character of the foreign immigration into this country has been undergoing a considerable change within the last few years; the German element now strongly predominates over the Irish, and perhaps the Protestant and infidel, over the Catholic. The disastrous issue of the revolutionary movements which convulsed all Europe in 1848-9, has thrown upon our shores masses of foreign political refugees, most of whom are infidels in religion, and red republicans, or destructionists of all social order, in politics. The greatest, and, in fact, the only real danger to the permanency of our republican institutions, is to be apprehended from this fast increasing class of foreigners, composed in general, of men of desperate character and fortune,—of outlaws from society, with the brand of infidelity upon their brow. Against the anarchical principles advocated by these men the Catholic Church takes open ground; and she feels honored by their bitter hostility. It could not be otherwise. Her principles are eminently conservative in all questions of religion and of civil polity; theirs are radical and destructive in both. Theirs is the old war of Satan Against Christ; of the sons of Belial against the keepers of the law; of false and anti-social against true and rational liberty—"the liberty of the glory of the children of God."

If the lately organized secret political association warred against the pernicious principles maintained by such foreigners as these, we would not only have no cause to complain, but we would rather applaud their patriotic efforts in the cause of true freedom, and bid them God speed. But what is our astonishment to find, that our boasted advocates of "American principles," instead of opposing, secretly or openly sympathize with these sworn enemies of all religion and of all social order—of God and man; as well as with the reckless and blood-stained Irish Orangemen! Say what you will, their efforts are directed almost solely against the Catholic element in the foreign immigration, and chiefly against the Irish Catholics. Their professions are belied by their acts, all of which point to Catholicity, as the victim whose ruin is to be accomplished, at all hazards, in this *free* and *republican* country. What else is indicated by the bloody riots gotten up by hired street brawlers against the Irish Catholics; what else by the wrecking and burning of Catholic churches? If the true policy of the country demands a revision or repeal of the naturalization laws, then bring about this result by fair, consistent, and honorable means; set about it in an open and manly manner, as men, as Americans, as Christians, not as cowards fearing the light of day, and skulking beneath the cover of darkness. If a new policy in regard to foreign immigrants is to be adopted, or if even the alien and sedition laws are to be re-enacted, let the country know your purpose in time, that all the true lovers of freedom may be prepared for the issue.

"For the sake of humanity—for the sake of your country . . . do not rally to the polls this living mass of moral putrescence and pitiable ignorance."

Immigrants Should Not Be Allowed to Vote

L.C. Levin (1808-1860)

L.C. Levin was a representative in Congress in the mid-nine-teenth century. He, like many Americans, deeply feared the impact the seeming invasion of foreigners would have on the country. Levin and many others viewed foreigners, particularly the Irish, as ignorant and corrupt. They feared that if foreigners were allowed to participate in the political process, they would take over American institutions and band together to ensure victory for their foreign causes.

The following viewpoint is excerpted from a speech Levin gave in Congress on February 1, 1847. In it, he details the despicable qualities of the immigrants and pleads with his congressional colleagues not to allow immigrants to vote until they have proven themselves good and loyal Americans.

The proposition of the Native Americans [is] a plain one. If, in the time of Mr. Jefferson it was deemed necessary, in self-defence, to pass a five-year law [that is, a requirement of five years' residence before naturalization]—when our western country was a wilderness—when educated and responsible men only came as emigrants—when only six or eight thousand annually landed at all the ports of the United States—and when they *melted* into the mass of American population, what ought to be the check now, in view of the change in the condition of our country—in view of the deteriorated character of the foreign population—in view of the fact that nearly two hundred thousand had landed *at the single port* of New York since the first day of March last, and that instead of amalgamating with the mass of the American population, they stand out as a distinct political organization, under the control of foreign leaders? Of these thousands of emigrants who annually flood our shores, how few are qualified to assume the functions of a republican voter, or discharge the duties of an American citizen in any of the political relations of life! In relation to their numbers, they present a frightful array of power, especially when we cast a prospective glance into the future, and contemplate what they will be, if not arrested by timely legislation.

The quantity of this foreign material, imported for political manufacture, [said Mr. Levin] was not less alarming than its quality, and its quality caused the American to shudder when he reflected that such elements would be brought to bear to accomplish the overthrow of our inestimable institutions. Can the tenants of the poor-houses of Europe land on our shores with faculties so formed by nature, or so fashioned by education, as to become the conservative element of our free institutions, whose very basis demands intelligence, patriotism, and virtue in the voter? This question answered itself. No American was willing to rest the conservation of his freedom on such a foundation, were he not attached to one or the other of the two old parties of the day, who rely on it as a necessary means of political aggrandizement. And herein resides the evil of foreign immigration, and the evil of the foreign vote which both the old parties so devoutly court, as the only means by which they can vanquish each other. . . .

Obsolete Laws

The foreign vote in the United States now amounted to nearly half a million, and was fully competent to turn the scale from Whig to Democrat, or Democrat to Whig, at every annual election. Both the old parties seemed to feel that their very existence depended on the continuance of the supply: the Democrats having possession of it—the Whigs hoping to secure it; and hence neither seemed willing to choke up the fountain that nourished the upas tree of their power. . . . Your naturalization laws are obsolete in principle—obsolete in object—obsolete in tendency and most destructive in practice. Their obvious and laudable design,

Samuel Busey, author of Immigration: Its Evils and Consequences, *published in 1856, points out the dangers of immigrants developing organizations strong enough to influence elections in a way to benefit immigrants and harm "native" Americans.*

In late years, immigration has greatly increased. Foreign organizations have become more numerous and formidable, and their attempts to obtain political power more frequent.

At a charter election, held in the city of New York, a few years ago, the following hand-bill was published by the Irish organization, and extensively circulated, to wit:

Irishmen to your posts, or you will lose America. By perseverance you may become its rulers. By negligence you will become its slaves. Your own country was lost by submitting to ambitious rulers. This beautiful country you gain by being firm and united. Vote the tickets Alexander Stewart, Alderman; Edward Flannigan, Assessor, both true Irishmen. . . .

Numerous instances could be cited where the leaders of political parties have been compelled to submit to the decision of the foreign population of their respective election districts. . . .

When foreigners enjoying our hospitality as they do, assume to set up a standard of "Democracy" which proscribes a portion of their benefactors, it is high time that the birth-right qualification for office and voting should be established.

when first passed, was to adopt a class of aliens as American citizens who were qualified by morals, manners, and education to aid in the expansion of our then wild country and the consolidation of our new and untried government. Wise in their generation, they have now become the political opprobrium of the nation. An enlightened policy conforming to existing circumstances appeals to us to wipe those antiquated laws from our statute books. Europe no longer drives her valuable and gifted sons, her useful and virtuous subjects from her domains by the persecutions of state policy, or the tortures of bigoted superstition.

No Vote for Foreigners

A new era has broken upon Europe. Famine and liberality seem to go hand in hand. One plague now settles upon Europe, and that reaches only the lowest class of her population. The potato rot has spread famine among that class of her population, who, born to labor, languish in want and die in ignorance of their right to the morsel which would have saved them from an agonizing death. The policy of their governments now is, to burden us with this refuse mass of wretchedness, and rid themselves of those who populate their poor-houses. To feed these unhappy beings when they come among us, is a work of humanity. God forbid, while we have bread, we should refuse it to the cravings of hunger! But that is not the question. An American never disputes a point of charity, or benevolence. You may increase your poor-rates, according to the extent of your humane sympathies, and none will blame you for your effort to hush the cries of suffering humanity. But there stop. Feed them, clothe them, shelter them; but for the sake of humanity—for the sake of your country—for the sake of your children, do not endow them with the attribute of sovereignty, do not rally to the polls this living mass of moral putrescence and pitiable ignorance. This is the point at which to suspend the further operation of your naturalization laws, and protect your country against the political influence of the starved-out refugees of European poor-houses and almshouses—hundreds of whom, as the memorials from New York assert, perish on our wharves as they land, and thousands of whom are driven to crime to obtain the first morsel they eat among us.

Shall such men, sir, compete with free Americans in the exercise of the right of suffrage? Shall we taint our institutions by political fellowship with such as these, who in the hands of artful and designing demagogues are banded together, to give the casting vote for the rulers of the land, whether those rulers be honest or culpable—competent or incapable—patriots or traitors? No logic can refute the truth of this position as a general position, that in proportion as the constituency are debased, the Government will be corrupt, incapable, and unscrupulous, and our organic institutions in danger of dissolution from the disgust and want of faith excited by their infraction. A government certain of election will rush headlong into all party excesses, calculating on impunity in the vices or ignorance of the people to apply the political penalty to its violators. This combination of foreign voters devoted to the party which favors its political franchise, amounts to impunity for official folly and administrative crime.

VIEWPOINT 7

"We shall never be able to bring about a homogeneity in the diverse elements of our alien population except through compulsory education in the national language."

Retention of Immigrants' Native Language Harms America

Rena Michaels Atchison

A persistent American debate has been whether immigrants should retain characteristics of their native cultures. These characteristics include language; family, social, political, and religious values and practices; and living standards. Many Americans feel that by retaining these traits, immigrants demonstrate their unwillingness or inability to become truly American. Others feel that these foreign traits threaten to degrade American society. In the minds of many Americans, language is the key trait that can make or break an immigrant's assimilation into American society.

In the nineteenth century, when a huge number of immigrants were German and a smaller number Scandinavian, debate raged over whether immigrants should be required to learn English and whether schools should be required to instruct in English only. (In some areas, notably the Midwest where many Germans and Scandinavians had settled, many schools taught bilingually; a few Catholic and Lutheran parochial schools taught exclusively in German, Norwegian, or Swedish.) Rena Michaels Atchison was one advocate of monolingual schooling. A sociologist, Atchison believed that bilingual education encouraged disloyalty to the United States and that, in effect, the United States was financing its own downfall by providing such schooling to immigrants. The following viewpoint is excerpted from her 1894 book *Un-American Immigration* (Chicago: Charles H. Kerr and Company).

No part of the public school funds should be applied to the maintenance of schools in foreign languages for the benefit of an alien population.

The most naturalizing and nationalizing influence that can be brought to bear upon our foreign population is the public school taught in the national language, and we shall never be able to bring about a homogeneity in the diverse elements of our alien population except through compulsory education in the national language. In all the States having a large foreign element, a large percentage of the foreign population can neither speak, read nor write the national language.

In some of the Southern States where the proportion of the foreign element is small we find a lower per cent, but in general the percentage is uniform relative to the foreign population. The following table gives the percentage of our alien population in each State and Territory of the Union, who cannot speak English:

North Atlantic Division and North Central Division.	Per cent of foreign element who cannot speak English.	North Atlantic Division and North Central Division.	Per cent of foreign element who cannot speak English.
Maine	17.30	Illinois	30.24
New Hampshire	27.66	Michigan	27.99
Vermont	12.52	Wisconsin	42.23
Massachusetts	13.38	Minnesota	34.26
Rhode Island	15.19	Iowa	29.02
Connecticut	21.76	Missouri	23.42
New York	37.76	North Dakota	21.07
New Jersey	34.19	South Dakota	33.21
Pennsylvania	41.40	Nebraska	34.30
Ohio	35.43	Kansas	29.12
Indiana	26.10		

South Atlantic Division and South Central Division.	Per cent of foreign element who cannot speak English.	Western Division.	Per cent of foreign element who cannot speak English.
Delaware	24.59	Montana	24.26
Maryland	33.76	Wyoming	36.83
District of Columbia	7.91	Colorado	31.15
Virginia	28.76	New Mexico	53.91
West Virginia	34.91	Arizona	63.66
North Carolina	8.35	Utah	21.16
South Carolina	6.52	Nevada	37.39
Georgia	8.04	Idaho	41.12
Florida	43.14	Washington	23.45
Kentucky	21.86	Oregon	56.27
Tennessee	12.45	California	48.83
Alabama	12.64		
Mississippi	13.22		
Louisiana	38.87		
Texas	60.54		
Oklahoma	9.76		
Arkansas	18.83		

In other words, 24.98 per cent, or in general terms very nearly 25 per cent of our alien population cannot speak the national language, and it should be remembered that these large numbers are mainly found in our large cities where this possible illiterate and irresponsible citizenship will be most dangerous in its effects.

The table above given does not take into account another rapidly growing element, i.e., children of foreign born parents, born on American soil, who are either not educated at all, or are educated in parochial schools, taught exclusively in their native languages, and who, when arraigned in courts of justice, have to be sworn through an interpreter. Cases of this character were cited before the Committee of the Fiftieth Congress, and any one familiar with Chicago knows that there are children born in that city, who cannot speak the English language. . . .

The prejudices of race and religion have conspired to oppose the right of the State, to insist upon bringing about the homogeneity of its citizenship by compulsory education in the national language. We have the strange spectacle of these historic foes in Europe, German Lutheranism and Roman Catholicism conspiring in America against our public schools.

German Lutherans, who have never raised a question as to the propriety of compulsory education in the schools and universities of the fatherland controlled by the imperial government, rise *en masse* to protest against compulsory education in the schools controlled by the State in their adopted country. Obviously there can be but one reason, and that is the wish to perpetuate, through their parochial schools, the German race in America with its language and racial and religious prejudices intact. . . .

We should remember, however, that no nation has become permanently great except through the crystallization of its highest ideals into a great national literature. But what national literature can spring up in America if we are to be divided into petty Germanies and Scandinavias, and little Italies, Bohemias, Hungaries and Russias, each fostering its lingual prejudices and race antipathies? We cannot lose sight of the fact that if we are ever to become a nation permanently great, we shall have to become a homogeneous nation, with a common patriotism, a common country, a common language and a common literature, and this can only be accomplished through the education of our widely diverse elements of citizenship in common schools taught in the national language.

Viewpoint 8

"It is no dependable sign that a man is a good citizen just because he can speak only English."

Retention of Immigrants' Native Language Does Not Harm America

Waldemar Ager (1869-1941)

While many Americans and immigrants believed that complete abandonment of old-country cultural traits was an essential step toward becoming American, others believed it was possible to keep the good aspects of the old culture while acquiring the good aspects of the new. Some saw the old traits in a sort of nostalgic, decorative way. Others thought they made a valuable contribution to the enrichment of America.

Norwegian-born Waldemar Ager was the editor of *Kvartalskrift*, a Norwegian-language quarterly published by the Norwegian Society of America. Ager militantly promoted the retention of Norwegian culture by immigrants. He believed that the old ways had shaped the immigrants and were an essential part of their being. To abandon the old ways was to kill a part of their self. Ager was particularly firm on the matter of retaining the old language. Speaking Norwegian as well as English, he believed, enabled immigrants to maintain the strength of their own characters, as well as to produce strong, hard-working, patriotic families that would be a credit to the United States.

Do we need to strive to preserve our mother tongue? This is a question which presents itself to us as an immigrant group. A goodly number seem to think that the Norwegian language is only suited for the "old man" or the "old woman," that the ones who want to advance in this country had better slip into the new conditions and become Americanized as quickly as possible. To do this they must shake off everything that reminds them of a foreign culture as soon as practicable. . . .

The Nature of Character

A character is not a single virtue or a single peculiarity, but several suited and joined on a firm base to result in a harmonious whole. One cannot form character by orders or recipes from cookbooks. It must have its deep origin in the child's inborn ability to attach itself to its own family and to its race. The education and the heritage which parents can give a child ought to stress that it should feel related to this larger family. And it must then become a further extension of its own racial inheritance.

To form a character which is worth much in life's struggle, a fundamental element is required: a mother tongue tied to pride in family and race. The greater part of the Norwegian youth who grow up in this country receive neither the one nor the other. That is the failure and fault of the parents, for no child is born, be it ever so poor, that does not possess a God-given right to a mother tongue accompanied by the love of a fatherland.

Researchers have hardly penetrated deeply enough into the importance of language in a person's spiritual life. One knows that a nation's language is its history and surely that refers back to the country's origin in its misty past. And the words through centuries-long adaptations and additions are naturally better suited to the characteristic dispositions and perceptions of the same race than are those of a hastily acquired language. When all is said, there is for each individual only one language which can reach the inner recesses of the mind—and that is the mother tongue. . . .

The majority of the Norwegian children who grow up here do not acquire a mother tongue. Mother has one; she got that from her mother, but she has a feeling that it is not good enough for her children. The women want "smart" children, and they tell each other proudly that their children do not understand a single word of Norwegian. Not a word—if they want to be really swank. What the women themselves can say is restricted to household words like "Shut your mouth," "Quit that monkey business," and the like. Then comes the day—a bitter day—when the parents discover that they cannot converse intelligently with their own children.

The children leave the home and go into the world without having learned to know their parents. They never got to know the soul of the mother or the heart strings of the father. They could have learned these things through the language—the language of the heart.

Others can—even if they are old and gray—close their eyes and hear their fathers' and mothers' voices after they are departed. One remembers their stories and advice. One really does not have any other storehouse of sustenance to draw upon when the world about threatens evil. We need just such a source of strength in life's struggle. This treasure, this heritage, the poorest mother can give to her son, her daughter. And it is a treasure that neither moth nor rust can destroy. It shall build a wall around the character and protect a younger person when evil days appear.

Under what influence do the smart Norwegian children of the even smarter Norwegian parents grow up? The answer is that of a stammering mother who couldn't make herself sufficiently understood—who couldn't express herself the way she wanted to, because she herself didn't understand the words she used. They were brought up by mother who could not in a motherly way express her words because they often became a hindrance. Such expressions as "What's the matter with you?", "Never mind that," and "Quit that monkey business" are not much to sustain a human soul in life's struggle. . . .

Haven't the Americanized Norwegian young people shown a strong tendency to scorn their parents? Not only do they often reject the father's Norwegian name—if he himself has not rejected it—but without the slightest compunction they sell the father's old homestead no matter how much toil has been exerted to create it. For these young people, the childhood home only represents so and so much per acre. The father is dead and often forgotten long before the preacher has thrown three shovels of dirt on him. Has anyone seen any person prosper who despised or did not honor his parents?

How is it possible for the "smart" Norwegian children to honor their even "smarter" parents? Since they do not understand the parents' mother tongue, they can never enter into their parents' thoughts. But they must experience something; so their first impressions are derived from the streets closest to the home. Because of their superior knowledge of the English language, it often becomes the children who lead the parents instead of the parents leading the children. Many parents learn their English from their children, who thus become their teachers. The children learn certain expressions on the streets and pass them on to their parents. The habits of the street penetrate the home. The children get the impression early that they are superior to their parents.

The most pitiful sight I know is that of a father who stammers and struggles to make himself understandable to his own child—like an awkward suitor who is at a loss for words. If the child doesn't get the impression that the father is a dullard, then it is because the child itself has a low mentality. Such childhood experiences do not serve to teach the youngster to honor his parents. . . .

Combine the Best of Old and New

Carl Schurz was a prominent German-American politician, journalist, orator, and patriot. Masterfully fluent in both German and English, he believed that it was possible for immigrants to retain their old language and still be loyal Americans. He believed that the foreign-language press enabled immigrants who had poor English skills to become more Americanized, because these immigrant newspapers transmitted much information about America. In this excerpt from a speech presented to the Deutscher Liederkranz of New York (a choral society), presented in German and translated by his daughter, Schurz extols the worth of retaining the German tongue.

We possess, in truth, a treasure which we cannot prize highly enough, especially we who have made a new home in a new world speaking another language. It is sometimes expected of our compatriots in America that they shall not only learn English, but that they shall entirely cast aside the old mothertongue. That is very unwise advice. Nobody will dispute that the German-American must learn English. He owes it to his new country and he owes it to himself. But it is more than folly to say that he ought, therefore, to give up the German language. As American citizens we must become Americanized; that is absolutely necessary. I have always been in favor of a sensible Americanization, but this need not mean a complete abandonment of all that is German. It means that we should adopt the best traits of American character and join them to the best traits of German character. By so doing we shall make the most valuable contribution to the American nation, to American civilization.

One cannot teach children to honor their parents in the way many well-meaning but stupid Norwegian parents raise them. From the time the child is old enough to understand, it learns that food which it does not like is old-country food, outmoded and ugly clothing is old-country style, peculiar people with crooked legs and hunchbacks are old-countrylike, awkward people who say grace at the table are of the old country. Two braids on the back or a patch on the pants are old-country style. To make use of hands, to patch, to darn, to exhibit ridiculous thrift are old-country ways. The quintessence of everything stupid, ill-bred, distasteful, intolerable is so because it exists in the old country. Mother is "peculiar" and in many ways "funny," an acquisition from the old country. Grandmother is even "funnier" and "queerer," for she is even more old-countrylike. That is the child's idea about mother and grandmother. In such a manner it learns to honor them.

And when the children early learn to scorn their parents, it is because something old-country is always attached to them. You may be sure that in just the way you taught your children to make fun of your parents, your offspring will teach their youngsters to make fun of you. The honor you denied your parents will also escape you. When children grow up under these conditions, they draw apart from their parents. Mother gets only the recognition which a waitress expects, and as regards "papa," his children are only interested in what he can earn.

I will note here that we as a race have just as much right to honor the memory of our forefathers who were Norsemen as the New Englanders have to honor their ancestors who were English. I believe the same about the citizens of the Southern states whose forebears were French or Spanish. Hopefully, a man can be just as good a citizen whether he knows one or two languages. We show our loyalty best in educating men and women with character. It is no dependable sign that a man is a good citizen just because he can speak only English.

Feelings of nationality, traditions, race are very important elements in the formation of a character that will leave its imprint. The great reformers like Luther and Melanchthon, authors like Goethe and Schiller, musicians like Mozart and Beethoven, or a philosopher like Kant—all are stamped with peculiarities belonging to the Germans. . . . The somber English sense of reality and energy that one finds in Darwin and Newton one also discovers in the dramas of Shakespeare as well as in the sermons of Spurgeon. The glow and color of the Italian do not leave him in Raphael's paintings, Dante's poetry, or Paganini's music. . . .

Their accomplishments were not only determined by their talent but also conditioned by the capacities they had absorbed from the peculiarities and advantages of their race.

And, therefore, many basic qualities are demanded to instill character in a man whether he be insignificant or be held in high regard in the world. The same courage and obstinacy which the Norwegians evidenced in 1814, when they wanted to build an independent state, are just as necessary today in the poor Norwegian who wants to clear a quarter section of land in the forests of Wisconsin or to build himself a future home on the great prairies.

CHAPTER 3

The New Immigrants: The Southern and Eastern Europeans

Chapter Preface

In the 1880s and 1890s immigration to the United States took a new direction. In the first seven decades of the nineteenth century, immigration had come largely from Britain, Ireland, and Germany. Suddenly, in the 1880s, as political and economic conditions began to change dramatically both in the United States and in Europe, streams of people began coming from southern and eastern Europe. Italy, Greece, Poland, Russia, and Albania were a few of these new countries of origin. In the first decades of the century, only about 2 percent, or 200,000 of the more than 10 million immigrants, had been from these countries. In the 1880s, of the approximately 5 million immigrants, 72 percent were still from Germany, Ireland, Britain, Scandinavia, and other European countries. But a whopping 20 percent—more than 1 million— were from the new sources. In the next three decades, the "new

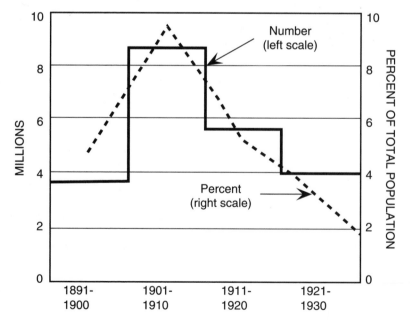

Immigrants Admitted: 1891-1930

Source: *The Ethnic Almanac.*

immigrants," as they came to be called, made up 60 percent of the more than 18 million newcomers, while northern and western Europeans shrank to less than 30 percent—only about 5 million.

This new wave of immigration had a character entirely different from the largely Irish and German immigration of the early and middle nineteenth century. While there had been cultural differences between the Irish and Germans and the "native" Americans, the differences were even greater with the new immigrants. Most of these people were of Mediterranean and Asian origin. Most spoke languages unintelligible to Americans. Most had dark skin, hair, and eyes, in contrast to the lighter skin and features of the northern and western Europeans who had come in the earlier nineteenth century. Most were Catholic or Jewish, and a few were Arab. The new immigrants were poor, and a large percentage were poorly educated, even illiterate. Many Americans—and many of the old immigrants—found all of these traits undesirable and threatening to American society.

As had immigrants in the past, the newcomers tended to congregate with their compatriots. This seemed a necessary first step for newcomers who could not speak the language of the new country and who depended on fellow immigrants for information about jobs, housing, and other aspects of getting along in the new land. These ethnic enclaves were offensive and frightening to Americans. They seemed to prove that the newcomers were not sincere about becoming Americans. They also seemed to indicate that the new immigrants would cling to their foreign lifestyles and languages and would intermingle with and degrade the "real" America.

The new immigrants, like the immigrants before them, faced discrimination in hiring, housing, and other aspects of American life. "No Italians need apply" became as common a sign over company doors as "No Irish need apply" had been a generation earlier. Settlement houses, social workers, and educators worked hard to help the new immigrants assimilate. But even among these people conflict was common: They could not agree on whether integrating immigrants into American life meant encouraging them to abandon all traces of their old cultures or to somehow adapt their customs to complement American ways.

As the United States entered its second century as a nation, Americans continued to debate the role of immigrants in their society.

VIEWPOINT 1

"History shows that it has usually been the peaceful migrations and not the conquering armies which have undermined and changed the institutions of peoples."

The New Immigrants Threaten America's Racial Stock

Prescott F. Hall (1868-1921)

Prescott F. Hall was the executive secretary of the Immigration Restriction League and a prominent spokesperson and frequent writer on the topic of immigration. Among his books are *Immigration and Its Effects* and *The Selection of Immigrants*. He strongly believed that the massive immigration between 1880 and 1920 was harmful to the United States in a number of ways.

The following viewpoint was first published in the January 1912 issue of the *North American Review*, a prominent monthly journal that has published articles on politics, social issues, and literature from 1815 to the present day. In this article, Hall asserts that the new immigrants, those predominantly from southern and eastern European nations, are of different racial stock than were those people who founded the United States and those who emigrated here in huge numbers earlier in the nineteenth century. These new immigrants, he says, will irretrievably weaken the racial stock of America and thus weaken America itself. He believed that nature (heredity) shapes character and that nurture (environment) cannot overcome inborn weaknesses. Thus, education, promoted by many as a way to make foreigners into good Americans, cannot succeed in making these new immigrants of positive value to the nation, Hall concludes.

Gobineau once said, "America is likely to be, not the cradle of a new, but the grave of an old race." Is there, indeed, a danger that the race which has made our country great will pass away, and that the ideals and institutions which it has cherished will also pass?

It seems to be generally agreed that down to the period of fifteen years or so after the close of the Civil War there was a fairly definite American type, which had expressed itself, not so much in literature or art, as in politics and invention, and in certain social ideals. Washington and Lincoln, however different in some respects, both represented a certain type of English civilization, and both stood for certain political, social, and ethical points of view. The original settlers of this country were mainly Teutonic, belonging to what is now called the Baltic race, from northern Europe, which has always been distinguished for energy, initiative, and self-reliance. Impatient of much government, relying upon self-help rather than the paternalism of the State, this race was none the less firm in its allegiance to certain pretty definite religious and social standards. It insisted from the beginning on general education, and where opportunities for schooling were wanting there was nevertheless a wide training given by interchange of ideas in the home, on the farm, in the church, and in the town meeting. In town affairs every citizen was expected to take part, and usually did so, thus conferring a benefit on the community and receiving something in exchange. The result of this common racial origin and of these relatively homogeneous institutions was, as I have said, the amalgamation of the people into a fairly definite national type.

(Perhaps the best statement of the proper conditions of race mixture is in Houston Stewart Chamberlain's *Foundations of the XIXth Century*, vol. i, chap. iv, "The Chaos." He points out that the successful cases of amalgamation have been those where there has been an immigration of kindred races only, and such immigration has continued for a comparatively brief period and then ceased. This was precisely the situation in the United States prior to 1880.)

What has happened since then? To-day, less than one-half of

"Native" American Threatened

Madison Grant, author of the 1916 book The Passing of the Great Race, *warned that America's racial strength was threatened by the influx of racially and genetically inferior "new" immigrants foisted off on our complacent country by a sly and grateful Europe.*

These new immigrants were no longer exclusively members of the Nordic race as were the earlier ones who came of their own impulse to improve their social conditions. . . . The European governments took the opportunity to unload upon careless, wealthy and hospitable America the sweepings of their jails and asylums. The result was that the new immigration . . . contained a large and increasing number of the weak, the broken and the mentally crippled of all races drawn from the lowest stratum of the Mediterranean basin and the Balkans, together with hordes of the wretched, submerged populations of the Polish Ghettos. Our jails, insane asylums and almshouses are filled with this human flotsam and the whole tone of American life, social, moral and political, has been lowered and vulgarized by them.

These immigrants adopt the language of the native American, they wear his clothes, they steal his name and they are beginning to take his women, but they seldom adopt his religion or understand his ideals. . . .

It is evident that in large sections of the country the native American will entirely disappear. He will not intermarry with inferior races and he cannot compete in the sweat shop and in the street trench with the newcomers.

One thing is certain: in any such mixture, the surviving traits will be determined by competition between the lowest and most primitive elements and the specialized traits of Nordic man; his stature, his light-colored eyes, his fair skin and light-colored hair, his straight nose and his splendid fighting and moral qualities, will have little part in the resultant mixture.

our people are descendants of the original stock and of the early settlers. Since 1820, we have received from Europe and Asia some twenty-eight millions of people. About one-third of these came prior to 1880 and were of races kindred to those already here; in other words, they had a common heritage of institutions if not of language, and were assimilated into the general population with comparative ease. The other two-thirds, the eighteen millions who have come since 1880, have been, on the other hand, of entirely different races—of Alpine, Mediterranean, Asiatic, and African stocks. These races have an entirely different mental make-up from the Baltic race; they bring with them an inheritance of widely differing political and social ideals, and a training under social and political institutions very different from ours. The Slavic races, for example, differ from the Teutonic in temperament as much as the emotional nations of the Mediterranean. The South Italian, which constitutes the largest element in our present immigration, is one of the most mixed races in Europe and is partly African, owing to the negroid migration from Carthage to Italy. The modern Greek is by no means the Greek of the time of Pericles, either in race or temperament. The Hebrew, which constitutes the next largest element of immigration, in spite of long residence in Europe is still, as it always has been, an Asiatic race; while the Syrians, Chinese, Japanese, and Hindus are still more removed from the civilization of northern Europe and America.

This movement of peoples from the Old World to the New is on a scale unprecedented in history, and its effects cannot fail to be profound and far-reaching. What will they be?

Americans have hitherto paid very little attention to this question: first, because they have not considered the difference between hostile and peaceful invasions in history; and second, because they fail to observe that recent immigration is of an entirely different kind from that which our fathers knew. The earlier immigration having been of kindred races and having produced no profound changes, our people became used to the phenomenon and took it as a matter of course. At the present time, most of us consider that the movement now going on is similar to that which has been, and anticipate results no different from those previously observed.

An Invading Hostile Army

If the million people coming every year came not as peaceful travelers, but as an invading hostile army, public opinion would be very different to what it is; and yet history shows that it has usually been the peaceful migrations and not the conquering armies which have undermined and changed the institutions of peoples. To take the classical error on this subject, we have been told repeatedly that, on the one hand, it was the conquering Goths and Vandals, and on the other hand, their own vice and luxury, which cost the Romans their empire. The real cause of the fall of Rome was neither of these things. It was the constant infiltration into Roman citizenship of large numbers of "barbarians"—that is, of races alien in instincts and habits of thought and action to the races which had built up the Roman Empire. For a time, indeed, the mold of political structure and social habit, though cracking, did not break; but the new-comers assimilated the Romans faster than they were themselves assimilated, and in time the mold broke in pieces. In precisely the same way some provinces of France are to-day becoming German, and others Italian, while the Germans are consciously making use of this method in their attempt to Prussianize Poland.

The "barbarians" of the present time, however, do not come from the plateaus of central Asia or from the jungles of Africa; they are the defective and delinquent classes of Europe—the individuals who have not been able to keep the pace at home and

---

Melting Pot Analogy Is False

In his 1920 book, The Rising Tide of Color Against White World Supremacy, *Lothrop Stoddard warned of the dangers facing the white race from increasing numbers of colored people of various races. In addition, he (and others of his time) divided the white race into three groups (Nordic, Alpine, and Mediterranean), of which the Nordic are most superior and the Mediterranean least so. In America, Stoddard warned, the huge influxes of immigrants of color and of the lower Mediterranean races, through strength of numbers and through intermarriage, threatened to dangerously degrade the white race and even to destroy its political power.*

Contrary to the popular belief, nothing is more *unstable* than the ethnic make-up of a people. Above all, there is no more absurd fallacy than the shibboleth of the "melting-pot." As a matter of fact, the melting-pot may mix but does not melt. Each race-type, formed ages ago, and "set" by millenniums of isolation and inbreeding, is a stubbornly persistent entity. Each type possesses a special set of characters: not merely the physical characters visible to the naked eye, but moral, intellectual, and spiritual characters as well. All these characters are transmitted substantially unchanged from generation to generation. . . .

Two things are necessary for the continued existence of a race: it must remain itself, and it must breed its best. Every race is the result of ages of development which evolves specialized capacities that make the race what it is and render it capable of creative achievement. These specialized capacities (which particularly mark the superior races), being relatively recent developments, are highly unstable. They are what biologists call "recessive" characters; that is, they are not nearly so "dominant" as the older, generalized characters which races inherit from remote ages and which have therefore been more firmly stamped upon the germ-plasm. Hence, when a highly specialized stock interbreeds with a different stock, the newer, less stable, specialized characters are bred out, the variation, no matter how great its potential value to human evolution, being *irretrievably lost.* This occurs even in the mating of two superior stocks if these stocks are widely dissimilar in character. The valuable specializations of both breeds cancel out, and the mixed offspring tend strongly to revert to generalized mediocrity.

---

have fallen into the lower strata of its civilization.

Formerly, America was a hard place to get to, and a hard life awaited those who came, although the free and fertile land offered rich prizes to those with the energy to grasp them. To-day, the steamship agent is in every little town in Europe; fast steamers can bring thousands in a few days, and wages, often indeed not enough for an American to live decently on, but large in the eyes of the poor European peasants, await the immigrant on landing. There is, moreover, abundant testimony to the fact that much of the present immigration is not even a normal flow of population, but is artificially stimulated in every possible way by the transportation companies which have many millions invested in the traffic.

Now there are two hopeful attitudes with regard to the possible dangers from this "peaceful invasion." One of them is that we can continue, as we have in the past, to assimilate all this material and turn it into good American citizens. This was the general attitude until recently, and is still the attitude of the average man who does not fear the future. The other attitude is that, although perhaps we cannot do this, although the aliens may to some extent assimilate us, yet the seething of the melting-pot will remove the dross and turn out a product, possibly new, but at any rate as good, if not better, than the old.

Conservation of Ideals

It is important to consider the truth of these points of view, because the social and political institutions of any country depend upon the type of its citizenship and are molded by it. Ruskin long ago observed that the only real wealth is human character, and what boots an extended railroad mileage or the fact that all our coal and minerals are dug up or all our trees cut down some years or decades sooner, if at the end our democracy goes to pieces? We have heard much lately of the conservation of natural resources, but the conservation of ideals is surely much more important.

Those who believe that we can assimilate all the aliens who may come usually qualify their belief by saying that, although we may not succeed entirely with the parents, we can succeed with the children, and that the salvation of the situation is the public school. They also point out that many immigrants have had little opportunity for improvement in their own countries and may develop rapidly in a new environment. Now just as the Latin races make a fetish of the State, we Americans are apt to make a fetish of education, and we constantly fail to discriminate between education as the molding of character and education as the imparting of information. Far the larger part of a child's education comes from his home and his companions, rather than from his schooling. Emulation and imitation are the two mainsprings of his growth. We should never forget the somewhat hackneyed truth that education, in general, brings out what is in the man, be it good or bad, and seldom puts much there which was not there before. For this reason it is very questionable whether the small amount of schooling the children of most aliens receive plays a very large part in the total of influences brought to bear upon them; and it is still more debatable whether it appreciably alters their characters, or does anything more than bring out their inherited instincts and tendencies. Undoubtedly immigrant children crowd our schools because it aids them in the struggle for existence, and is usually paid for by some one else. Undoubtedly, also, many of them obtain high marks and show considerable capacity for storing up information.

Education Cannot Compensate for Heredity

Nevertheless, as has been said, schooling is but a small part of the influences to which the child is subject, and the tendency of recent immigrants to crowd into the cities and to settle in racial groups means that a very large part of the influences affecting the children will be those of their neighbors and co-workers of the same race. As in John Bunyan's parable, a small quantity of oil poured secretly and steadily upon a fire will cause it to withstand a large quantity of water poured upon it from all directions. Moreover, to a great extent this water of public-school education will fail to quench hereditary passions, because the latter are so strong that the former will be vaporized, so to speak, and pass off without closely touching them. Dr. Gustav LeBon in his *Political Psychology*, has thus expressed this phase of the matter:

> Education merely sums up the results of a civilization; the institutions and the beliefs representing the needs of such civilization. If, then, a civilization does not harmonize with the ideas and sentiments of a people, the education setting forth this civilization will remain without effect upon it; in the same way that institutions corresponding to certain needs will not correspond to different needs.

The result in such a case will be, not a true amalgamation of races, but a mixture of peoples as in Austria-Hungary, living side by side, sharing certain interests in common, but never wholly merging into a general national type.

This is, indeed, what many educators like Dr. Charles W. Eliot expect and rejoice in. Dr. Eliot does not share in the second view—that the melting-pot will fuse the various races into one. And he rejoices because, in his view, half-breeds of any races are inferior to their parents, just as alloys of metals are not as valu-

Some Americans feared that the "new" immigrants, most from southern and eastern Europe, would degrade the American physical type.

able as the metals themselves. And he is right. The evidence on this point is convincing. Dr. Alfred P. Schultz, in his *Race or Mongrel*, gives numerous examples drawn from history, one of the most conspicuous being that of the Jews, who, wherever they have kept their racial purity, have kept also their fine qualities of energy, push, and mental alertness, but have deteriorated rapidly when intermarried with other races. Humboldt and Darwin have declared the same truth. Agassiz, in a well-known passage, says:

> Let any one who doubts the evil of the mixture of races and who is inclined from mistaken philanthropy to break down all barriers between them come to Brazil. He cannot deny the deterioration consequent upon the amalgamation of races, more wide-spread here than in any country in the world and which is rapidly effacing the best qualities of the white man, the Indian, and the negro, leaving a mongrel nondescript type deficient in physical and mental energy.

Evils of Race Mixing Foreseen

The same thing has happened in Cuba, in Mexico, and other countries to the south of us. But is there any danger of this occurring in the United States? It has not occurred in the past because the only race outside of the Teutonic immigrants present in large numbers has been the negro, and the Baltic races have an insurmountable prejudice against intermarriage with the black races.

112

The Mediterranean and Asiatic races, on the other hand, have much less of this feeling. The negro strain in the South Italians has been already mentioned, and there are some examples of intermarriage between negroes and Jews. What would happen if a large Mediterranean population should be colonized in our Southern States and should interbreed with the negro population it finds there? This is not an imaginary possibility, for the dark-skinned races are more likely to settle in the southern part of this country; indeed, it must be so if Major Woodruff is correct in his view that the blond races cannot permanently live south of the fortieth parallel on account of the effects of the light on their nervous systems. Let us assume that some interbreeding with the negroes takes place. Will the descendants of the emotional, fiery Italians submit to the social judgment that a man with a sixteenth or a thirty-second part of negro blood is a colored man who must occupy a position socially, if not politically, inferior? Assuredly not, and thoughtful Southerners are already alarmed by this prospect and have announced through many of their industrial conventions that they do not desire the immigration of southeastern Europeans. The Western States feel the same way about Asiatics, both for racial and economic reasons.

Even if the result of the immigration of southeastern Europeans to the South should not immediately be an interbreeding, the result may be to add other problems to the one we already have there. Mr. Booker T. Washington, who has recently been investigating conditions in Europe, expresses this view when he says:

> I greatly fear that if these people should come in large numbers and settle in colonies outside the cities, where they would have comparatively few educational advantages, and where they would be better able and more disposed to preserve their native customs and languages, we might have a racial problem in the South more difficult and more dangerous than that which is caused by the presence of the negro.

(The first part of this quotation is almost the exact language used by George Washington in a letter to John Adams, November 27, 1794. Of course, he was speaking of the relatively homogeneous immigration of his day.)

But whether the result be an amalgamation or a mixture, it is evident that the nation will be profoundly altered by the addition of large numbers of persons with alien habits and ideals, and that the social and political structure will be changed accordingly. Dr. LeBon, in the work above quoted, says:

> A preponderating influence of foreigners is a sure solvent of the existence of States. It takes away from a people its most precious possession—its soul. When aliens became numerous in the Roman Empire it ceased to be.

113

And again:

> It was a very sure instinct which taught the ancients the fear of strangers: they well knew that worth of a country is not measured by the number of its inhabitants, but by the number of its citizens.

Can we not already see certain effects of the newer immigration upon our social life? In many places the Continental Sunday, with its games and sports, its theatrical and musical performances, and its open bars, is taking the place of the Puritan Sabbath. In some of our factory towns there are many operatives living under the system of free marriage, and in at least one place the method of building tenements has been altered to correspond to this system. Professor Commons notes that we have already begun to despotize our institutions in order to deal with large masses of citizens not capable of intelligently supporting representative government. We see, also, the phenomena of political parties and groups on racial lines, with their own newspapers in foreign languages, seeking representation as racial units precisely as in Austria. These groups have already taken a conspicuous part in opposing immigration legislation, already existing or proposed, which makes it more difficult for their friends and relatives to come here; and, under our political system, these foreign-born groups already hold the balance of power in many places. This means that they often divide, not on public policy, but on some matter of racial advantage. In any case they do not and cannot combine to make parties like those of the older population.

Profound Changes

All these changes may be good or bad, but they cannot fail to impress us; and, if these changes rise above the swirling mass of events and catch our eyes, we may be sure that more profound changes are in process beneath the surface.

We have to contend not only with alien habits and ideals, and with the fact that these differences cannot be effaced by education in one or even two generations, but also with the fact that we are getting a great many immigrants who are below the mental, moral, and physical average of both our country and their own. A recent writer in a leading German review has said: "The immigration of the last decade has increased the number of hands, but not the number of heads, in the United States." While this may be an extreme statement, there is the unanimous testimony of the Commissioner-General of Immigration, the Commissioner at the Port of New York, and the Immigration Commission, which has recently spent several years studying the matter, to the fact that for one immigrant whose defects are so marked as to put him in the classes excluded by law there are hundreds, if not thousands, who are below the average of our people, and who, as George William Curtis put it, are "watering the nation's life blood."

Heredity More Influential than Environment

Recent investigations in eugenics show that heredity is a much more important factor than environment as regards social conditions—in fact, that in most cases heredity is what makes the environment. This is confirmed by the practice of the insurance companies which attach the chief importance to the hereditary characteristics of an individual. If this position is sound, education and distribution can only palliate the evils and delay fundamental changes. As Professor Karl Pearson says: "You cannot change the leopard's spots, and you cannot change bad stock to good; you may dilute it, possibly spread it over a large area, spoiling good stock, but until it ceases to multiply it will not cease to be."

Intelligent foreigners, like Bourget, H. G. Wells, and LeBon, are continually surprised that Americans pay so little regard to these matters. Already our neighbor to the north has become much more strict as to those she admits than we are; and, in fact, the Dominion is now rejecting at the border many whom we have admitted. And in our own practice we are not very logical, for we are much more stringent in regulations as to importing cattle, sheep, hogs, dogs, and horses than we are as to human beings. The English sparrow and the gypsy moth were not considered dangerous when first imported, but by their multiplication have done serious damage. The history of the Jukes family in New York State shows how much harm can be done by immigration of a single pair of defectives.

The foregoing is not intended to be a pessimistic wail. Our people are successful in part because they are optimistic, and in general they have little use for prophets of evil. Nor has the writer forgotten for a moment either what the country owes to past immigration, or that much of the present immigration is desirable and valuable. But our optimism should not be blind. Sumner once said of Garrison that he would go straight ahead even if the next step were over a precipice. If there is a precipice ahead we should avoid it while there is time, not merely for our own sake, but that the United States may continue strong to uphold the cause of democracy and liberty throughout the world.

VIEWPOINT 2

"Our apprehension of harm to American ideals from race mixture is nothing but prejudice."

The New Immigrants Do Not Threaten America's Racial Stock

Percy Stickney Grant (1860-1927)

Percy Stickney Grant, an author and member of the clergy, wrote several works on social issues, notably *Fair Play and the Workers, Socialism and Christianity*, and *Religion of Main Street*. Unlike H. Prescott Hall and others who wanted to dramatically curtail if not altogether stop immigration, Grant did not believe the new immigrants were detrimental to American society. He maintained that people's fears of the new immigrants "weakening" the American racial stock were based on irrational prejudices. He pointed to scientific thought supporting the idea that mixing the "races" (for the immigrants under discussion were with few exceptions Caucasian) results in a stronger breed of human.

In the following viewpoint, excerpted from the April 1912 issue of *North American Review*, Grant concedes that many of the new immigrants come to America with poor working and social skills, but he asserts that education can help them become sound and contributing citizens. He cites many authorities of his day to show that nurture is more important than nature.

The most impressive sight to be seen in America is the stream of immigrants coming off ship at Ellis Island. No waterfall or mountain holds such awesome mystery; no river or harbor, embracing the navies of the world, expresses such power; no city so puts wings to the imagination; no work of art calls with such epic beauty. But there are spectators who behold in the procession from overseas an invading army comparable to the Gothic hordes that overran Rome, who lament this meeting of Europe and America as the first act in our National Tragedy.

Undoubtedly we have a situation unknown to any other nation, past or present. In 1910 the total population of the United States was 91,972,266; of these 13,343,583 were foreign-born whites; 10,239,579 were negroes, Indians, and Asiatics. Between 1900-1910, 9,555,673 immigrants came in from over fifty races. Of the native whites forty-seven per cent. are the children of foreign-born parents. Of our entire population 43,972,185 were born of native white parents—that is, only forty per cent.

A recent writer in *The North American Review*, Prescott F. Hall, secretary of the League for Limiting Immigration and author of a volume on immigration, stated in the January number the case against the future of American ideals under the influence of race mixture. He began by quoting Gobineau: "America is likely to be not the cradle of a new, but the grave of an old race." Mr. Hall sought to sustain this prophecy.

I belong to no immigration league, "limiting" or "liberal"; I have had no admixture of blood in my own family, outside the original area of Massachusetts, for two hundred years, but I wish to suggest considerations that may calm the fears of Mr. Hall and his friends. . . .

Fears Caused by Prejudice

Broadly speaking, our apprehension of harm to American ideals from race mixture is nothing but prejudice. Much of our dread of a deterioration of the American stock by immigration is a survival of ancient jealousy and alarm which once characterized the contact of all "natives" everywhere with all "foreigners." The sight of a foreigner meant ordinarily a raid or a war. This real dread, as it was of old, lingers in our subconsciousness. The destruction of the trait will yield only to intelligence, sympathy, and civilization.

Another element in our fear is the fetish of Teutonic superiority and the dogma of Latin degeneracy. Races that have produced in our lifetime a Cavour, a Mazzini, a Louis Pasteur, that have fought and defeated ecclesiastic and feudal enemies in their own households, have much to teach us.

In the Conference on Immigration held in New York a few years ago, there were delegates scarcely able to speak the English language who orated against later arrivals in this country than themselves and predicted our downfall if they were admitted. In short, every race considers itself superior; its diatribes against other races are sheer vanity. We Americans, in conceit of superiority, are in the same class as the Chinese. William Elliot Griffis, a writer on Asiatic people, recently declared that

> after an adult lifetime of study of the peoples of the Far East, I find few or no novelties in their history or evolution as compared with that of our own rise from savagery to civilization; nor is their human nature by a hair's-breadth different from our own. What we need now to have cast in the world's melting-pot is the colossal conceit common to the white and the yellow man with more scientific comparative history.

At any rate, our free government is a standing invitation to the oppressed of other countries, and our undeveloped wealth makes a constant appeal for strong arms and hard workers. What can we do, then? We cannot shut out "foreigners" and still be true either to our own ideals or to our practical requirements. Nor can we pick and choose. There is no accepted standard of excellence except health and "literacy." Moreover, there are not enough of one foreign stock, were we to select one as the best, to do the work in the United States waiting to be done. . . .

Scientific Attitude Toward Heredity

The scientific attitude toward heredity is to-day different from a generation ago. Darwin's theory of slowly acquired characteristics and of the transmission by heredity of acquired characteristics was attacked by August Weismann, whose germ-plasm theory of heredity seriously weakened Darwin's hypothesis. Then came the botanist, De Vries, with his theory of spasmodic progress, amounting to "spasmodic appearance of species at a given time under the influence of certain special conditions."

Francis Galton brought forward the theory of mathematical inheritance, which, modified by Pearson, amounts to this: That of all the heritage which an individual possesses one-half on the average comes from his parents, one-fourth from his grandparents, and so on. Meanwhile the studies of Gregor Mendel, Abbot of Brünn, neglected for thirty-five years after their publication in 1865, came to light, with a specific body of botanical experiments leading to certain general principles of heredity. The essential part of Mendel's discoveries is the principle of the segregation of characters in the fusion of the reproductive cells or gametes, with its natural corollary, the purity of the gametes. Mendel did not believe in blends, but in the unit character of heredity.

Two theories of heredity are now current:

1. Children show a tendency to revert to a type intermediate between the types of the two parents, or in cases of changes of types to another type, dependent upon the mid-parental type. In other words, the characteristics of the parents are blended in the children.

2. Either the father's or the mother's type, or the type of a more remote ancestor, is reproduced, and certain parental traits may be dominant over others—i.e., on particular trait, either father's or mother's, to appear with greater frequency in the children than the corresponding but different trait of the other parent. (*Change in Bodily Form of Descendants of Immigrants*, by Franz Boas.)

An inquiry into the values of a cephalic index (that is, the ratio of the width of the head to the length) has shown clearly that the type of heredity in intermarriages in the same race is that of alternating heredity. Children do not form a blend between their parents, but revert either to one type or the other.

American "Race" Still Evolving

John Palmer Gavit, author of Americans by Choice, *from which this excerpt is taken, strongly believed that immigrants had a great deal to contribute to American society. Unlike many people of his time who were enthralled with the relatively new science of eugenics, Gavit believed the immigrant "races" would only strengthen the American.*

Let us come straight to the fact that this absence of exclusive racial marks is the distinguishing physical characteristic of the American. True of him as of no other now or ever in the past, is the fact that he is, broadly speaking, the product of *all* races. It is of our fundamental history and tradition from the beginning that in America all peoples may find destination, if not refuge, and upon a basis of virtual race equality mingle, and for good or ill, send down to posterity in a common stream their racial values—and their racial defects. Whether we like it or not, this is the fact. We are not a race, in any ethnic sense. At most, we are in the very early stages of becoming one. . . .

We are in the midst of the making of the "American." It does not yet appear what he shall be, but one thing is certain, he is not to be of any particular racial type now distinguishable. Saxon, Teuton, and Kelt, Latin and Slav—to say nothing of any appreciable contribution by yellow and brown races as yet negligible in this aspect of the question—each of the races that we now know on this soil will have its share of "ancestorial" responsibility for the "typical American" that is to be.

Mendel's law attaches so much value to "dominant" and so much danger to "recessive" units that under his theory, it would be natural to try to divide races into the old categories of sheep and goats. But even under the operation of his law a mixed race has advantages over a pure race. [Charles B. Davenport writes in the *Annals of American Academy*:]

> The clear lesson of Mendelian studies to human society is this: That when two parents with the same defect marry—and there is none of us without some defect—*all* of the progeny must have the same defect, and there is no remedy for the defect by education, but only, at the most in a few cases, by a surgical operation. The presence of a character in one parent will dominate over its absence in the other parent; . . . the advanced position masters the retarded or absent condition.

[He adds:] *"The mating of dissimilars favors a combination in the offspring of the strongest characteristics of both parents and fits them the better for human society."* A strong argument for miscegenation.

Environment More Important than Heredity

Environment to-day is considered a most important factor in heredity by students outside the ranks of pure biologists. Take such a fact as this, that the intellectual classes among the Magyars, the Uralo-Altaic peoples, the Slavs or German races, furnish us with identical measurements of trunk, extremities, etc., whereas individuals of the same race differ considerably when once distinctly separated by their occupations. Another fact in the same direction is that the measurements of Austrian Jews correspond entirely with those that Gould mentioned in the case of cultivated persons in the United States. The Austrian Jews are not engaged in mercantile work, but almost exclusively are money-lenders, small shop-keepers, lawyers, and doctors [according to Jean Finot in his book *Race Prejudice*].

We all agree with Professor Ripley that

> the first impression from comparison of our original Anglo-Saxon ancestry in America with the motley crowd now pouring in upon us is not cheering. It seems a hopeless task to cope with them, to assimilate them with our present native-born population.

But listen further:

> Yet there are distinctly encouraging features about it all. These people, in the main, have excellent physical qualities, in spite of unfavorable environment and political oppression for generations. No finer physical type than the peasantry of Austro-Hungary are to be found in Europe. The Italians, with an out-of-door life and proper food, are not weaklings. Nor is even the stunted and sedentary Jew—the third greatest in our present immigrant hordes—an unfavorable vital specimen. Their care-

ful religious regulations have produced in them a longevity even under most unfavorable conditions. Even to-day, under normal conditions, a rough process of selection is at work to bring the better types to our shores. We receive, in the main, the best, the most progressive and alert of the peasantry that the lower classes which these lands recently tapped are able to offer. This is a feature of no mean importance. Barring artificial selection by steamship companies and police, we need not complain in the main of the physique of new arrivals.

"The great problem for us in dealing with these immigrants is not that of their nature, but that of their nurture," [writes Ripley].

[E.A. Ross writes in the *Annals of American Academy*:]

We Americans who have so often seen the children of underfed, stunted, scrub immigrants match the native American in brain and brawn ought to realize how much the superior effectiveness of the matter is due to social conditions. The cause of race superiority is a physiological trait—namely, climatic adaptability.

The races coming to America show power of adaptation. But as this power of adaptation must be slow, we must be patient. It was slow among the best of the early colonists. [Jenks and Lauck write in *The Immigration Problem*], *"The adaptability of the various races coming together on our shores seems, if these indications be borne out by further study, to be much greater than had been expected."*

[E.A. Ross agrees:]

Not merely do the children of immigrants in many instances show greater height and weight than the same races in their mother country, but in some instances even the head form, which has always been considered one of the most stable and permanent characteristics of races, undergoes very great changes.

But the important fact to be kept in mind is that whatever the cause may be, and whether the change in type is for the better or worse, the *influence of the new environment is very marked indeed, and we may therefore expect that the degree and ease of assimilation has probably been somewhat greater than has been heretofore assumed. . . .*

Professor Earl Finch presents "some facts tending to prove that race blending, especially in the rare instances when it occurs under favorable circumstances, produces a type superior in fertility, vitality, and cultural worth to one or both of the parent stocks."

This view was maintained, on the whole, in the preliminary discussion of the last Congress of Races, the manifest exceptions to the statement being explicable mainly by the unsatisfactory social conditions of the half-breeds—in other words, *the problems of miscegenation are sociological rather than physiological.*

All Races Equal in Mental Ability

Professor Franz Boas, of Columbia University, in a recent volume, *The Mind of Primitive Man,* defends the proposition that there is a substantial equality in the native mental ability of all races of mankind; that the inferiority of races is not due to any lack of native ability, but to the accidents which have prevented them from sharing in the fruits of the discoveries made by individual geniuses. He finds that "the characteristics of the osseous, muscular, visceral, and circulatory system have practically no direct relation to the mental ability of men" (Manouvrier); and that the size of the brain is so nearly alike in all races that no inferences can be drawn from the facts collected. "It is not impossible that the smaller brains of males of other races should do the same work as is done by the larger brain of the white race." He contends that "the civilizations of ancient Peru and Central America may well be compared with the ancient civilizations of the Old World." *In view of his investigations, the author does not fear the effects of the intermingling of races in America.*

Says Professor Ripley: "Going back far enough, it is clear that all the peoples of Europe are a hodge-podge of different stocks." Going back as far as we please to the Aryans, we find, some scholars claim, a mixed race. *"Le terme d'Aryen est de pure convention,"* [quotes Chamberlain]. In addition to this sort of general evidence, there is material of a more definite kind. Distinguished men have an ancestry of a mongrel sort.

Alexandre Dumas (West-Indian negro blood); Alexander Hamilton (French and English); Du Maurier and St.-Gaudens,

Dante Gabriel Rosetti, stand for still greater strains of bonds of nationality. Lafcadio Hearn (Greek and Irish). These few examples show that intermixture is, at all events, not destructive in its effect.

Take, too, such a case as Robert Browning, who was rather proud of the fact that he was the product of four strains of European blood.

No Pure Races Exist

Drs. von Luschan and Haddon agree that there are practically no pure races still existing, and that a discussion of races is mainly of academic interest. The former goes so far as to state that the old Indo-European, the African, and the Asiatic all branched off from the same primitive stock, perhaps hundreds of years ago, but all three forming a complete unit, intermarrying in all directions without the slightest decrease of fertility.

Even American families have been much beholden to "foreign" blood. Wendell Phillips and Phillips Brooks would be regarded by most people as fine products of the Anglo-Saxon stock. Both had Du Maurier's "drop of Hebrew blood." Professor Sombart credits the Jews with furnishing one frontiersman to every four in the era of American beginnings.

The unfavorable mixture of South-American races with Indians and negroes cited by Prescott F. Hall is not a fair parallel with the mixture of European races. It leaves out of account the European and American *milieu*—education, marriage, the home, and high political institutions.

There seems some distinct limits put by nature upon the mixture of certain races, just as there is to the blending of blood which has become badly vitiated. Nature puts a final veto upon propagation in such directions. There would seem to be, then, a friendly hand held out by nature itself to prevent disastrous results in race admixture.

Another interesting side to this question, however, is seen particularly in the Orient, where the Chinese have mixed with many peoples, as, for instance, the Hawaiians, Filipinos, and Malays. These Mestizos are recognized in the Orient as particularly clever, the reason often assigned being that the Chinese protect and educate their children, no matter what the other blood may be, whereas the Eurasian (white and Asiatic mixed) is crippled by the lack of support and education—that is, practical desertion by the white father. . . .

The Roman Empire did not fall on account of racial degeneracy, due to the infiltration of Huns, Goths, and Vandals, but on account of the weakness of its political and industrial institutions, and the enervation of the people in the hands of the patrician class. The Roman land laws and Roman slaves, as well as the Roman system of government, which had no method of true amalgamation, but was a loose sort of confederacy, are responsible for the breakup of the Roman Empire.

Immigrants Quickly Adapt to American Ideals

The rapidity with which the democratic ideas are taken on by immigrants under the influence of our institutions is remarkable. I have personally had experiences with French-Canadians, Portuguese, Hebrews, and Italians. These races have certainly taken advantage of their opportunities among us in a fashion to promise well for their final effect upon this country. The French-Canadian has become a sufficiently good American to have given up his earlier programme of turning New England into a new France—that is, into a Catholic province or of returning to the Province of Quebec. He is seeing something better than a racial or religious ideal in the freedom of American citizenship; and on one or two occasions, when he had political power in two municipalities, he refrained from exercising it to the detriment of the public-school system. He has added a gracious manner and a new feeling for beauty to New England traits.

The Portuguese have taken up neglected or abandoned New England agricultural land and have turned it to productive and valuable use. Both the French-Canadian and the Portuguese have come to us by way of the New England textile mills.

The actual physical machinery of civilization—cotton-mills, woolen-mills, iron-mills, etc.—lock up a great deal of human energy physical and mental, just as one hundred years ago the farms did, from which later sprang most of the members of our dominant industrial class. A better organization of society, by which machinery would do still more and afford a freer play for mental and physical energy and organization, would find a response from classes that are now looked upon as not contributing to our American culture; would unlock the high potentialities in the laboring classes, now unguessed and unexpended.

The intellectual problems and the advanced thinking of the Hebrew, his fondness for study, and his freedom on the whole from wasteful forms of dissipation, sport, and mental stagnation, constitute him a more fortunate acquisition for this country than are thousands of the descendants of Colonial settlers. In short, we must reconstruct our idea of democracy—of American democracy. This done, we must construct a new picture of citizenship. If we do these things we shall welcome the rugged strength of the peasant or the subtle thought of the man of the Ghetto in our reconsidered American ideals. After all, what are these American ideals we boast so much about? Shall we say public schools, the ballot, freedom? The American stock use private schools when they can afford them; they too often leave town on Election Day; as for freedom, competent observers believe it is disappearing. The conservators and believers in American ideals seem to be our immigrants. To the Russian Jew, Abraham Lincoln is a god. If American ideals are such as pay honor to the intellectual and to the spiritual or foster human brotherhood or love culture and promote liberty, then they are safe with our new citizens who are eager for these things.

Not only do these races bring with them most desirable qualities, but they themselves are subjected to new environment and strongly influential conditions. Just here arise duties for the present masters of America. Ought they not to create an industrial, social, and educational environment of the most uplifting sort for our foreign-born citizens?

Immigrant Adaptation

If working-people are obliged to live in unhealthful tenements situated in slums or marsh land, if the saloon is allowed to be their only social center, if they are fought by the rich in every effort to improve their condition, we may expect any misfortune to happen to them and also any fate to befall the State.

What improved *milieu* can do to improve the physique is easily seen on all sides. The increase in the height and weight of Americans in the last few decades is conspicuous. Even the size of American girls and boys has increased, and this increase in size is commonly attributed to the more comfortable conditions of life, to better food, and especially to the popularity of all forms of athletics, and the extension, as in the last twenty-five or thirty years, of the out-of-door and country life. If these factors have made so marked and visible a change in the physique of the children of native-born Americans, why may not the same conditions also contribute an improvement to the more recent immigrant stock?

Our question, then, as to the effect of race mixture is not the rather supercilious one: What are we admitting into America that may possibly injure American ideals? but, What are the old American races doing to perpetuate these ideals? And is not our future as a race, largely by our own fault, in the hands of the peasant races of Europe?

After all, for those who pin their faith to the Baltic and northern European races, there is reason for hope to be found even in current immigration. From 1899 to 1910, the Hebrew, southern Italian, Polish, and Slovak period, of the nine millions who landed in the United States, while there were 377,527 Slovaks and 318,151 Magyars, there were 408,614 English, 586,306 Scandinavians, and 754,375 Germans, and even 136,842 Scotch, 151,774 Finnish,

439,724 Irish, and 20,752 Welsh. Two millions and a half from northern Europe—over twenty-six percent. One million seventy-four thousand are Hebrews, mostly from Russia; and the Russian Jews, according to a most distinguished German Jew, are intellectually the ablest Hebrews in America. If, on the other hand, nearly two millions of the immigrants of the last decade have been southern Italians, let us show them gratitude for their invaluable manual labor, for their willingness, their patience, their power for fast work, and their love of America. Their small stature does not argue their degeneracy. The Romans were small compared to the Goths—small, but well formed and strong. The Japanese are also small.

Indifference, prejudice, illiteracy, segregation of recent immigrants by parochial schools, by a native colonial press, bad physical and social environment, and the low American ideals of citizenship held by those the immigrant sees or hears most about, obstruct race assimilation; but all these can be changed. Yes, it is the keeping up of difference and class isolation that destroys and deteriorates. Fusion is a law of progress.

Optimistic Thought on Race Mixture

Lastly, let us observe that the men who hold a brief for the "foreigner" are largely men of science from the faculties of our American colleges. Ripley of Harvard, Giddings and Boas of Columbia, and Mayo-Smith (now dead), Jenks of Cornell, Patten and Kelsey of the University of Pennsylvania. The best thought and the best teaching of the country on race mixture is optimistic and constructive. Is it not also significant that an alienist like Dr. Dana is not dismayed by the immigrant, but is hopeful of his contribution? All these are scientific witnesses and are on the spot.

Every act of religious or civil tyranny, every economic wrong done to races in all the world, becomes the burden of the nation to which the oppressed flee for relief and opportunity. And the beauty of democracy is that it is a method by which these needs may freely express themselves and bring about what the oppressed have prayed for and have been denied. Let us be careful not to put America into the class of the oppressors. Let us rise to an eminence higher than that occupied by Washington or Lincoln, to a new Americanism which is not afraid of the blending in the western world of races seeking freedom. Our present problem is the greatest in our history. Not colonial independence, not Federal unity, but racial amalgamation is the heroic problem of the present, with all it implies in purification and revision of old social, religious, and political ideals, with all it demands in new sympathy outside of blood and race, and in a willingness to forego old-time privileges.

The familiar words of Israel Zangwill will bear repeating—that modern prophet from the race that gave to the world Jesus—when, from a steamer in New York Harbor, he broods over America:

> There she lies, the great Melting Pot. Listen! Can't you hear the roaring and the bubbling? There gapes her mouth—the harbor where a thousand mammoth feeders come from the ends of the world to pour in their human freight. Ah, what a stirring and a seething! Celt and Latin, Slav and Teuton, Greek and Syrian—black and yellow. Yes, East and West, and North and South, the palm and the pine, the pole and the equator, the crescent and the cross—how the great Alchemist melts and fuses them with his purging flame! Here shall they all unite to build the Republic of Man and the Kingdom of God. Ah, what is the glory of Rome and Jerusalem where all nations and races come to worship and look back, compared with the glory of America, where all races come to labor and look forward.

If America has done anything for an American, it ought to have made him helpful and hopeful toward mankind, especially the poor and oppressed; but science to-day comes to the assistance of democracy and finds the lyric cry of brotherhood in the laws of nature:

> Open thy gates, O thou favored of Heaven,
> Open thy gates to the homeless and poor.
> So shalt thou garner the gifts of the ages—
> From the Northlands their vigor,
> The Southlands their grace,
> In a mystical blending of souls that presages
> The birth of earth's rarest, undreamable race.

VIEWPOINT 3

"One need not question the fundamental worth of the immigrants or their possibilities in order to argue that they must act as a drag on the social progress of the nation."

The New Immigrants Harm American Society

Edward Alsworth Ross (1866-1951)

Edward Alsworth Ross was professor of sociology at the University of Wisconsin for many years and a well-known writer on social issues. Among his many books are *Social Control, Social Psychology, The Changing Chinese, Changing America in Contemporary Society, The World Adrift,* and *The Old World in the New* (New York: The Century Co., 1914), from which the following viewpoint is taken.

Ross believed that the new immigrants were generally detrimental to American society. Largely uneducated, impoverished, unskilled, and in many instances strongly under the control of Catholic and Jewish religious beliefs, these new immigrants, Ross believed, could not be easily assimilated into American culture. In addition, their health, standards of hygiene, psychological status, and social mores were inferior to American standards. Ross believed these people were responsible for increasing crime, disease, poverty, and unemployment in America. He even believed their inevitable intermarriage with "native" Americans would cause Americans to become less attractive.

The Old World in the New was written at the height of the immigration influx; it was published in 1914. Ross believed that if immigration continued unchecked both quantitatively and qualitatively, America could expect its society to deteriorate.

There is a certain anthracite town of 26,000 inhabitants in which are writ large the moral and social consequences of injecting 10,000 sixteenth-century people into a twentieth-century community. By their presence the foreigners necessarily lower the general plane of intelligence, self-restraint, refinement, orderliness, and efficiency. With them, of course, comes an increase of drink and of the crimes from drink. The great excess of men among them leads to sexual immorality and the diffusion of private diseases. A primitive midwifery is practised, and the ignorance of the poor mothers fills the cemetery with tiny graves. The women go about their homes barefoot, and their rooms and clothing reek with the odors of cooking and uncleanliness. The standards of modesty are Elizabethan. The miners bathe in the kitchen before the females and children of the household, and women soon to become mothers appear in public unconcerned. The foreigners attend church regularly, but their noisy amusements banish the quiet Sunday. The foreign men, three-eighths of whom are illiterate, pride themselves on their physical strength rather than on their skill, and are willing to take jobs requiring nothing but brawn.

Barriers of speech, education, and religious faith split the people into unsympathetic, even hostile camps. The worst element in the community makes use of the ignorance and venality of the foreign-born voters to exclude the better citizens from any share in the control of local affairs. In this babel no newspaper becomes strong enough to mold and lead public opinion. On account of the smallness of the English-reading public,—the native-born men number slightly over two thousand and those of American parentage less than a thousand—the single English daily has so few subscribers that it cannot afford to offend any of them by exposing municipal rottenness. The chance to prey on the ignorant foreigner tempts to cupidity and corrupts the ethics of local business and professional men. The Slavic thirst, multiplying saloons up to one for every twenty-six families, is communicated to Americans, and results in an increase of liquor crimes among all classes. In like manner familiarity with the immodesties of the foreigners coarsens the native-born.

With the basest Americans and the lowest foreigners united by thirst and greed, while the decent Americans and the decent for-eigners understand one another too little for team-work, it is not surprising that the municipal government is poor and that the taxpayers are robbed. Only a few of the main streets are paved; the rest are muddy and poorly guttered. Outside the central por-tion of the city one meets with open sewage, garbage, dung-heaps, and foul odors. Sidewalks are lacking or in bad repair. The police force, composed of four Lithuanians, two Poles, one Ger-man, and one Irishman, is so inefficient that "pistol-toting" after nightfall is common among all classes. At times hold-ups have been so frequent that it was not considered safe for a well-dressed person to show himself in the foreign sections after dark. In the words of a prominent local criminal lawyer: "We have a police force that can't speak English. Within the last few years there have been six unavenged murders in this town. Why, if there were anybody I wanted to get rid of, I'd entice him here, shoot him down in the street, and then go around and say good-by to the police."

Here in a nutshell are presented the social effects that naturally follow the introduction into an advanced people of great num-bers of backward immigrants. One need not question the funda-mental worth of the immigrants or their possibilities in order to argue that they must act as a drag on the social progress of the nation that incorporates them. . . .

Illiteracy

While sister countries are fast nearing the goal of complete adult literacy, deteriorating immigration makes it very hard to lift the plane of popular intelligence in the United States. The for-eign-born between twenty and thirty-four years of age, late-com-ers of course, show five times the illiteracy of native whites of the same age. But those above forty-five years of age, mostly earlier immigrants, have scarcely twice the literacy of native whites above forty-five. This shows how much wider is the gulf between the Americans of to-day and the new immigrants than that be-tween the Americans of a generation ago and the old immigrants.

Thanks to extraordinary educational efforts, the illiteracy of na-tive white voters dropped a third during the last decade; that is, from 4.9 per cent. to 3.5 per cent. But the illiteracy of the foreign-born men rose to 12 per cent.; so that the proportion of white men in this country unable to read and write any language declined only 9 per cent. when, but for the influx of illiterates, it would have fallen 30 per cent.

In the despatches of August 16, 1912, is an account of a gather-ing of ten thousand afflicted people at a shrine at Carey, Ohio, re-puted to possess a miraculous healing virtue. Special trains brought together multitudes of credulous, and at least one "miracle" was reported. As this country fills up with the densely ignorant, there will be more of this sort of thing. The characteristic features of the Middle Ages may be expected to appear among us to the degree that our population comes to be composed of persons at the medieval level of culture. . . .

In the South Side of Pittsburgh there are streets lined with the decent homes of German steelworkers. A glance down the paved passage leading to the rear of the house reveals absolute cleanliness, and four times out of five one glimpses a tree, a flower garden, an arbor, or a mass of vines. In Wood's Run, a few miles away, one finds the Slavic laborers of the Pressed Steel Car Company huddled in dilapidated rented dwellings so noisome and repulsive that one must visit the lower quarters of Canton to meet their like. One cause of the difference is that the Slavs are largely transients, who do nothing to house themselves because they are saving in order to return to their native village.

The fact that a growing proportion of our immigrants, having left families behind them, form no strong local attachments and have no desire to build homes here is one reason why of late the housing problem has become acute in American industrial centers.

Overgrowth of Cities

Not least among the multiplying symptoms of social ill health in this country is the undue growth of cities. A million city-dwellers create ten times the amount of "problem" presented by a million on the farms. Now, as one traverses the gamut that leads from farms to towns, from towns to cities, and from little cities to big, the proportion of American stock steadily diminishes while the foreign stock increases its representation until in the great cities it constitutes nearly three-fourths of the population. In 1910 the percentage distribution of our white population was as follows:—

	Native White Stock	Foreign Stock	Foreign-Born
Rural districts	64.1	20.8	7.5
Cities 2,500-10,000	57.5	34.5	13.9
Cities 10,000-25,000	50.4	42.0	14.4
Cities 25,000-100,000	45.9	46.7	20.2
Cities 100,000-500,000	38.9	53.4	22.1
Cities 500,000 and over	25.6	70.8	33.6

It is not that the immigrants love streets and crowds. Two-thirds of them are farm bred, but they are dropped down in cities, and they find it easier to herd there with their fellows than to make their way into the open country. Our cities would be fewer and smaller had they fed on nothing but country-bred Americans. The later alien influx has rushed us into the thick of urban problems, and these are gravest where Americans are fewest. Congestion, misliving, segregation, corruption, and confusion are seen in motley groups like Pittsburgh, Jersey City, Paterson, and Fall River rather than in native centers like Indianapolis, Columbus, Nashville, and Los Angeles.

Pauperism

Ten years ago two-fifths of the paupers in our almshouses were foreign-born, but most of them had come over in the old careless days when we allowed European poorhouses to send us their inmates. Now that our authorities turn back such as appear likely to become a public charge, the obvious pauper is not entering this country. We know that virtually every Greek in America is self-supporting. The Syrians are said to be singularly independent. The Slavs and the Magyars are sturdy in spirit, and the numerous indigent Hebrews are for the most part cared for by their own race.

Nevertheless, dispensers of charity agree that many South Italians are landing with the most extravagant ideas of what is coming to them. They apply at once for relief with the air, "Here we are. Now what are you going to do for us?" They even *insist* on relief as a right. At home it had been noised about that in foolish America baskets of food are actually sent in to the needy, and some are coming over expressly to obtain such largess. Probably none are so infected with spiritual hookworm as the immigrants from Naples. It will be recalled that when Garibaldi and his thousand were fighting to break the Bourbon tyranny in the South, the Neapolitans would hurrah for them, but would not even care for the wounded.

Says the Forty-seventh Annual Report of the New York Juvenile Asylum:

> It is remarkable that recently arrived immigrants who display small adaptability in American standards are by no means slow in learning about this and other institutions where they may safely leave their children to be fed, clothed, and cared for at the public expense. This is one of the inducements which led them to leave their native land.

Charity experts are very pessimistic as to what we shall see when those who come in their youth have passed their prime and met the cumulative effects of overwork, city life, drink, and vice. Still darker are their forebodings for a second generation, reared too often by ignorant, avaricious rustics lodging in damp cellars, sleeping with their windows shut, and living on the bad, cheap food of cities. Of the Italians in Boston Dr. Bushee writes:

> They show the beginnings of a degenerate class, such as has

been fully developed among the Irish. . . . If allowed to continue in unwholesome conditions, we may be sure that the next generation will bring forth a large crop of dependents, delinquents and defectives to fill up our public institutions.

Says a charity superintendent working in a huge Polish quarter:

It is the second generation that will give us trouble. The parents come with rugged peasant health, and many of them keep their strength even in the slum. But their children often start life weakened physically and mentally by the conditions under which they were reared. They have been raised in close, unsanitary quarters, in overlarge families, by parents who drunk up or saved too much, spent too little on the children, or worked them too soon. Their sole salvation is the open country, and they can't be pushed into the country. All of us are aghast at the weak fiber of the second generation. Every year I see the morass of helpless poverty getting bigger. The evil harvest of past mistakes is ripening, but it will take twenty years before we see the worst of it. If immigration were cut off short to-day, the burden from past neglect and exploitation would go on increasing for years.

In 1908 nine-tenths of the 2600 complaints of children going wrong made to the Juvenile Protective Association of Chicago related to the children of immigrants. It is said that four-fifths of the youths brought before the Juvenile Court of Chicago come from the homes of the foreign-born. In Pittsburgh the proportion is at least two-thirds. However startling these signs of moral breakdown in the families of the new immigrants, there is nothing mysterious about it. The lower the state from which the alien comes, the more of a grotesque he will appear in the shrewd eyes of his partly Americanized children. "Obedience to parents seems to be dying out among the Jews," says a Boston charity visitor. "The children feel it is n't necessary to obey a mother who wears a shawl or a father who wears a full beard." "Sometimes it is the young daughter who rules the Jewish family," observes a Pittsburgh settlement head, "because she alone knows what is 'American.' But see how this results in a great number of Jewish girls going astray. Since the mother continues to shave her head and wear a wig as she did in Poland, the daughter assumes that mother is equally old-fogyish when she insists that a nice girl does n't paint her face or run with boys in the evening."

Through their knowledge of our speech and ways, the children have a great advantage in their efforts to slip the parental leash. The bad boy tells his father that whipping "does n't go" in this country. Reversing the natural order, the child becomes the fount of knowledge, and the parents hang on the lips of their precocious offspring. If the policeman inquires about some escapade or the truant officer gives warning, it is the scamp himself who must interpret between parent and officer. The immigrant is braced by certain Old-World loyalties, but his child may grow up loyal to nothing whatever, a rank egoist and an incorrigible who will give us vast trouble before we are done with him.

Immigrants Swell Prisons

The Reverend Joseph Cook believed immigrants were the cause of increased crime and other ills in American society. In this excerpt from his introduction to Rena Atchison's book called Un-American Immigration *(1894), he comments on the high proportion of criminals in the immigrant population.*

Incredible as the fact appears, it has been proved by Congressional investigation that several foreign countries, including Italy, Austria, Germany and even England, have societies to aid criminals and paupers to emigrate to America, and sometimes give them governmental assistance. Voluntary or assisted emigration of paupers and criminals from Europe is making America in some respects an international Botany Bay.

The proportion of criminals among our foreign-born population is startlingly greater than among the native born. Directly, or indirectly in the persons of their immediate descendants, this element contributes considerably more material for our State prisons and penitentiaries than the entire native white population. . . .

Unrestricted immigration is doing much to lower the wages of American labor, besides causing a deterioration of the quality of American citizenship.

Still, the child is not always to blame. "Often the homes are so crowded and dirty," says a probation officer, "that no boy can go right. The Slavs save so greedily that their children become disgusted with the wretched home conditions and sleep out." One hears of foreign-born with several boarders sending their children out to beg or to steal coal. In one city investigation showed that only a third of the Italian children taken from school on their fourteenth birthday were needed as bread-winners. Their parents thought only of the sixty cents a week. In another only one-fourteenth of the Italian school children are above the primary grades, and one-eleventh of the Slavic, as against two-fifths of the American school children in grammar grades or high school. Miss Addams tells of a young man from the south of Italy who was mourning the death of his little girl of twelve. In his grief he said quite simply: "She was my oldest kid. In two years she would have supported me, and now I shall have to work five or six years longer until the next one can do it." He expected to retire permanently at the age of thirty-four.

Not only do the foreign-born appear to be more subject to insanity than the native-born, but when insane they are more likely to become a public charge. Of the asylum population they appear to constitute about a third. In New York during the year ending September 30, 1911, 4218 patients who were immigrants or of immigrant parents were admitted to the insane hospitals of the State. This is three-quarters of the melancholy intake for that year. Only one out of nine of the first admissions from New York City was of native stock. The New York State Hospital Commission declares that "the frequency of insanity in our foreign population is 2.19 times greater than in those of native birth." In New York City it "is 2.48 times that of the native-born."

Excessive insanity is probably a part of the price the foreign-born pay for the opportunities of a strange and stimulating environment, with greater strains than some of them are able to bear. America calls forth powerful reactions in these people. Here they feel themselves in the grasp of giant forces they can neither withstand nor comprehend. The passions and the exertions, the hopes and the fears, the exultations and the despairs America excites in the immigrant are likely to be intenser than anything he would have experienced in his natal village.

In view of the fact that every year New York cares for 15,000 foreign-born insane at a cost of $3,500,000 and that the State's sad harvest of demented immigrants during the single year 1911 will cost about $8,000,000 before they die or are discharged, there is some offset to be made to the profits drawn from the immigrants by the transporting companies, landlords, real-estate men, employers, contractors, brewers, and liquor-dealers of the State. Besides, there is the cost of the paupers and the law-breakers of foreign origin. All such burdens, however, since they fall upon the public at large, do not detract from or qualify that private or business-man's prosperity which it is the office of the true modern statesman to promote.

Immigration and the Separate School

In a polyglot mining town of Minnesota is a superintendent who has made the public school a bigger factor in Americanization than I have found it anywhere else. The law gives him the children until they are sixteen, and he holds them all. His school buildings are civic and social centers. Through the winter, in his high school auditorium, which seats 1200 persons, he gives a course of entertainment which is self-supporting, although his "talent" for a single evening will cost as much as $200. By means of the 400 foreigners in his night schools he has a grip on the voters which his foes have learned to dread. Under his lead the community has broken the mine-boss collar and won real self-government. The people trust him and bring him their troubles. He has jurisdiction over everything that can affect the children of the town, and his conception is wide. Wielding both legal and moral authority, he is, as it were, a corporation president and a medieval bishop rolled into one.

This man sets no limit to the transforming power of the public school. He insists that the right sort of schooling will not only alter the expression, but will even change the shape of the skull and the bony formation of the face. In his office is a beautiful tabouret made by a "wild boy" within a year after he had been brought in kicking and screaming. He scoffs at the fear of a lack of patriotism in the foreign-born or their children. He knows just how to create the sentiment. He has flag drills and special programs, and in the Fourth of July parade and the Decoration day procession the schools have always a fine float. He declares he can build human beings to order, and will not worry about immigration so long as the public school is given a chance at the second generation.

But is the public school to have this chance?

Multitudes of the new immigrants adhere to churches which do not believe in the public schools. "Their pupils," observed a priest to me, "are like wild children." Said a bishop: "No branches can be safely taught divorced from religion. We believe that geography, history, and even language ought to be presented from our point of view." Hence with great rapidity the children of Roman Catholics are being drawn apart into parochial schools. In Cleveland one-third of the population is supposed to be Catholic, and the 27,500 pupils in the parochial schools are nearly one-third of all school children. In Chicago there are 112,000 in the parish schools to 300,000 in the public schools. In New York the proportion is about one-sixth. In twenty-eight leading American cities the attendance of the parish schools increased 60 per cent. between 1897 and 1910, as against an increase of from 45 to 50 per cent. in the attendance of the public schools. The total number of children in the parochial schools is about 1,400,000. Separate education is a settled Catholic policy, and the bishops say they expect to enroll finally the children of all their people.

To bring this about, the public schools are denounced from the pulpit as "Godless" and "immoral," their product as mannerless and disobedient. "We think," says a Slovak leader, "that the parochial school pupils are more pious, more respectful toward parents and toward all persons in authority." The Polish, Lithuanian, or Slovak priest, less often the German or Bohemian, says bluntly: "If you send your children to the public school, they will go to hell." Sometimes the priest threatens to exclude from the confessional parents who send their children to the public school. An archbishop recently decreed that parents who without permission send their children to the public school after they have made their first communion "commit a grievous sin and cannot receive the sacraments of the church." Within the immigrant groups there is active opposition, but it appears to be futile. In the soft-coal mining communities of Pennsylvania 9 per cent. of the children of native white parentage attend the parochial schools, whereas 24 per cent. of the Polish children and 48 per cent. of the Slovak children are in these schools. In a certain district in Chicago where the public-school teachers had felt they could hold their own, the foreign mothers came at last to take away their children's school-books, weeping because they were forced to transfer their children to the parish school.

Now, the parish school tends to segregate the children of the foreign-born. Parishes are formed for groups of the same speech, so a parish school will embrace children of only one national-ity—German, Polish, Bohemian, Lithuanian, Croatian, Slovak, Magyar, Portuguese, or French Canadian, as the case may be. Often priest and teachers have been imported, and only the mother-tongue is used. "English," says a school superintendent, "comes to be taught as a purely ornamental language, like French in the public high school." Hence American-born children are leaving school not only unable to read and write English, but scarcely able to speak it. The foreign-speech school, while it binds the young to their parents, to their people, and to the old country, cuts them off from America. Says a Chicago Lithuanian leader: "There are 3000 of our children in the parochial schools here. The teachers are ignorant, illiterate spinsters from Lithuania who have studied here two or three years. When at fourteen the pupils quit school, they are no more advanced than the public-school pupils of ten. This is why 50,000 Lithuanians here have only twenty children in the high school."

When, now, to the removal of the second generation from the public school there is added, as is often the case, the endeavor to keep them away from the social center, the small park field-house, the public playground, the social settlement, the secular American press and welfare work in the factories, it is plain that those optimists who imagine that assimilation of the immigrant is proceeding unhindered are living in a fool's paradise.

Social Decline

"Our descendants," a social worker remarked to me, "will look back on the nineteenth century as our Golden Age, just as we look back on Greece." Thoughtful people whose work takes them into the slime at the bottom of our foreignized cities and indus-trial centers find decline actually upon us. A visiting nurse who has worked for seven years in the stock-yards district of Chicago reports that of late the drinking habit is taking hold of foreign women at an alarming rate. In the saloons there the dignified *stein* has given way to the beer pail. In the Range towns of Minnesota there are 356 saloons, of which eighty-one are run by native-born, the rest chiefly by recent immigrants. Into a Pennsylvania coal town of 1800 people, mostly foreign-born, are shipped each week a car-load of beer and a barrel of whisky. Where the new foreign-born are numerous, women and children frequent the saloons as freely as the men. In the cities family desertion is growing at a great rate among foreign-born husbands. Facts are justifying the forecast made ten years ago by H. G. Wells: "If things go on as they are going, the great mass of them will remain a very low lower class—will remain largely illiterate, industrialized peasants."

The continuance of depressive immigration will lead to nothing catastrophic. Riots and labor strife will oftener break out, but the country will certainly not weaken nor collapse. Of patriotism of the military type there will be no lack. Scientific and technical advance will go on the same. The spread of business organization and efficiency will continue. The only thing that will happen will be a mysterious slackening in social progress. The mass will give signs of sluggishness, and the social procession will be strung out.

We are engaged in a generous rivalry with the West Europeans and the Australians to see which can do the most to lift the plane of life of the masses. Presently we shall be dismayed by the sense of falling behind. We shall be amazed to find the Swiss or the Danes or the New Zealanders making strides we cannot match. Stung with mortification at losing our erstwhile lead in the advancement of the common people, we shall cast about for someone to blame. Ultimate causes, of course, will be overlooked; only proximate causes will be noticed. There will be loud outcry that mothers, or teachers, or clergymen, or editors, or social workers are not doing their duty. Our public schools, solely responsible as they obviously are for the intellectual and moral characteristics of the people, will be roundly denounced; and it will be argued that church schools must take their place. There will be trying of this and trying of that, together with much ingenious legislation. As peasantism spreads and inertia proves unconquerable, the opinion will grow that the old American faith in the capacity and desire of the common people for improvement was a delusion, and that only the superior classes care for progress. Not until the twenty-first century will the philosophic historian be able to declare with scientific certitude that the cause of the mysterious decline that came upon the American people early in the twentieth century was the deterioration of popular intelligence by the admission of great numbers of backward immigrants.

VIEWPOINT 4

"Our powers as a nation and our prosperity as individuals would only have been a fraction of what they are had immigration been prevented."

The New Immigrants Do Not Harm American Society

A. Piatt Andrew (1873-1936)

A. Piatt Andrew, congressman and economist, did not agree with immigration restrictionists who said the new immigrants would damage American society. Writing in the June 1914 issue of *North American Review*, a monthly journal of letters and politics, he pointed out that Americans have always feared the impact of immigrants and that their fears have always been groundless. In the early nineteenth century, for example, many Americans were certain the large influx of Irish immigrants would cause America to crumble. Instead, the Irish became mainstays of the labor market and influential in politics and other areas of American life.

In this excerpt, Andrew points out that the Immigration Commission's massive study of immigrants, done between 1907 and 1910 and resulting in a forty-one volume report, turned up no hard evidence of inferiority on the part of the new immigrants in the areas of health, crime, and dependency on social welfare. He argues that the educational and economic opportunities offered by this country soon turn rough immigrants into productive members of society.

A. Piatt Andrew was a professor of economics at Harvard University and expert assistant and editor of publications at the National Monetary Commission. He also served as director of the mint, secretary of the treasury, and treasurer of the American Red Cross.

The subject of immigration we have always with us in this country. It has been a topic of contentious interest and legislation almost continuously since the first Englishman set foot in the Western World. The Pilgrims and Puritans of Massachusetts Bay were scarcely settled in their log huts before they began planning a policy of exclusion, and already in 1637 they voted to keep out those who were not members of their own religious sect. So in the very earliest decades of the English settlement, immigration began to be restricted, and Quakers and Baptists, Episcopalians and Catholics, were banished and proscribed from the Commonwealth on the ground that American standards were apt to be impaired by their admission. From that day to this the older immigrants and their descendants have tried to keep this country for those already here and their kindred folk. They have looked upon themselves as a kind of aristocracy, their supposed superiority being proportioned to the length of time that they and their ancestors have lived upon this continent, and each successive generation of immigrants newly arrived has tended with curious repetition to adopt the same viewpoint, to believe that the succeeding immigrants were inferior to the former in religion, habits, education, or what not, and ought to be kept out. Then for more than a hundred years a further motive for exclusion has found constant iteration. Each generation has been taught to believe that the country was rapidly filling to the brim, and that on that account also the doors of entry ought to be closed.

In the very first decade of our Federal Government, in 1797, when the first Alien Act was under consideration, we find passages in the records of Congress which sound much like the utterances of certain Congressmen in 1914:

> When the country, said Otis (in 1797), was new it may have been good policy to admit all. But it is so no longer. A bar should be placed against the admittance of those restless people who cannot be tranquil and happy at home. We do not want a vast horde of wild Irishmen let loose upon us. (McMasters' *History of the People of the United States*, Vol. II, page 332.)

Passage after passage of similar tenor could be cited from every subsequent decade, but I shall only quote one or two examples,

140

beginning with a report made in 1819 by the Managers of the Society for the Prevention of Pauperism in the City of New York. In this report of nearly a hundred years ago the fear is expressed that through immigration

> pauperism threatens us with the most overwhelming consequences. . . . The present state of Europe contributes in a thousand ways to foster increasing immigration to the United States. . . . An almost innumerable population beyond the ocean is out of employment. . . . This country is the resort of vast numbers of these needy and wretched beings. . . . They are frequently found destitute in our streets: they seek employment at our doors: they are found in our almshouses and in our hospitals: they are found at the bar of our criminal tribunals, in our bridewell and our penitentiary and our State prison. (*Reports of the Industrial Commission*, Vol. XV, page 449.)

This was in 1819. Coming down another score of years, we find the next generation once more extolling the immigration up to its own time, but once more greatly perturbed by the supposedly inferior character of the immigrants then beginning to come. In a paper published in 1835, entitled "Imminent Dangers to the Institutions of the United States through Foreign Immigration," we read that formerly

> our accessions of immigration were real accessions of strength from the ranks of the learned and the good, from enlightened mechanic and artisan and intelligent husbandmen. Now immigration is the accession of weakness, from the ignorant and vicious, or the priest-ridden slaves of Ireland and Germany, or the outcast tenants of the poorhouses and prisons of Europe. (*Hearings before the Committee on Immigration, Sixty-first Congress*, page 327.)

In the course of the twenty years that followed came the great increase of Irish immigrants during the famine in Ireland, and then again many Americans became panic-stricken at the thought of the possible consequences. A great secret order and a new political party, the so-called Know-Nothings, were organized to overcome the dire results that were apprehended. The abject squalor and wretchedness to which these Irish immigrants had for generations been accustomed, it was urged, could not but result in the degradation of American standards, and many seemed to fear that on account of their religion the immigrants would try to overthrow our democratic government and establish an ecclesiastic hierarchy in its stead. Feeling in some places was so bitter that the immigrants were mobbed in the streets, their churches were desecrated, and their children were persecuted in the public schools. One could spend hours reading passages from speeches and pamphlets of this period denouncing the Irish immigration.

Yet the American government still lives and, notwithstanding the abject condition of these Irish settlers and the fears and apprehensions which they aroused, we have absorbed and assimilated some four millions of them and no one has yet observed any deterioration of American standards and ideals in consequence. We and they have flourished and prospered, and we reckon their descendants among our best citizens. The names of many of them are daily on our lips and before our eyes in the headlines, for they are our political magnates, our aldermen and mayors and governors.

Passing on to the next generation, during the later seventies and early eighties came a great migration of Germans and Scandinavians, and once more racial prejudice found a new objective. The previous immigrants had for the most part spoken our language, were akin, it was said, to our original stock and familiar with our traditions, but the new immigrants, ignorant of English and with different modes of thought and practice, were held to be unassimilable and to menace our standards and institutions. The apprehension was so great and the objection became so general as to induce in 1882 the first general immigration law. Nevertheless, we have absorbed over four million Germans and over two million Swedes and Norwegians, and to-day we count no more valuable factors in our national stock than their descendants.

The New Immigrants

But once again the racial currents shifted, and during the last fifteen years new vast streams have flowed to this country from Russia, Italy, and Austria-Hungary, and new smaller streams from Portugal and from Greece, Rumania, and other parts of Eastern Europe. During 1913 Russia, Italy, and Austria-Hungary offered each nearly a quarter of the year's total inflow. So once again the familiar clamor of alarm has been turned in another direction. It is now admitted that the millions of Irish and Germans and Scandinavians who have come into the country have been absorbed without any degradation of our standards, that they have rendered invaluable service in developing the country, and that the earlier fears have proven groundless. But it is said that the new immigrant is of a type radically less desirable than that of the earlier periods, and once more we hear the warning that the situation to-day is different in that the country is now thickly settled and land and opportunities are no longer available. As I recall the similar assertions and fears of earlier periods I must confess that I sympathize with the gentleman from Missouri who expressed a desire to have some evidence submitted. It looks as if in the eyes of some Americans the only good immigrants were the dead immigrants, and that the only opportunities for the country's development lay in the past. I want to know and you want to know in what sense the immigrants of to-day are thought to be inferior to those who preceded them, and on what grounds it is claimed that the country has reached the limit of profitable increase in population.

Immigrants and Crime

Kate Halladay Claghorn, a prominent immigration analyst, wrote in the October 1900 issue of the Atlantic Monthly *that statistics do not bear out the notion that immigrants increase crime in America.*

Several detailed statistical studies recently made confirm our expectations on this point, and agree in showing, pretty conclusively, that when like sex and age classes are made the basis for comparison in the different race groups, the rate of crime for the foreign-born white population of all races is no higher, to say the least, than that of the native white population of native parentage; and that the difference in crime rate still remaining after sex and age have been allowed for, between the different race groups, to be attributed to race tendency, is so slight as to be negligible as a social factor.

Are the new immigrants less sound of body and mind than those of earlier generations? Do they more frequently evince criminal proclivities? Are they more apt to become a charge upon the State? Is their standard of living lower? Are they less capable of becoming loyal, worthy American citizens? We may well inquire what the Immigration Commission, with their exhaustive investigations published in forty-one volumes, have to say in answer to these questions, and in this connection we may also turn to the volume upon *The Immigration Problem* prepared by Professors Jenks and Lauck, the reputed authors of the Immigration Commission Report, which summarizes the data and conclusions of the Commission.

Are the new immigrants wanting in bodily vigor and health? The authors of the Immigration Commission Report deny this.

Our later immigration laws have forbidden the entrance of those afflicted with any loathsome or contagious disease, or of those in such a condition of health as is likely to make them become a public charge. Under these laws, too, the steamship companies are held responsible and are compelled to return free of charge passengers rejected by our immigration officials, and in the case of the insane or diseased they are fined in addition one hundred dollars for each such passenger brought to this country. This legislation has brought about a very great change in the matter of inspection and exclusion, and the representatives of the Immigration Commission declare that the careful inspection abroad, sometimes by representatives of the United States Government, otherwise by inspectors of the steamship companies, and the final examination at the port of entry, have brought about the result that with very rare exceptions every immigrant admitted to this country is now in good health, and is not bringing with him the germs of any disease that might prove detrimental. (Jenks and Lauck, page 28.)

And they add that

as far as one can judge from the records kept, the races of the recent immigration, those from Southern and Eastern Europe, are not so subject to diseases that seem to be allied with moral weaknesses as some of those of the older immigration races. (Jenks and Lauck, page 47.)

Are the new immigrants more addicted to crime? Again the authors of the Immigration Commission Report assert that there is no proof of this.

No satisfactory evidence has yet been produced to show that immigration has resulted in an increase in crime disproportionate to the increase in the adult population. Such comparable statistics of crime and population as it has been possible to obtain indicate that immigrants are less prone to commit crime than are native Americans. (*Reports of the United States Immigration Commission*, Vol. XXXVI, page 1.)

Are the new immigrants more likely to become charges upon the community? The authors of the Immigration Commission Report declare the contrary.

The Immigration Commission, with the assistance of the Associated Charities in forty-three cities, including practically all the large centers excepting New York, reached the conclusion that only a very small percentage of the immigrants now arriving apply for relief. (Jenks and Lauck, page 50.)

Is the standard of living of the new immigrants lower than that of the old? Any one who has read the contemporary descriptions of the living conditions of the Irish and German immigrants in the periods from 1840 to 1880 will hesitate to believe that the standard of living of the immigrants of our day is lower than the standard of living of the immigrants in the earlier period. Nothing could be more pitiful and depressing than the pictures of the poverty and wretchedness of the Irish settlers at the time of the great migration from Ireland. The majority of the Irish people for centuries had been forced to live in hovels with only the barest necessities in the way of furniture and clothing, and many of the thousands who came to this country were in serious danger of actual starvation if they remained at home. The authors of the Immigration Commission Report state that "practically none of our immigrants of the present day are in such a condition" (Jenks and Lauck, page 12).

In a very few years, with our free and compulsory schools, our free libraries, and the economic opportunities which this country has to offer, these people were transformed into ambitious, self-respecting, public-spirited citizens. And so it is with the Italians and Poles, the Russian Jews, and other poor immigrants of more recent times. They are often very poor in this world's goods when they enter our gates. One sees the mothers coming in with shawls in place of hats, often without shoes or stockings, and with all their worldly belongings in a rough box or tied in a single hand-kerchief. But it is one of the miraculous phases of our history how quickly we are able to transform, enrich, and absorb them. A few years later one sees the children of these same immigrants well dressed and ambitious, well educated, and literally undistinguishable in manners, morals, or appearance from the descendants of those who came over in the *Mayflower*. Such is the Aladdin-like power of the great American melting-pot.

It is easy to echo the cry of prejudice if you happen to be of An-

---

Immigrants Do Not Increase Pauperism and Crime

In an article in the February 8, 1912, issue of the Independent, W. F. Willcox *wrote that many of the popular delusions about immigration are false. He uses statistics to show that immigrants do not degrade American society.*

The third objection is that "immigration seriously increases the amount of pauperism and crime in the United States." I grant that the 13,000,000 foreign born add to the *amount* of pauperism and crime. To make an effective argument the word *amount* should be changed to *proportion* and no doubt this is meant. Do the foreign-born population contribute disproportionately to the crime and pauperism of the country?

I have found nothing to prove that the foreign born contribute more largely to the almshouse population or the prison population than do the native whites of the same sex and age residing in the *same part* of the country. . . . When we consider that more than nineteen-twentieths of the foreign born in almshouses have been in the United States longer than ten years it cannot be claimed that recent immigrants are contributing disproportionately to the burden of pauperism.

As to crime, when attention is confined to major, or serious, offenses, the proportion of foreign-born whites committed to prison is almost exactly the same as the proportion of native whites of the same age. For example, among 100,000 native whites thirty to thirty-four years of age, forty-nine were committed to prison for serious offenses in 1904, and among the same number of foreign-born whites, forty-eight.

glo-Saxon descent, and to assume an air of superiority and denounce the Italians, Greeks, Poles, Bohemians, and Russian Jews, as if they ranked somewhere between man and the beast, but were not yet wholly human. The same intolerant attitude of mind among the Anglo-Saxon Puritan settlers of early colonial days led to the whipping, imprisonment, banishment, and even hanging of Quakers and others of unlike religious beliefs. If you share these prejudices to-day, walk some Sunday afternoon through the galleries of the art-museums in our large cities and note who are the people most interested in their treasures; inquire at the public libraries who are their most appreciative patrons; visit the night schools and observe who constitute their most eager classes; study the lineage of the ranking students in our universities and you will find that our libraries, art-galleries, universities, and schools often find their best patrons among the offspring of these despised races of Southern and Eastern Europe. Or if you seek your information in books, I would commend you to authorities who have studied the new immigrants at first-hand. If you will examine the volume on *The Italian in America*, by Messrs. Lord, Trenor, and Barrows, you will be reminded of what America owes to the Italians from Columbus down to our own day. And if you will read the study of *Our Slavic Fellow-Citizen*, by Dr. Balch, you will be reminded of what we owe to the Poles and Bohemians from the time of Pulaski and Kosciuszko down to our time. And if you will read the story of *The Promised Land* and *They Who Knock at Our Gates*, by Mary Antin, you will find descriptions of what we may expect from the Russian Jews. Incidentally you will also discover that the traditions and heroes of American history find their most ardent admirers to-day among these same people who but recently were aliens.

There is no evidence that the newer immigrants are inferior to the old. It is only the recurrence of a groundless prejudice which makes some people feel so. But even if the new immigration is not inferior in character to the old, we have still to ask whether there is not a menace in the very numbers of the immigrants now coming in. We hear a great deal these days about the alarming increase in immigration. We are told that more than a million foreign-born are coming into this country every year, that the number is increasing as never before, and that the country cannot absorb so great an influx. What are the facts in this regard?

As to the amount of recent immigration, the tide ebbs and flows with the alternating advances and recessions of business, and the tendency is for each successive wave to reach a higher level than its predecessors. In 1854 a record of 428,000 arrivals was established; then there was a great recession, and in 1873 a new high level of 460,000 was reached. The next wave culminated in 1882 with 789,000, and in 1907 the highest of all immigrant records was reached, 1,285,000. During the last ten years the average number of immigrants arriving in this country has not fallen much short of a million per year, and this figure considered by itself does look portentous. One must bear in mind, however, that it represents only one side of the ledger and is subject to very heavy deductions. If you are reckoning the extent to which your property has increased during a given period, it does not suffice merely to count up the income. You must also deduct the outgo. And if you are reckoning the actual addition to our population which results from immigration, if you would have in mind the actual number of immigrants that we have had to absorb, you must take account of both sides of the ledger, of the outgo as well as of the income. During the last six years the number of departing aliens has been carefully collated, and it appears that from 400,000 to 700,000 aliens depart from the United States every year. This leaves a net balance of arriving aliens of only about 550,000 per year, or only about one-half of the total that is commonly cited as representing the annual influx. Even this figure may look precarious, however, until we have considered it in its appropriate relations and comparisons.

America's Capacity

The capacity of the country to assimilate the incoming thousands without any serious modification of our institutions or standards depends in part upon two conditions: first, upon the proportion which the aliens bear to the resident population by which they are to be absorbed, and, second, upon whether the country is already approaching the saturation point as regards the density of its population. Now the proportion of foreign-born in our total population has not varied much in recent decades, and even in the record year of 1907 the percentage of immigrants to population was lower than it has been on several other occasions during the past sixty years. As compared with the population of the country the immigration of recent years has not bulked as large as the immigration of the early fifties, and if we consider only the net immigration, it makes to-day an addition to the total population of the country of only a little more than one-half of one per cent. per year.

Nor need one fear that we are reaching the point in this country where population presses upon the means of subsistence. The number of our people will have to be multiplied sixfold to equal the density of the population of France, to be multiplied tenfold to equal that of Germany or that of Italy, and to be multiplied eighteenfold to equal that of England. If the present population of the whole United States were located in the State of Texas alone,

147

there would still not be two-thirds as many inhabitants per square mile in that State as there are to-day in England. One must, indeed, have little faith in the future of the United States who, in the face of such comparisons, believes that the population of this country as a whole is approaching the saturation point, or that from the standpoint of the country as a whole we need be terrified by the dimensions of present immigration. It amounts in annual net to little more than one-half of one per cent. of our present population, and that population will have to increase many hundred per cent. before we have reached a density remotely approaching that of any of the leading countries of Europe.

There will, of course, always be timid Americans who will wonder how we can possibly hope to assimilate foreigners to the extent of as much as one-half of one per cent. of our population per year and who would prefer to see the country relatively weak and undeveloped than run the risk of continuing the experiment. When Jefferson proposed to purchase all of the great territory west of the Mississippi known as Louisiana, the citizens of Boston organized a public meeting to protest against the project. They thought it would destroy the relative influence of New England in the country's affairs, and they thought that the United States could not assimilate so vast a territory; and though their fears have been proven not only groundless but absurd by subsequent history, there are many still in Boston and elsewhere in the country who feel that our powers of assimilation have now reached their limit of capacity and ought not to be further taxed.

There will, of course, always be Americans absorbed in history and genealogy who will sigh for the good old days when America was only a sparsely settled fringe of seaboard States, and who will wish that the population of the country might still consist of the Sons and Daughters of the Revolution, the Colonial Dames, and the Sons of Colonial Wars. This might, indeed, have been a pleasant condition from certain points of view, but of one thing we may be certain: this country to-day would not be settled from coast to coast; our cities would not be a fifth of their present size; our powers as a nation and our prosperity as individuals would only have been a fraction of what they are had immigration been prevented.

VIEWPOINT 5

"That there is an inseparable relation between un-employment and immigration is demonstrated by the statistics which are available upon the subject."

The New Immigrants Harm the American Worker

John Mitchell (1870-1919)

An active spokesperson for labor and president of the American Federation of Labor, John Mitchell frequently wrote for the *American Federationist*, the official organ of the AFL, the country's first association of independent trade unions. Mitchell is also the author of *The Wage Earner and His Problems* and *Organized Labor: Its Problems, Purposes and Ideals and the Present and Future of American Wage Earners*. Established in 1886, the AFL, under the leadership of Samuel Gompers, exhorted its members to use their votes to protect American workers rather than to slavishly follow a political party. Its large membership gave the AFL considerable lobbying power, and one of the issues on which it frequently lobbied was immigration.

Most unionists believed immigrants harmed the American worker in several ways: In many cases, the newcomers, desperate to make a living or to get a start on the fortune they expected to make in the new land, were willing to work for low wages under sometimes criminally substandard working and living conditions. This meant the "native" American worker had to accept similar conditions and wages or be unemployed. In addition, huge numbers of the immigrants were unskilled or did not speak English and were therefore unable to put higher skills to work; consequently, they were available to fill unskilled positions. This, unionists felt, put Americans who would otherwise hold these jobs out of work.

In this viewpoint, originally published in the October 1909 *American Federationist*, Mitchell discusses the plight of the American worker in the wake of widespread immigration, and he supports a Congressional proposal for an immigrant head tax; that is, to help keep out impoverished people who would become a drag on society (and take American menial jobs), each immigrant would be required to pay a sum of money for the privilege of entering this country.

Certain steamship companies are bringing to this port many immigrants whose funds are manifestly inadequate for their proper support until such time as they are likely to obtain profitable employment. Such action is improper and must cease. In the absence of a statutory provision, no hard and fast rule can be laid down as to the amount of money an immigrant must bring with him, but in most cases it will be unsafe for immigrants to arrive with less than $25 besides railroad ticket to destination, while in many cases they should have more. They must, in addition, of course, satisfy the authorities that they will not become charges upon either public or private charity.

No official bulletin upon the subject of immigration has attracted more attention or caused more discussion than that issued under date of June 28, 1909, by the Commissioner of Immigration at the port of New York, from which the above excerpt is taken. It is both interesting and significant to observe the expressions of approval and disapproval of the principle laid down by Commissioner Williams for the guidance of prospective immigrants and the steamship companies through whose instrumentality large numbers of aliens are induced to leave the countries of their nativity and seek temporary or permanent homes upon our shores.

While this article is written from the standpoint of a wage earner, the subject is approached from the viewpoint of an American, because, fundamentally, no governmental policy can be of permanent value to the wage earners as such that is not beneficial to our country and all our people. And it is because a high standard of living and a progressive improvement in the conditions of life and labor among workingmen are essential to the prosperity of the whole people that the wage earners believe in a reasonable and effective regulation of immigration.

The commissioner at the port of New York in serving timely notice upon steamship companies, and indirectly upon the people of the Old World, that "in most cases it will be unsafe for immigrants to arrive with less than $25, besides railroad ticket to destination," has laid down a rule that, if followed, will not only afford some measure of protection to American labor, but will also protect the poor and oppressed of other countries by deterring them from coming here without adequate means to enable them to maintain themselves until such time as they can secure employment at a rate of wages comparable to the standard prevailing in the trade in which they seek work. When it becomes known in the countries of Europe that it is necessary for an immigrant to have in his possession a sufficient amount of money to pay his own way to the interior of the United States and to live until he can secure work at the prevailing rate of wages, only such immigrants will seek admission as are of the better class, and the danger of lowering the American standard of living will be materially reduced. It goes without saying that it is no advantage to society when an alien gains admission to our country and is forced by his necessities to accept employment at a rate of wages lower than the established or prevailing rate in the class of work he undertakes to do. And it is real hardship to the American workman and a loss to society if the newly arrived immigrant underbids him and secures the job held by one of our own citizens.

Maintaining American Wage Standards

The standard of wages for both skilled and unskilled labor in the United States has been built up as a result of years and years of energetic effort, struggle, and sacrifice. When an immigrant without resources is compelled to accept work at less than the established wage rate, he not only displaces a man working at the higher rate, but his action threatens to destroy the whole schedule of wages in the industry in which he secures employment, because it not infrequently occurs that an employer will attempt to regulate wages on the basis of the lowest rate paid to any of the men in his employ. Any reduction in wages means a lowering of the standard of living, and the standard of living among a civilized people can not be lowered without lowering in the same ratio the physical standard and the intellectual and moral ideals of that people.

Of course it may be said that this observation is not borne out by the experience and the history of our country. It is admittedly true that our population is largely an immigrant population, and that the standard of living has gradually tended higher; but in considering the influence and effects of stimulated immigration it is necessary to contrast conditions now with conditions prevailing in the past, and also to keep in mind the change that has taken place in the extent and the character of the immigration.

If the number of aliens coming annually to the United States were no greater now than in any year between 1820 and 1880, there would be, and could be, no reasonable ground for complaint; indeed, there would be little demand from wage earners for the enactment of laws restricting immigration if the number of aliens arriving did not exceed the number admitted in any year up to 1900, provided, of course, that such aliens were not brought here as contract laborers, or were not physically, mentally, or morally defective.

New Immigrants Demoralize Labor

W. Jett Lauck, a member of the 1907-1910 Immigration Commission and co-author of The Immigration Problem: A Study of American Immigration Conditions and Needs, *wrote in the February 1912 issue of* North American Review *that a major effect of the huge influx of "new" immigrants was to demoralize American labor.*

Another significant result of the extensive employment of southern and eastern Europeans in mining and manufacturing is seen in the general weakening and, in some instances, in the entire demoralization of the labor organizations which were in existence before the arrival of the races of recent immigration. This condition of affairs has been due to the inability of the labor-unions to absorb within a short time the constantly increasing number of new arrivals. The southern and eastern Europeans, as already pointed out, because of their tractability, their lack of industrial experience and training, and their necessitous condition on applying for work, have been willing to accept, without protest, existing conditions of employment. Their desire to earn as large an amount as possible within a limited time has also rendered the recent immigrant averse to entering into strikes which involved a loss of time and a decrease in earnings. . . .

The impossibility of competing with the recent immigrants or of educating them to demand their own standards of living and conditions of employment has voluntarily or involuntarily led to the displacement in many industries and occupations of native Americans and older immigrants from Great Britain and northern Europe.

That immigration in recent years has been stimulated beyond the line of assimilative possibility will be apparent even to the casual observer when the volume of immigration at the present time and in the recent past is compared with the number of immigrants who arrived here during the first eighty years for which statistics have been tabulated. For illustration, more aliens were admitted through our ports in one year, 1907, than were admitted during the entire twenty-four years from 1820 to 1843, inclusive; and nearly as many aliens were admitted in the five years from 1904 to 1908, inclusive, as were admitted during the forty years from 1820 to 1859, inclusive.

It is important to an intelligent understanding of this subject that at this point consideration be given not only to the extent of present immigration as compared with the immigration of early times, but also to the character and intention of many aliens who in recent years have gained admission to our country. It is safe to say that prior to 1880 nearly every immigrant, except contract laborers, left his own country for the purpose of making a permanent home for himself and his posterity in the country of his adoption. The immigrant of those days was a sturdy, adventurous pioneer, who was willing to undertake and withstand the struggles and the hardships incident to the development of a new and ofttimes dangerous country. He expected to carve out a career for himself, to build his home, and to find employment on ground and in fields upon which no other man had claim. The avenues and the opportunities of employment and home building of early times have largely passed away. To-day the alien has not the chance, even though he have the inclination, to be a constructive factor in the development of a new and high civilization. Large numbers of the immigrants of recent years regard our country simply as a foraging ground, in which they expect to make a "stake," and when they have done so, to return to their own countries and spend the remainder of their lives there; and this "stake" is too often accumulated by eating and living in a manner destructive of physical and social health. An immigration of this character is of absolutely no benefit to us. The alien who enjoys the advantages and protection of our Government, and afterwards takes or sends his accumulated savings back to the country of his birth, is not unlike our butterflies of fashion whose parents invest American millions in the purchase of foreign titles.

The Plight of the American Worker

That the question of immigration presents a real problem, which is rapidly approaching a crisis, is evidenced by many circumstances, all of which point in the same direction—not the least of these being the act of Congress creating a commission to make an exhaustive investigation into the effects of immigration upon our national life. From public and private institutions of charity comes the ominous warning that the means at hand are insufficient to relieve the cry of distress; the bread line, that standing indictment against society which has been duplicated in other cities and in other sections of the city of New York, proclaims louder than words that something is radically wrong. Trade-unions, ever jealous of their prestige and of the dignity and self-respect of their members, have given out millions of dollars to buy bread for those of their number who can not find work to do. And all this time, during which able-bodied men anxious and willing to work are tramping the streets and the highways in idleness, hundreds of thousands of immigrants are pouring in upon us—some to make the struggle of the American worker more difficult to bear, and others to be recruited into that army of unemployed which threatens to become a permanent institution of our national life.

It is not sufficient to say that these are abnormal conditions, the result of a temporary industrial depression, or that the evils will vanish with the return of "good times." While there can be no doubt that a revival of industrial activity will relieve, in a measure, the strain of the situation, and perhaps the cry of want and the mutterings of discontent will be less frequently heard, nevertheless a cure will not be effected and the problem will remain unsolved. The world does not owe a living to an able-bodied man, but society does owe its workmen an opportunity to earn a living under fair and reasonable conditions. The first duty of a community is to give its own members the opportunity of being employed at decent wages; then, and not until then, its arms should be held wide open to welcome the less favored of every nation and of every clime.

The American wage earner, be he native or immigrant, entertains no prejudice against his fellow from other lands; but, as self-preservation is the first law of nature, our workmen believe and contend that their labor should be protected against the competition of an induced immigration comprised largely of men whose standards and ideals are lower than our own. The demand for the exclusion of Asiatics, especially the Chinese and the Hindus, is based solely upon the fact that, as a race their standard of living is extremely low and their assimilation by America impossible. The American wage earner is not an advocate of the principle of indiscriminate exclusion which finds favor in some quarters, and he is not likely to become an advocate of such a policy unless he is driven to this extreme as a matter of self-preservation. He fails, however, to see the consistency of a legislative protective policy which does not, at the same time that it protects industry, give equal protection to American labor. If the products of our mills and factories are to be protected by a tariff on articles manufactured abroad, then, by the same token, labor should be protected against an unreasonable competition from a stimulated and excessive immigration.

And it is highly important to the peace and harmony of our population, whether it be native or alien, that discrimination against Americans shall not be permitted. Every good citizen will view with regret and foreboding the publication of advertisements, such as the following, which appeared in the Pittsburgh papers a few days ago:

> Men wanted. Tinners, catchers, and helpers, to work in open shops. Syrians, Poles, and Roumanians preferred. Steady employment and good wages to men willing to work. Fare paid and no fees charged.

The suggestion that American labor is not wanted is likely to arouse a sentiment of hostility against the foreign workers whose labor is preferred by the companies responsible for advertisements of this character. Nothing but evil can come from discord and racial antagonism. At the same time that the American workman recognizes the necessity of reasonable restriction upon the admission of future immigrants, he realizes that his own welfare depends upon being able to work and to live in harmony and fellowship with those who have been admitted and are now a part of our industrial and social life.

There is perhaps no group in America so free from racial or religious prejudice as the workingmen. It is a matter of indifference to them whether an immigrant comes from Great Britain, Italy, or Russia; whether he be black, white, or yellow; whether he be Christian, Mohammedan, or Jew. The chief consideration is that, wherever he comes from, he shall be endowed with the capacity and imbued with the determination to improve his own status in life, and equally determined to preserve and promote the standard of life of the people among whom he expects to live. The wage earners, as a whole, have no sympathy with that narrow spirit which would make a slogan of the cry, "America for the Americans"; on the contrary, we recognize the immigrant as our fellow worker; we believe that he has within him the elements of good citizenship, and that, given half a chance, he will make a good American; but a million aliens can not be absorbed and converted into Americans each year; neither can profitable employment be found for a million newcomers each year, in addition to the natural increase in our own population.

That there is an inseparable relation between unemployment and immigration is demonstrated by the statistics which are available upon the subject. There are, of course, no complete data showing the extent and effects of unemployment, but from the records of 27 national and international trade unions it is found that during the year 1908 from 10 to 70 per cent of the members of various trades were in enforced idleness for a period of one month or more. These 27 unions are selected from the highly skilled trades, in which organization is most thorough and systematic. Their records show that an average of 32 per cent of the total membership was unemployed. If this ratio applied to other organizations it would indicate that approximately 1,000,000 organized workmen were without employment during the past year. Assuming that unemployment affected the unskilled and unorganized wage earners in the same proportion, it would mean that 2,500,000 wage earners were unemployed; and while there has been a marked improvement in industrial conditions during the past few months, it will not be contended that unemployment is not still a serious problem and the cause of great and general suffering. Indeed, it is perfectly safe to say that the unskilled and unorganized workmen suffered more from unemployment, both as to the proportion who were so unemployed and in actual physical and mental distress, because the organized workman, in most instances, had built up in normal times a fund upon which he could draw to tide him over his emergency; whereas the unskilled and unorganized workmen—many of whom are recently arrived immigrants—were forced to depend upon charity or upon the munificence of their friends to carry them over the industrial crisis.

Unskilled Immigrants

In connection with this subject, a significant feature of our immigration problem presents itself. Of the 113,038 aliens admitted in March, 1909, which figures are typical of all other periods in recent years, only 10,224 were skilled workmen, while 77,058 were unskilled laborers; the remaining 25,756 being women and children, professional men, and others having no definite occupation. In other words, these figures show that less than 10 per cent of the aliens admitted in the month of March were equipped and trained to follow a given line of employment, whereas 77,058 were thrust upon us, in most cases so situated that they would be compelled to accept the first job, and at any wages, offered to them. It is true that many thousands of these laborers are classed as "farm hands," but it requires no exhaustive inquiry to discover that a farm hand from continental Europe rarely seeks employment as a farm laborer in America. Farming in Europe and farming in America are two separate and distinct propositions; in this country farming is done with modern machinery, in continental Europe the work is done by hand, and the European farm laborer is little better equipped to operate the machinery on an American farm than is a section hand to drive a locomotive. The facts are that the immigrant who was a farm laborer in his own country seeks employment in America in the unskilled trades. He becomes a mill hand, a factory worker, an excavator, a section hand, and in large numbers he becomes a mine worker. It is only necessary to visit the mining districts of the Eastern and Central Western States, the mill towns, and the centers of the textile industry to find these erstwhile European farm laborers. They have been colonized, and because of the large numbers who are congregated together, the opportunity for or the possibility of their assimilation is greatly minimized. The temptation to establish and perpetuate the customs and standards of their own countries, instead of adopting the standards of our country, is so great that if the system of colonization continues it will take several generations to amalgamate these races and blend them into an American people. This condition is not best for them; neither is it good for us; it is simply the result of an unregulated immigration and an unwise distribution of aliens.

While wage earners will undoubtedly indorse the principle laid down by the Commissioner of Immigration at the port of New York, the enforcement of that policy should not be discretionary with him. If we are going to regulate immigration at all, we should prescribe by law definite conditions, the application of which would result in securing only those immigrants whose standards and ideals compare favorably with our own. To that end wage earners believe:

First. That, in addition to the restrictions imposed by the laws at present in force, the head tax of $4 now collected should be increased to $10.

Second. That each immigrant, unless he be a political refugee, should bring with him not less than $25, in addition to the amount required to pay transportation to the point where he expects to find employment.

Third. That immigrants between the ages of 14 and 50 years should be able to read a section of the Constitution of the United States, either in our language, in their own language, or in the language of the country from which they come.

While the writer holds no commission that gives him authority to speak in the name of the American wage earners, he believes that he interprets correctly in this article their general sentiment upon the subject of immigration.

VIEWPOINT 6

"Wages have advanced more rapidly and hours of labor have been shortened more during the periods of our greatest European immigration than in any previous period in our industrial history."

The New Immigrants Help America

Harris Weinstock (1854-1922)

Born in London, Harris Weinstock moved to the United States while a very small child. He ultimately became a prominent merchant and philanthropist in California. He was active in military, educational, economic, and legislative affairs and was particularly active in promoting California commerce. In 1916, while he was the state market director of California, he wrote an article for the *Annals*, a publication of the American Academy of Political and Social Science, that took the often unpopular stance that America needs immigrants in order to get all its work done. Far from depriving the American laborer of jobs and wages, Weinstock asserts, the immigrant fills a void unfilled by the American laborer. Immigrants take jobs Americans do not want, and they fill jobs in less populous areas where there are not enough Americans to fill them. Weinstock also asserts that both wages and working conditions improved during the period of heavy immigration in the early part of the twentieth century.

Most of us are opposed to all monopolies except our own. The

officials of organized labor, being a part of us, can
hardly be blamed for being opposed to the encouragem
migration. These officials feel exactly as merchants an
sional men would feel if they were asked to help to inc ___ ___ ___
number of their competitors, and to that degree to invite decreased earnings.

The natural feeling on the part of organized labor officials is
that a large influx of immigrants brings lowered wages and more
hands to do the work, and thus less work for each pair of hands
to do. When hard times come, they claim that these conditions
simply aggravate the problem of unemployment.

The officials of organized labor are the leading proponents in
the claim that immigration has largely been responsible for the
existing state of industrial unrest; that it has been the largest
single factor in preventing the wage scale from rising as rapidly
as food prices; that it has done much to prevent the development
of better relations between employers and employees; that it has
greatly hampered the formation of trade unions and has increased the problem of securing responsible organizations.

I said that the officials of organized labor are opposed to immigration. No man knows what is the attitude on this question on
the part of the rank and file of the three million trade unionists,
since to my knowledge there has never been a trade union referendum taken to learn their attitude. It is quite likely that if such
referendum were taken it would be found that the great body of
trade unionists, many of whom are immigrants or the immediate
descendants of immigrants, would favor giving the same opportunities for betterment to their European kith and kin that they
have been permitted to enjoy.

What the worker in this country needs is the widest opportunity for employment and the greatest demand for the output of
his handiwork.

Imagine the population of this nation reduced from one hundred million to say fifty million. It must be plain that under such
circumstances the home consumption for the output of American
labor would be cut in half and opportunities for employment on
the part of the remaining 50 per cent of the population would be
reduced accordingly.

On the other hand, imagine the population of the nation in due
course doubled. This would double the home demand for labor's
output. The increased output would lessen cost of production
and thus tend to widen our world markets.

A great cry over the scarcity of labor comes from the farmer,
more especially of the West. This very harvest season has seen a
call for harvest hands at offers of wages almost prohibitory to the
farmer, and yet the farm labor demand was not supplied. Let this

condition go on and in the near future farming would become so unprofitable as to cut down the acreage under cultivation, not only because of the scarcity of new labor, but also because much of the present farm labor would be lured to the cities on account of the higher wages offered and the greater city attractions. This in turn would spell yet higher costs for food, putting a still greater burden on the consumer.

Impact of World War I

The European War has revolutionized world conditions. When it shall have been brought to an end, Europe will find herself poor indeed.

The world's greatest asset is its men. This most valuable of all assets is being steadily decimated by being killed off and crippled in Europe by the hundreds of thousands. When peace shall have been restored, the nations will find themselves handicapped not only by the loss of millions of able-bodied workers carried off by the bullet and by disease, but also by other millions of men who through loss of limb and of productive power will have become

Immigrants Do Not Displace American Workers

In statistician Isaac A. Hourwich's study of immigration called Immigration and Labor: The Economic Aspects *(1912), he wrote that immigration had not caused an oversupply of labor.*

There is absolutely no statistical proof of an oversupply of unskilled labor resulting in the displacement of native by immigrant laborers. No decrease of the number of common laborers among the native white of native or foreign parentage appears in any of the great states which serve as receptacles for immigration. The same is true of miners. In none of the states affected by the new immigration has there been a decrease in the number of native miners. Such states as Pennsylvania and Illinois showed large increases in the number of native miners, both of foreign and native parentage. . . .

The effect of immigration upon the occupational distribution of the industrial wage-earners has been the elevation of the English-speaking workmen to the status of an aristocracy of labor, while the immigrants have been employed to perform the rough work of all industries. . . . The rapid pace of industrial expansion has increased the number of skilled and supervisory positions so fast that practically all the English-speaking employees have had the opportunity to rise on the scale of occupations. This opportunity, however, was conditioned upon a corresponding increase of the total operating force. It is only because the new immigration has furnished the class of unskilled laborers that the native workmen and older immigrants have been raised to the plane of an aristocracy of labor.

burdens.

There will be the greatest scarcity of able-bodied men to carry on the great work of restoring European industry and the ravages of war.

It is plain to foresee that the governments of Europe must establish conditions that will conserve for themselves what remains of their brawn and muscle. Every possible step will most likely be taken to put a ban upon emigration of the able-bodied, and anyone who will encourage such emigration will be regarded as an enemy to the country and doubtless treated as such.

Meanwhile, while the warring countries of Europe are impoverishing themselves in men and in money, the United States is waxing rich as never before in its history. Its wealth will keep on growing to proportions never dreamed of by the wildest visionary. This vastly increased wealth must be profitably employed and can best be profitably employed by the development of our many yet undeveloped natural resources.

How are these great resources to be developed without an adequate labor supply? How are we to build our canals, our reservoirs and our railways? How are we to develop our mines, cut down our forests, build our ships, colonize our lands and conduct the potential great industrial enterprises now in sight, without added supply of brawn and muscle? Unless all this is done, the opportunities for still greater betterment on the part of the labor now with us are minimized.

Americans Disdain Manual Labor

We may deplore the fact, but the fact nevertheless remains, that our American-born workers look with more or less disdain upon the handling of the pick and shovel. Whatever the causes may be, they do not and will not perform the unavoidable tasks inseparable from the development of great natural resources by being "hewers of wood and drawers of water."

Imagine how impossible it would have been, for example, to build the Panama Canal within even a lifetime, if none but American citizens were to have been employed as common laborers. Had there not been available a supply of Jamaican negroes, Spanish, Mexican and other common labor, the completion of the Canal in all likelihood would have been postponed for a decade or more, to the loss of the entire world. As it was, remunerative employment for several years was afforded thousands of American citizens during the construction of the Canal as foremen, as engineers, and in all the positions of trust and responsibility.

Another problem affected by immigration is that of domestic service. Cut off the supply of house servants by restricting immigration and you further aggravate, more especially in the West, the great existing problem of securing domestic help. Already the cry of the American housewife has gone abroad that the supply is entirely inadequate to meet the demand. The lack of efficient servants and the great increase in their wage have caused a famine in this line of activity. Again the fact remains that for social and other reasons American girls will not, as a rule, enter domestic service. The shorter hours, the alleged higher social standing, the greater freedom offered by the shop, the store and the office are decimating the ranks from which domestics were formerly recruited. This change in conditions is in the nature of a menace to the American home.

Untold thousands of salaried men and small tradesmen who could formerly afford to employ one or more domestic servants find that these have become luxuries beyond their means. The home is therefore in thousands of instances being abandoned all over the land for the boarding-house or the hotel. Children, formerly reared in private, surrounded by proper home influences, are now destined to be reared in cheap hotels or boarding-houses, with all their consequent ills on childhood. Conditions such as these must in time cause "our new graves to become more numerous than our cradles." The only recruiting ground for domestic help remains in Europe.

Minimize immigration and you still further aggravate the existing problem of domestic service.

A Labor Famine

There is today throughout industrial centers a labor famine, caused partly by the cessation of immigration and partly due to many able-bodied men of foreign birth leaving the United States to fight the battles of their native land. This labor famine is limiting the possibilities of industrial and agricultural development and is simply a forecast of what would follow a still further limitation of immigration. The unprecedented industrial and agricultural expansion which has taken place in this country in recent decades is primarily due to immigration. Without it, development along such lines would long since have ceased.

The possibilities in all directions in this country are as yet limitless. We can better appreciate this when we realize that the State of Texas with England's density of population could alone accommodate the people of the entire United States.

Every able-bodied male or female producer, literate or illiterate, that can be brought to this country with sound body and good character is an added asset.

It has been pointed out that a first class black slave was worth before the Civil War, $1,500. How much more then should a healthy, able-bodied, free, white man be worth to the country?

162

It is true that at times our congested centers are seemingly overloaded with labor. A goodly percentage of this overload will be found to be among seasonal workers, temporarily out of employment because of climatic conditions, as well as the disabled, the incompetent, the unwilling, or the victims of drink, drugs or disease.

These conditions could in a measure be minimized if we were to follow the plan pursued by the Argentine Republic and other South American countries, which furnish free transportation within their borders to new arrivals in order to minimize labor congestion.

Immigrants Good for America's Welfare

It is not a question so much of giving population across the sea so large a place in our regard and in our hospitality, as it is a question of seeking the welfare and development of our own nation, and all its wonderful resources.

We are told that immigration tends to beat down wages; but the fact remains that wages have advanced more rapidly and hours of labor have been shortened more during the periods of our greatest European immigration than in any previous period in our industrial history.

It has been pointed out that

> eighty-five per cent of all labor in the slaughtering and packing industries is done by alien laborers. They mine seven-tenths of our bituminous coal. They do 78 per cent of the work in the woolen mills, nine-tenths of all the labor in the cotton mills, and make nineteen-twentieths of all the clothing. Immigrants make more than half the shoes in the country. They turn out four-fifths of our furniture, half the tobacco and cigars and nearly all of our sugar. In the iron and steel industries, immigrants share all the risks.

The workman at one time looked upon the invention of every labor-saving device as a menace and a competitor likely to rob him of his job. Time has shown that, instead of robbing men of labor, these devices have created untold new avenues of labor. The lessened cost of production made possible by labor-saving devices has greatly increased consumption and thus in turn tremendously increased the demand for labor.

The immigrant, by furnishing the needed labor, opens out new productive possibilities that otherwise would remain closed, so that instead of robbing those here of work, his presence makes new and still more abundant work possible.

Despite the alleged excessive immigration of recent decades, the fact remains that the ratio between foreign- and native-born during the past fifty years remains substantially the same. The census shows that in 1860 the foreign-born were 13.2 per cent of the population, and in 1910 were but 14.7 per cent. Wages are higher, working hours shorter, and standards of living far in advance in the United States today compared with 1860.

It has been pointed out that immigrants have a passion for educating their children. The United States Commissioner of Education tells us in a Bulletin that

> the least illiterate element of our children is the native-born children of foreign-born parents. The illiteracy among the children of native-born parents is three times as great as that among the native-born children of foreign-born parents.

Welcome the Immigrant

We find then that labor leaders and those who sympathize with their point of view are not warranted by the facts in opposing immigration. We find that our industrial needs, our agricultural needs, our domestic needs, all demand that we shall continue to extend the hand of welcome to every decent, able-bodied man and woman who is willing to come and work among us. We find that the greatest progress we have made in trade, in industry, in commerce, in agriculture, in education, in the arts and sciences and in social welfare has been made during the decades when immigration in this country has been greatest. We believe that ample provision has been made by law to keep out the mentally, morally, and physically unfit. We believe that these laws should be rigidly enforced and that if the present machinery for doing so is inadequate it should be bettered and perfected. We believe that in order to make still greater progress along all lines of human endeavor, we can with perfect safety and advantage to ourselves and to our children, as well as to the advantage of the fit immigrants and their children, invite them to be of us and with us for their good and for ours.

VIEWPOINT 7

"However rapidly the difficulties of Americanization may be increasing, the efficiency and activity of the forces of Americanization are increasing even more rapidly."

Forces in American Society Aid Assimilation

Grover G. Huebner (1884-1964)

During the height of the "new" immigration in the first part of the twentieth century, many people were concerned with how the newcomers would fit into America. They believed the huge numbers of immigrants from cultures far different from that of the United States would destabilize the nation. Many people envisioned a future America with language, customs, and beliefs degraded by these foreigners.

Grover G. Huebner disagreed. He believed many forces in American society were helping bring about successful assimilation. Professor of transportation and commerce at the prestigious Wharton School at the University of Pennsylvania, Huebner was the author of many books on topics in his field. The following viewpoint is excerpted from an article published in Volume XXVII of *The Annals of the American Academy of Political and Social Science* (1906). In it, Huebner comments on several forces in American society that help immigrants assimilate.

"Americanization" is assimilation in the United States. It is that process by which immigrants are transformed into Americans. It is not the mere adoption of American citizenship, but the actual raising of the immigrant to the American economic, social and moral standard of life. Then has an immigrant been Americanized only when his mind and will have been united with the mind and will of the American so that the two act and think together. The American of to-day is, therefore, not the American of yesterday. He is the result of the assimilation of all the different nationalities of the United States which have been united so as to think and act together.

Again, Americanization is very different from amalgamation. Amalgamation is but one force which appears in the Americanization process and that an unimportant one, as it usually occurs only after the immigrant has been at least partly Americanized. Furthermore, "to think and act together" does not necessitate that race ties are wholly lost. That is its usual meaning, but nationalities such as the Jews, Italians, Bohemians and even Scandinavians often settle in practically exclusive settlements. Such settlements are Americanized in as much as the immigrants learn to think and act like Americans. "To think and act together" in some cases is, therefore, to think and act like Americans, and in others it is the actual uniting of the minds and activities of the immigrants with those of the Americans by actual, permanent association.

Finally, it is essential to recognize degrees of Americanization. Some immigrants will adopt certain American methods, customs and ideas, but will refuse, or prove themselves unable, to adopt others. Some will, quite fully, adopt the industrial methods of American industry and yet be unable to speak the English language. While they are not fully Americanized, they are at least to a greater or less degree. . . .

The question now to determine is: . . . What are the Americanizing forces? How do they affect the immigrant? . . . What forces are doing most to meet the problem?

The School

The importance of the school as an Americanization force lies chiefly in its effect upon the second generation; yet indirectly it affects the adult immigrant himself, in as much as his children, consciously and unconsciously, influence him in the same direction. A considerable number of immigrants, also, come as children and can and do attend school. . . .

The following are some of the main Americanizing activities of the public school:

Economics Helps Assimilation

Edward A. Steiner, a professor at Grinnell College in Grinnell, Iowa, himself an immigrant, wrote about the immigrant experience in his 1909 book The Immigrant Tide: Its Ebb and Flow. *In this excerpt he comments on how economic aspirations aid the immigrant's assimilation.*

Like their forerunners in the migratory movement of European races, the present immigrants respond quickly to the American higher standards of living, and in many cases much more quickly than some of the older groups responded.

When we speak of the horrors of the East Side of New York, the crowded Ghetto and Mulberry Street with its Italian filth, we forget the days when the Irish possessed the land, "squatting" wherever they could, and living in wretched huts; when the American used to sing:

"The pig was in the parlour, and that was Irish too."

The pig and the goat have gone, and instead, the Irish have pianos and phonographs in their parlours; but in one generation, many Slavs and Italians, under less favourable conditions, have achieved the same results, minus the pig and goat period.

To-day, the merchants in Wilkes-Barre, Scranton, Connelsville and Pittsburg regard the Slav as a great "spender"; and if the Italian is not now like his predecessors, he soon will become so imbued by the American spirit, that, like us, he will live up to his income and beyond it.

1. It at once throws the children of different nationalities into mutual relationship. This inevitably breaks up the habits of any one of the foreign nationalities. The next step is, then, to adopt a common way of thinking and acting, which practically means the adoption of the American standard. This does not, however, apply to exclusive foreign colonies where schools may consist of a single nationality. In many cases it not only means the forced association of different nationalities, but of an immigrant child with children who are already Americanized. It is evident that in this case, which is the normal one, the immigrant child necessarily loses its foreign ideas and unconsciously adopts the thoughts and activities of the American companions. . . .

2. The public school teaches the children the English language. This enables them to associate with the various nationalities in their community, even outside of the school. . . .

3. The public school tends to break up hostility between nationalities. Not only is this the natural consequence of the close association between the children of different nationalities in the

school, but the teacher prevents its open appearance and teaches the existence of common interests. Social solidarity is secured.

4. It teaches American traditions and the history of our institutions. This again means a breaking up of race ties and a building up of social solidarity. Under this comes, also, the growth of American patriotism, which, while not important industrially, is a step toward the assimilation of minds and wills.

5. The public school is the first and chief trainer of the immigrant child's mind to fit it for originality and inventiveness. It enlarges the child's capacity.

6. The introduction of machinery makes it essential that labor shift from one kind of work to another. The public school, in training the minds of the children, fits them to meet this versatility in American industry.

7. The American characteristic of aspiration to reach a higher plane of production is transmitted to the immigrant child. This Americanizes the thoughts of the immigrant.

8. Finally, the public school, by the introduction of manual training, not only tends to give the child some idea of American industrial methods, but teaches him that manual work is here the universal rule and is not a stamp of inferiority. . . .

Trade Unionism

While the school is the greatest Americanization force for the second generation, it has but an indirect effect upon the adult. The problem of how to induce this adult immigrant to adopt American life is rapidly coming to be a function of trade unionism. Professor Ripley says: "Whatever our judgment is as to the expediency of the industrial policy of our American trade unions, no student of contemporary conditions can deny that they are a mighty factor in affecting the assimilation of our foreign population.". . .

The most pronounced instance of union Americanization is the activity of the United Mine Workers. There are twenty-six nationalities now working in the coal fields, with a growing difficulty in the form of a movement away from the mines by the Irish, Welsh, English, Germans, and Scotch, and the coming in of an increasing number of Poles, Ruthenians, Hungarians, Italians, and Bohemians. To-day the union members consist of over 90 per cent. of foreign birth, one-half of whom cannot speak the English language. Before the union entered, these people were formed into hostile groups, which made Americanization impossible. The Lithuanians, for example, were bitter enemies of the Poles; the Magyars were the enemies of the Slovaks. At first separate nationalities had separate unions, because they could not be induced to organize together. In this form they were first taught that they had common interests. Then it was that men of the common nationalities and districts were organized together. Now it is not so much a question as to whether a man is Polish or Italian, as to whether he is union or non-union.

Addresses are made in two, three or even more languages, but the association of the various nationalities must inevitably result in the adoption of the English tongue. The union is also breaking up the domination of the priest. Again, it teaches the immigrant that he is not working because of the generosity of the boss. It also teaches these men the power to sacrifice something for a cause, and consequently leads them to recognize something more than private interests. Finally, it has increased wages, reduced hours, and improved other working conditions. Without this the pauper immigrant would not have the ability to adopt the American standard of life.

The unions of the clothing trades have also done much to Americanize the immigrants. The present weakness of the United Garment Workers is but temporary, and their history indicates what can be expected in the future. In New York City the union began twenty years ago, and, with periods of success and failure, although controlled by the Jews, finally abolished the sweatshop and task system, increased wages and reduced hours of labor, secured large factories in many instances and steam power instead of foot power. Thus it Americanized the industry itself, and made the Americanization of the immigrants in other directions a possibility.

Then it was that assimilation advanced in other directions. In the 1904 strike, while many of the immigrants did not know exactly why there was a strike, they struck because they thought their union was in danger. In other words, they knew how to fight for a cause. Those union men who worked for independent employers paid from 15 to 20 per cent. of their wages to support the strikers, many of whom were non-union men and not even Jews, but Italians and Lithuanians. When a Jew voluntarily does that, one can say that he is no longer a Jew. He is at least partly Americanized. Ties of nationality are being broken. Americans, Germans, Lithuanians, Italians, Irish and Scotch are in the same union, and are harmonious. Furthermore, when the Jews arrive they, more than any other nationality, are timid and fear the employer. During the recent strike, however, they considered their union as unconquerable, and expressed confidence and fearlessness. This leads to participation in the control of business by the employee, a great step toward Americanization. . . .

Some of the most important activities in this direction are the following:

1. The union teaches the immigrants self-government. It is the

first place where they learn to govern their own activities and to obey officers whom they themselves elect, where each has a vote, and each can state his grievances, not to be remedied by some superior force, as in his native country, but by himself and his fellow-workmen.

2. The union gives the immigrant a sense of common cause, which leads to a sense of public, not merely private, interest.

3. It throws different nationalities into united groups, so that the foreign nationality of any one of them becomes lost. The next step is to adopt a common way of thinking and acting, which is Americanization.

4. It often brings foreigners into direct association with members of unions who have already been partly or wholly assimilated. These foreigners then learn to see the difference between the customs of these assimilated workmen and their own.

5. The union usually requires every member to be a citizen of the United States, or to have declared his intention of becoming one.

6. It develops foresight in the immigrant. In fact, the very act of joining a union is an evidence of foresight.

7. It does away with the arbitrary dictation of bosses and employers, and introduces the idea of partial control of the industry by the employee.

8. The union shows the immigrant that he does not hold his "job" solely because of the generosity or personal favor of the employer, but because he has an inherent right to work.

9. It does away with priest rule.

10. It raises the immigrant's wages, reduces his hours and improves his physical working conditions. In other words, it enables him to adopt the American social and moral standard of living.

11. It breaks up hostilities between nationalities. This is not only in itself a step toward Americanization, but is essential before the immigrants can begin to adopt the thoughts and activities of Americans. . . .

Physical Environment and the Presence of American Life

Not a little Americanizing influence is exerted by the physical conditions in which the immigrant lives after he arrives in the United States. Climate, for example, compels a change of dress, manner of living and kind of occupation. Physical environment tends to destroy his old habits and customs, and he adopts in their place American habits and customs, because they are better suited to American physical conditions.

In the beginning of our history, the strongest Americanizing force was "frontier life," which is a form of physical environment.

Under its influence the immigrants were transformed so rapidly and silently that there was not until recently such a problem as modern Americanization. This force is, of course, diminishing in importance, but in the country of to-day there exists something very much like it. Even when immigrants live in colonies, they frequently become Americans, in the first generation. Still there are no unions in the country, and the schools are inferior to those of the city. Why is it that they Americanize? Quite probably it is because of this force of physical environment in the form of frontier life, slightly modified. These immigrants do not Americanize as rapidly or as completely as they did years ago, but they Americanize in a similar way. It is slower than in the city—but it is permanent. It is the distinguishing feature of Americanization in the country.

In the city it is essential to note the Americanizing influence which is exercised by the mere presence of American life. There is a continual rush of industry. In order to live the immigrant must work largely at American occupations, and this, either through the boss or through competition, compels him to adopt American industrial methods. He sees the American system of government, the American way of living, American activity and American ideals. The difference between them and his own must influence him in the direction of those he sees all about him on the streets and at his work. . . .

The Church and Other Influences

The action of the church as an Americanization force is much like that of the parochial school. It does something to Americanize the immigrant; but, also, in another sense, acts as a hindrance. Its greatest influence is in molding the morals of the immigrant. In a certain sense, also, it acts as a co-ordinating force. Many nationalities comprising the great bulk of immigration belong to the same denomination—the Catholic. So it is with the Italians, the Bohemians, the Irish, Spanish, Portuguese, Hungarians, Lithuanians, Slavonians, Polanders, and most of the people from southeastern Europe. . . . The church, in some instances, tends to bring Americanized immigrants into association with unamericanized immigrants. It also tends to prevent lawlessness. It informs the immigrant what the new laws are and how they differ from those of his native country. It tells him what the new country expects of him socially, politically, and industrially. Finally, the church does something to obliterate slum conditions, thus not merely raising the immigrant's standard of life, but making it possible for other Americanization forces to permanently affect him. . . .

In 1900 56.8 per cent. of the foreign born males of voting age in the United States were naturalized, 8.3 per cent. had filed their first papers, 14.9 per cent. were unknown, and 20 per cent. were aliens. Thus, politics directly affects considerably more than the majority of the immigrants.

In the past this influence of politics upon the immigrants has done much to assimilate them. Its effect to-day depends upon its local conditions. . . . In the case of those immigrants who are not in the power of the political boss of the immigrant colonies, politics is one of the most striking differences between American life and life in their native country. When they vote it is an expression of their will, and inevitably spurs them on to learn how to express that will more intelligently. It tells them that they are part of society; that they have a voice in the control of their actions, and that their interests are not merely private, but are public. Every important step in our political system, to them, means further adoption of American life. . . .

Municipal governments are beginning to undertake activities which tend to assimilate the immigrants, at least from the social standpoint. They prevent unsanitary tenement houses, thus forcing a change in the home life of some of the immigrants and improving their social condition. They introduce public playgrounds, which tend to throw the children of the immigrants into association with other children. They establish baths, they minimize drunkenness and make efforts to prevent pauperism. All this aids in the movement of assimilation.

The *theaters, popular amusements, "boys' clubs," private societies* of various kinds, even *American slang* and the street life which prevails in the large cities, all act as assimilators. There is no more potent factor in the lives of some of the immigrant children than the influences which they meet on the streets.

Finally, it is necessary to consider, briefly, the activity of the *employer* as an Americanizer. In this respect, employers must be considered as individuals and not as a class, for many care nothing about Americanization, and others actually oppose it. Some of them, however, voluntarily give their workmen high wages, reasonable hours, and good physical and sanitary conditions of labor. In this way employers enable the immigrant to adopt the American standard of life, at least in the economic field. Again, in many instances employers have adopted the factory in preference to the sweatshop. The factory takes the immigrant out of his home and compels him to work with other workmen, many of whom are already Americanized and of different nationalities. Sometimes employers purposely employ men of different nationalities to prevent clannishness. Besides, the factory system is in itself a revelation to the immigrant from southern Europe. It means the compulsory adoption of American methods.

Many employers are in favor of the organization of their work-

Becoming American

Economics and politics are two strong assimilating influences, according to Richmond Mayo-Smith, author of Emigration and Immigration: A Study in Social Science *(1898).*

There are, fortunately, certain forces which tend to counteract this exclusiveness on the part of the immigrants and gradually to fuse the different elements into one American nationality. Two of these we have already mentioned, viz., economic prosperity and the practice of free political institutions. The former widens the circle of wants of the new citizen and leads him to imitate the higher style of living which he sees about him. This separates him from the habits and traditions of his native country and he adopts new standards which are associated in his mind with the new domicile, and which produce a feeling of superiority when he revisits the old home or comes into contact with later arrivals. It differentiates him, so to speak, from the immigrant, and gives him a feeling of attachment to the country where he has prospered. This feeling increases with his children and grandchildren until they become fully identified with our customs, manner of living and habits of thought, and are thoroughly Americanized.

The exercise of political rights, to which many of the immigrants are strange, tends to differentiate them in much the same way. It makes them of importance to the political leaders. It gives them a higher position than they were accustomed to at home, and this naturally attaches them to the new country. However much our politics may suffer from the addition of this vote, much of it ignorant and some of it depraved, there is no doubt as to the educational and nationalizing effect of the suffrage on the immigrants themselves. However attached the Irishman may be to the cause of home rule for Ireland, or however proud the German may be of the military glory of the empire, his feelings must gradually and unconsciously gravitate to the country where he has found economic prosperity and political recognition. He may still observe the national feast days and wave the old flag, but if it ever came to a contest, he would probably find that he was more of an American than an Irishman or a German.

men, and are, therefore, entitled to some of the credit given to trade unionism. The movement of the so-called "welfare work," but recently established on an organized basis, is also significant. Many of the private libraries and the industrial and evening schools are the work of employers. Not a few employers recognize the principle that the workmen have a right to participate in the control of industry, as is seen in the growth of the joint agreement. Correlative with this is the growing practice of certain employers to encourage originality and inventiveness. Finally, the railroads, who must be classed as employers, carry immigrants from one region to another that is entirely different, thus introducing influences which tend to break up their foreign characteristics. Some railroads distribute immigrants by transporting whole colonies out of the cities into the country.

The problem of the Americanization of the immigrant is very huge in proportion, and is becoming increasingly complex. The number of immigrants, together with the population of foreign parentage, might seem threatening to Americanism. This large bulk is annually increasing, and a greater and greater proportion of the increase each year consists of nationalities who are inherently more difficult to Americanize than were the immigrants of the past.

But, however rapidly the difficulties of Americanization may be increasing, the efficiency and activity of the forces of Americanization are increasing even more rapidly. The most promising field for Americanization is with the second generation, and it is here that the public school stands pre-eminent. The chief hope of Americanizing the adult immigrant lies with trade unionism, whose rapid adoption of Americanization as a function is applauded even by those who condemn most of its policies. Physical environment, the church, politics, the employer, and also numerous miscellaneous forces exert an Americanizing influence to a greater or less degree.

New forces are being developed; old methods are, with some exceptions, being increasingly perfected. The problem, both in its increasing scope and complexity, is being met by the forces of Americanization.

VIEWPOINT 8

"It is doubtful whether . . . any adult immigrant to any country is ever completely assimilated."

Assimilation of Immigrants Is Almost Impossible

Henry P. Fairchild (1880-1956)

Henry P. Fairchild, a prominent sociologist and prolific writer on the topic of immigration, thought the notion of America as a melting pot into which people of all different races and backgrounds could be indiscriminately poured and stirred together, resulting in a homogeneous American soup, was fallacious. He was particularly critical of the "Americanization" programs popular during the early twentieth century, programs set up in settlement houses, schools, and other public and private organizations that were designed to turn foreigners into Americans by teaching them English, American values, and patriotism. Fairchild believed this process of Americanization, though well-meaning, did not work. Americanization, he believed, is a soul-changing process that can only be achieved by those immigrants with a strong will to assimilate and who live in the midst of America, not in foreign colonies within America. He maintained that attempts by Americans to Americanize foreigners resulted in cardboard citizens whose souls remained very different from those of real Americans. Ultimately such attempts would lead to disaster for the United States because the falsely Americanized foreigners would cause and increase disunity in the country.

In the following viewpoint, excerpted from his book *The Melting-Pot Mistake* (Boston: Little, Brown, 1926), Fairchild expresses some of his misgivings about assimilation and the so-called Americanization process.

The most significant unity of the American people is national unity, and the outstanding problem involved in immigration has been the problem of preserving national unity in the face of the influx of hordes of persons of scores of different nationalities. The process by which a nationality preserves its unity while admitting representatives of outside nationalities is properly termed "assimilation" and this process now demands consideration. . . .

In the case of an organic being, assimilation is a part of the nutritive process. The process as a whole consists in taking into the body various extrinsic substances, subjecting them within the body to certain transforming forces by which they are reduced to uniformity, and then incorporating this uniform matter into the very body of the organism. As the content of the word itself suggests, the portion of this process included in the idea of assimilation is the process of transformation, the changing of the heterogeneous into the homogeneous, the unlike to the like. In this process there are several features of remarkable utility in promoting an understanding of the nature of social assimilation. In the first place, no organism—not even an ostrich—has the capacity of achieving the necessary transformation in the case of every conceivable kind of external object. Only certain types of substances will respond to the assimilative agencies in the body of any given organism, and the wise organism will see to it that other substances are not admitted except in strictly limited quantities. There is also a difference in the readiness with which assimilable substances yield to treatment. Those which are especially resistant can be taken less often and in smaller quantities than the opposite type. In the second place, even appropriate substances can not undergo the process of assimilation except as they come in contact with those organs of the body which are endowed with assimilating power, and under conditions which promote assimilation. In the third place—and this, as we shall see, is perhaps most significant of all—the final destiny of all assimilated material is to be transformed into the particular kinds of cells of which the organism is composed and eventually to be incorporated into the body of the organism itself. All trace of diverse origin is completely lost. If it be, for instance, a human organism, there is no suggestion that certain cells have originated in a slice of beefsteak, others in a cut of mince pie, and still others in a plate of pistachio ice cream. They have all become human cells. Nor do assimilated materials of a given origin arrange themselves in definite locations in the body, preserving an independent and separate identity. Neither the foot, nor the hand, nor the eye says, "I am not of the body." There is one common type to which all the assimilated materials conform,—that of the body itself. In the fourth place, the organism undergoes no change to correspond to the different sources from which its food substances come. Different substances doubtless play somewhat different rôles in the bodily economy, but because a human being has eaten sugar there is no tendency for his cells to take on a resemblance to those of the sugar cane, nor because he eats chicken does he therefore become like a fowl. Finally, in order that the assimilative processes may take place, the organism itself must be sound, healthy, and well organized.

Good Analogy

The application of these elemental facts to the processes of social assimilation has doubtless already suggested itself. As remarked above, the analogy is remarkably close. The assimilating body is an organization, not an organism, but with striking resemblances to a true organism. It is a society—in the present sense a society of the type defined as a nation. Into this body are received extraneous elements, foreign individuals, persons of a different nationality. It is axiomatic that as long as these differences persist unity is diminished by just so much, and that if unity is to be restored, these differences must be harmonized in some way.

There are three conceivable methods or processes whereby a nation may maintain its unity in the face of constant incoming streams of persons of other nationalities. The first is symbolized by the analogy of assimilation, and since this term is in practice loosely used to designate harmonization by any means it will be well to examine this process first. On this basis, foreign immigrants coming to a receiving country are to be regarded as analogous to food particles taken into the body of a living organism. They are to be considered as the materials out of which the organism is to build up its future body. In order that this may take place, they must undergo a transformation into cells uniform in type with those which make up the body, and have always made it up from the beginning of its independent existence.

Just what does this mean in terms of nationality? It has already been shown that genuine immigrants—that is, those who come for permanent residence—inevitably become incorporated into the *population* of the receiving country. That is the racial aspect of the matter; it is a physical process involved in the very act of im-

Foreigners Remain Foreign

Walter E. Clark, president of the University of Nevada, addressed the National Education Association on July 6, 1920. In the course of his speech, he voiced his concern that immigrants tend to remain in ethnic and nationalistic enclaves and resist becoming assimilated Americans.

I stood in Mulberry Street one day as the children thronged from the doors of one of the great city schools. As they ran to their play in the street I heard a group of well-grown boys begin to chatter Italian. I turned to a big blue-coated guardian of the peace, stationed to protect the children from reckless drivers, and commented to him upon the fact that boys coming from an American schoolroom should begin to speak a foreign tongue the minute they reached the school yard. He was a free-born American, scornful of this language treason, and in the perfection of his own American speech said to me something like this:

"Dat's nuttin', young feller. I knows a girl wot graduated from this school three years ago and she can't speak a word of English today!" Caught in that great Italian city of half a million between Bleeker Street and Chinatown, the Bowery and Broadway, many a lass graduates from an American common school to drop back into almost total ignorance of the American tongue while living in the greatest of American cities! American city, did I say? If, when walking down Broadway, you were to meet a racially representative one hundred New Yorkers, you would meet forty who had been born on foreign soil and eighty-three who had either been born on foreign soil or whose fathers and mothers were born abroad. Only *seventeen* out of every one hundred in that which we call our greatest American city are real Americans even in the limited sense that only one generation back of them is American born.

Granting that the most promising factor in the development of a real American culture is our public school, with its great army of self-sacrificing teachers, what chance has even this great school system in our industrial cities so congested with recent aliens that it is difficult for the school children to acquire American speech?

migration. There is no way of preventing it. But we have seen that nationality is a very different thing from population. Nationality is a spiritual reality, existing in the realm of the sentiments, emotions, and intellect. The act of migration does not in any sense make the foreigner a member of the receiving nationality. In fact, no immigrant immediately after arrival is ever a member of the new nationality, any more than a morsel of food that has just passed the lips is at once a portion of the body. The foreign immigrant brings his nationality with him. He is still a member of the Greek nationality, or the Danish nationality, or whatever it may be, even though separated by thousands of miles from the bulk of those who compose that nationality.

The transformation that must take place, then, before the process of social assimilation is complete, must be a transformation in the elements or qualities of nationality. We have already seen what the most important of these are—language, religion, political ideas, moral standards, economic abilities, dress, recreation, food, ornamentation, family customs, all sorts of habits, traditions, beliefs, and loyalties. In all of these particulars the immigrant must be transformed into the type of the receiving nationality. He must react to social stimuli and respond to social situations in exactly the same way as if he had always lived in the midst of this nationality. Before assimilation is complete he must have lost all trace or suggestion of his foreign origin. A crisis in his native country must arouse no different sensations in his heart than in the case of any native of his new country. He must feel no sense of alienation with reference to his new compatriots, nor they any sense of distinction from him, because of his origin. He must rise to the appeals of loyalty and patriotism just as if he had never known a different nationality. He must have become completely one with the receiving body.

Defined in these terms, assimilation appears as a task of tremendous, almost insuperable, difficulty. In fact, it is doubtful whether, according to this conception, any adult immigrant to any country is ever completely assimilated. Generally speaking, the lower the age at which immigration takes place, the greater is the ease of assimilation, and therefore the greater the possibilities of its being accomplished. This is for two reasons. First, because the younger the immigrant is the less firmly has his original nationality been established, and so the easier it is to throw it off. Second, the younger the immigrant is the more plastic is his emotional nature and the more receptive to the impressions of the new environment. Complete assimilation may be possible if commenced at an early age and carried on under the most favorable circumstances.

To carry this analogy to its conclusion, it must be observed that in all this process the receiving nationality undergoes no alteration to correspond to the qualities of the foreign elements. There is one central standard, the existing national type, which is constantly preserved, and to which all the different types are made to conform. This does not mean at all the "standardizing of the immigrant" in the sense that is often claimed. It does not mean that all foreign-born members of the nationality must become individually exactly alike, any more than all the native-born are identical. Personal variety is not only unavoidable but wholly desirable. But it does mean that the differences which the foreign individual exhibits shall be those of personality, not the characteristic differences of a foreign nationality.

The second of the conceivable processes of national harmonization is symbolized by the melting pot. This, as has already been shown, involves the idea of mixture. It is an idea which applies with much accuracy to racial unification. The present question is: Does it apply to national unification? Can diverse nationalities be harmonized by mixing them together?

Melting Pot Fallacy

The nature of a mixture is that while each individual particle retains its original qualities unaltered the separate particles are so intimately associated and so evenly distributed that the general aspects of the whole mass appear as a uniform blending of the characteristics of the different kinds of components in the proportions in which those components exist. The crux of the whole question is whether the qualities of nationality are of such a sort that the human particles who embody them can be intimately mingled together, so that the various features of the group will be the composite representation of the qualities of the individuals.

This problem requires a further examination of the elements of nationality. Let us take up a few of the more important in turn. At the top stands language. Can languages be mixed? In one sense, possibly yes. It may be that under primitive conditions, when nationality is as yet amorphous, two or more different languages may be blended together into an entirely new language showing some of the characteristics of each of the components. Thus it is said that the modern Turkish language is built up out of three distinct sources. The English language itself obviously derives from several sources. But in the sense that the mixing of languages may be a device for group harmonization under modern conditions the answer is emphatically no! Well-established languages do not mix. They may borrow words, and perhaps some idioms, from each other, but each language remains distinctly itself. In many ancient cities diverse linguistic groups have lived in close association with each other for centuries without the formation of a composite medium of communication. In the city of Smyrna, for instance, the Turkish, Greek, and Armenian languages, not to mention innumerable minor tongues, have been spoken for many generations, yet there is no "Smyrna blend," nor is a knowledge of one of these languages as spoken in that city of the slightest use in conversing with a person who knows only one of the others. It would probably be impossible to find a single instance among the civilized countries of the world for hundreds of years past where group unity has been achieved by the fusing of languages.

Next comes religion. Here the principle applies with equal

strength. The very nature of religion is exclusive and particularistic. It must be one thing or the other. It is true that religions are influenced by each other. Particularly when a group of people is converted from one religion to another they may carry over some of the forms and ritual of the old into the new. But the cleavage is none the less absolute between the two. In fact, a group of converts to a new religion is likely to be more intolerant toward the old belief than to some faith with which they have never been allied. Thus Mr. Wells observes: "Religious cults and priesthoods are sectarian by nature; they will convert, they will overcome, but they will never coalesce.". . .

The same is emphatically true of moral codes. The very nature of moral standards is that they are absolute. They cannot be mixed, combined, or blended. The almost inevitable effect of attempting to harmonize two diverse moral codes is to break down moral sanctions altogether. This is strikingly illustrated in the case of the second generation of immigrants in this country who appear to be, by all tests, the most nearly unmoral of any of the commonly recognized groups in the entire population. . . .

Another very important element in nationality is the family organization, and family customs and standards. Differences in this field are among the most serious obstacles to group coöperation, and harmonization is particularly difficult. It certainly can not be achieved by blending. The outlook of the Greek father who regards his ten-year-old son simply as a source of financial gain through the operation of the padrone system is too far removed from that of the typical American to leave any hope for adjustment through compromise. The Italian father who refused to let his daughter go to a hospital for a needed operation because she would have been forever dishonored by spending a night away from under his own roof saw no middle ground, and was only reconciled when a bed was provided for him in the same institution. Neither member of a Slavic couple engaged in the periodic exercise of wife-beating welcomes the intrusion of an outsider bent on mollifying the custom.

So we might go on down the long list of major and minor national traits. . . .

Traits of Nationality Do Not Combine

The simple fact is that, with negligible exceptions, the traits of nationality will not combine, and so nationalities as a whole can not be mixed. The reason is not difficult to comprehend. National traits are mass realities, existing in groups, not in individuals. We speak of the nationality of an individual. It is more accurate to speak of an individual as belonging to a nationality than as having a nationality. In the case of a mixture a single particle can slip

Immigrants flocked to the United States in the last two decades of the nineteenth century and the first two of the twentieth. Most of them hoped to become Americans in every sense of the word. Henry Fairchild and others maintained that most would fail.

into the mixture and become a part of it, keeping its own character and affecting the nature of the mixture by just so much. But in the case of a nationality the foreign particle does not become a part of the nationality until he has become assimilated to it. Previous to that time he is an extraneous factor, like undigested, and possibly indigestible, matter in the body of a living organism. That being the case, the only way he can alter the nationality is by injuring it, by impeding its functions. He can not produce a normal, healthy modification in his own direction.

It follows, then, that the attempt to mix nationalities must result not in a new type of composite nationality but in the destruction of all nationality. No one of the components can survive the process if it is carried too far.

This is the outstanding fallacy of the melting pot. . . .

If the truth were otherwise in this matter the history of the Balkans would have been very different from what it has been. The Balkan populations are often referred to as a racial conglomeration, and to a considerable extent the designation is accurate. But the heart of the Balkan tangle is not racial, but national. The inhabitants of this unfortunate area are broken up into incompatible groups not by racial differentiations—most of which they would be quite unable to detect—but by languages, religions, customs, social habits, and, perhaps most of all, by traditional group loyalties, the origin of which few would be able to trace and the nature of which few would be able to explain. In fact, the history and present situation of the Balkans suggests as the ultimate truth the conclusion that the contact of diverse nationalities, far from tending to produce a coalescing, actually tends to accentuate the differences and to intensify the unreasoning tenacity with which each group clings to its own particular traits.

When, as a result of the revelations of the War, it became clear that the figure of the melting pot was an anomaly, an attempt was made to develop a third conception of the process of national harmonization which had been envisaged by a few observers for some time previously. As a symbol of this idea the figure of a "weaving machine" was suggested:

"We have heard much, in the past, of the great American 'Melting Pot.' Why not think, instead, of a great American 'Weaving Machine'? Which kind of an America do you prefer: an America whose many national strains have been so merged into a common mass as to resemble nothing so much as the colorless drab which results from mixing many colors, or an America which resembles, rather, a brilliant fabric into which these national strains have been so woven that, like colors, none have been destroyed but all preserved in their original hues and so harmonized that each has gained lustre by the new association and contrast? Do you want a living and a growing America?"

The Weaving Machine Fallacy

The figure of the weaving machine never achieved much popularity. Probably few readers of this page ever heard of it. Undoubtedly this was due in part to the fact that it lacked the intangible qualities of an appealing symbol. It was artificial and labored, not picturesque. But another reason must have been its utter absurdity when subjected to a critical examination and analysis. At first blush it may seem like both a broad-minded and a constructive program that the traits of all the nations of Europe—only the best traits, we may assume; the others, by some undescribed social necromancy, having been sloughed off—should be woven together into a uniquely rich national pattern. But the moment one stops to consider exactly what is involved in such a program the futility of it becomes obvious enough. What kind of a nation would the United States be if we were to succeed in "weaving" in among our own traits the languages of Poland, Turkey, and Portugal, the family institutions of Bulgaria, Italy, and Sweden, the political ideas of England, Russia, and Greece, the sanitary customs of Roumania, Switzerland, and France, the economic systems of Albania, Spain, and Belgium, the moral codes of the Balkan States and Scandinavia, and so on *ad infinitum?* The very essence of nationality is uniformity throughout the entire body in important particulars. And in just what way are the strands of different nationalities to be represented? By individuals? By local groups? By organizations affiliated on a national scale?

The absurdity of this whole conception becomes especially clear when it is recalled how large a part of nationality consists in loyalties. To what is the individual to be loyal in this national coat-of-many-colors? How much loyalty of any sort would survive such a process? . . .

Reviewing these three proposed methods of unification, it becomes clear that the only one which can survive a close comparison with the facts of nationality is that symbolized by the metabolic analogy of assimilation. If this interpretation is accepted, it must be confessed that the implications with reference to the stranger in our midst are rigid and harsh enough. It is he who must undergo the entire transformation; the true member of the American nationality is not called upon to change in the least. The traits of foreign nationality which the immigrant brings with him are not to be mixed or interwoven. They are to be *abandoned*. The standard to which he must conform has been already fixed by forces quite outside himself, quite outside any individual, native or foreign, fixed by all the factors, topographical, climatic, racial, historical, fortuitous, which have worked together to make the American nationality what it is. A harsh situation, indeed! but a situation the harshness of which is determined not by the inclination or wish of any person or group of persons, but by the inherent qualities of human nature and social organization. It can therefore not be eliminated by any sentimental aspiration, however generous or altruistic. If immigration is to continue, and if our nation is to be preserved, we must all, natives and foreigners alike, resign ourselves to the inevitable truth that unity can be maintained only through the complete sacrifice of extraneous national traits on the part of our foreign elements. There is no "give-and-take" in assimilation.

CHAPTER 4

The Golden Door Narrows

Chapter Preface

Until the late nineteenth century, U.S. policy regarding immigration remained largely true to George Washington's assertion that the "bosom of America is open to receive not only the opulent and respected stranger, but the oppressed and persecuted of all nations and religions, whom we shall welcome to a participation of all our rights and privileges." The exceptions were the Alien and Sedition acts passed by Congress in 1798 authorizing the refusal of entry or the deportation of people who might endanger the security of the United States. However, these acts lapsed after only two years.

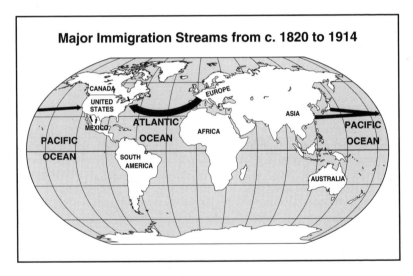

Number of Immigrants

From Asia 700,000   **From Canada**..........2,200,000
Main groups:
   Chinese 370,000   **From Latin America**..900,000
   Japanese 275,000

From Europe ..30,000,000
Main groups:
   Germans 5,000,000   Irish 4,500,000
   Italians 4,500,000   Poles........................2,600,000
   English.............2,600,000   Jews 2,000,000

Source: Roger Daniels, *Coming to America.*

The tremendous influx of immigrants in the mid-eighteenth century, however, made many Americans extremely nervous, particularly when large groups began to arrive from non-northern European nations. Those Americans concerned about immigration in the mid-nineteenth century worried primarily about competition for jobs and resources and moral and political corruption from people whose religious and personal values were extremely different from those of the mostly white Anglo-Saxon Protestants (WASP) who peopled the United States. Movements of various kinds attempted to restrict the opportunities of immigrants and even to get Congress to restrict or eliminate their entrance to the country. In 1875 those concerned about the evils they associated with immigrants were able to get the first restrictive legislation passed. It prohibited the immigration of convicts and prostitutes. In 1882, Congress further barred "idiots, lunatics, and persons likely to become public charges." More important, in that same year Congress passed the first law discriminating against immigrants on the basis of their race. They forbade the further immigration of Chinese laborers.

Americans had tolerated the Chinese, who first arrived at the time of the Gold Rush, as long as they were only a small number of alien workers. But when it appeared that their numbers were increasing rapidly, that they might pose a threat to the jobs and wages of "native" Americans, and that eventually they were going to want the benefits of citizenship, many Americans—particularly in California where the Chinese were settling—began a movement to restrict or even forbid Chinese from entering the United States. Their activism resulted in the passing of the 1882 Chinese Exclusion Act, forbidding the immigration of Chinese laborers to America and forbidding the naturalization of any Chinese.

On the East Coast, Americans objected to the new waves of southern and eastern European and Near Eastern immigrants. Many of these people—Italians, Jews, Poles, Greeks, Russians, and others—had dark skins, spoke foreign languages, and were non-Protestant (most were Catholics and Jews). Between 1880 and 1920, nearly 24 million foreigners entered the United States, the majority of them from these "undesirable" groups. The dominant American classes—mainly WASP—were alarmed. They feared that these people would lower wages, corrupt the "American race," and overwhelm American society with their unassimilable foreign ways. People from both the working and the moneyed classes lobbied to restrict the immigration of these undesirables. They first achieved restrictions of certain types of laborers, including European contract laborers and Korean and Japanese workers. They were able to add additional restrictions based on undesirable characteristics, including mental diseases, pauperism, anarchic political philosophies, certain physical diseases, and illiteracy. This last trait was a matter of controversy for more than twenty years, as groups such as the Immigration Restriction League battled to make literacy a requirement for the admission of male immigrants. (Many restrictionists viewed children and females as "accessories" to the more important males, who would be the ones potentially participating in the work force, in politics, and in other important aspects of American life.)

The culmination of the immigration restriction efforts came in 1921 when the first Quota Law was enacted. Like the Chinese Exclusion Act, it restricted immigration based on national origin. While it did not *exclude* any nationality, it put strict limits on the number of people who could enter the United States from any particular foreign country. Essentially, the quotas were based on a percentage of each nationality's population in the United States in 1910. Once people realized, however, that the great waves of 1890 to 1910 had already allowed large numbers of "undesirables" into the United States, they revised the law with the 1924 National Origins Quota System Act, which based its limitations on the 1890 census. This ensured that the largest number of new immigrants after 1924 would come from the less threatening northern and western European countries.

Since 1924, many other immigration laws have been passed. Notably, a law repealing the Chinese Exclusion Act was passed in 1943, and the National Origins Quota System Act was replaced in 1965. Today, immigration into the United States is largely determined by the 1965 act, which established numerical ceilings for each of the world's hemispheres: 120,000 immigrants are allowed from the Western Hemisphere and 170,000 from the Eastern Hemisphere. Although entrance is on a first come, first served basis, the law also established a hierarchy of preferences (relatives, 74 percent; scientists and artists, 1 percent; skilled and unskilled labor, 10 percent; and refugees, 6 percent).

To many people it seems ironic that in America, a nation built on the toil of immigrants, the debate over who should be allowed to populate it remains such a controversial issue.

VIEWPOINT 1

"It will be a serious mistake to allow this tide of [Chinese] immigration to continue without restriction."

The Chinese Should Be Kept Out of the United States

James Harvey Slater (1826-1899)

The Chinese were the first people to have immigration restrictions aimed at them because of their nationality. They began immigrating to the United States at the time of the California gold rush of 1849. In succeeding years, increasing numbers came, many hoping to acquire wealth and return to their homeland. They worked in all kinds of occupations, primarily as unskilled labor. At first, their presence was welcomed, for they were known as industrious workers willing to work for small wages. In support of Chinese immigration, the United States and China signed the Burlingame Treaty in 1868, which, among other things, guaranteed the right of immigration between the two nations to both Americans and Chinese.

Because of its proximity to China (as well as its promise of fields and mountains filled with gold), California was the primary immigration target of the Chinese. The large numbers of Chinese workers willing to work for low wages soon made California labor organizations (composed mainly of whites) uneasy, and so they lobbied to penalize Chinese workers with such things as head taxes. By the mid-1870s, enough Californians had become antagonistic toward the Asian immigrants to demand state and even federal restrictions against them. Many Californians asserted that the Chinese were damaging the wage structure for white workers, corrupting California society, and increasing at a rate that could enable them to take over the state at some time in the future.

In 1876, after several of California's restrictive measures were deemed unconstitutional, members of the California congress persuaded the federal government to investigate the situation. The U.S. Congress established the Joint Special Committee of Congress to Investigate Chinese Immigration. A small committee of senators traveled to San Francisco and Sacramento and listened for eighteen days to 129 witnesses. Although slightly more testimony favored the Chinese, the committee's conclusion was unfavorable.

Eventually, in 1882, Congress passed the Chinese Exclusion Act, the first immigration law forbidding entry to the United States by immigrants based on their nationality. Despite the fact that the Chinese made up only .002 percent of the U.S. population in 1882 (and less than 10 percent of California's population), Congress determined that Chinese laborers were enough of a threat to the well-being of the nation to void the 1868 Burlingame Treaty with China, which guaranteed unrestricted immigration between China and the United States, and the 1880 treaty which allowed for immigration regulation but not exclusion. The 1882 Chinese Exclusion Act forbade Chinese laborers to immigrate to the United States for a period of ten years. It also forbade naturalization for Chinese residents of the United States. Upon its expiration, the act was renewed and amended to have no expiration date. It remained in effect until 1943, when an act of Congress voided it and made Chinese immigration and naturalization subject to the same laws other nationalities were subject to.

The following viewpoint is taken from the remarks of Senator James Harvey Slater during one of the Senate's debates on the bill in 1882 (Congressional Record, vol. XIII, 1882). Slater, like the majority of Congress, was in favor of the bill.

I am in hearty accord with the promoters of this bill, and trust that it may pass substantially as it came from the hands of the committee. The only fear that I have is that it may not prove as effectual in checking the influx of Chinese laborers as its promoters hope and expect it will. It may turn out after a time that its provisions can be systematically evaded, but this will come not so much from the bill itself as from the provisions of the treaty under which it is drawn, the defect being one difficult to meet with legislative provisions.

The bill is drawn in accord with the provisions of the treaty, and whatever of defects there may prove to be in its provisions when it shall go into operation will have to be referred to the narrowness of the treaty stipulations in conformity with which it is constructed. It cannot be disguised that the treaty of 1880 is so constructed that there is danger that no legislation, however carefully prepared, if kept strictly within its provisions, will be certain to save it from proving to be a snare and a delusion. Under the treaty we may suspend for a limited period the coming of laborers from China to the United States, but the coming of other classes for other purposes is unrestricted, and the rights which they may enjoy are made even greater than they were under the Burlingame treaty. They may come without limit as teachers, professors, traders, and merchants, and when here are to enjoy all the privileges of the citizens and subjects of the most favored nation, and being lawfully within the United States under treaty stipulations may they not change their vocations and become laborers? As citizens and subjects of other nations they would certainly have this right.

Possibly the treaty carries with it the power to extend legislation to the prohibiting of any Chinese other than laborers from engaging in the labor avocations of the country during the suspension of the coming of Chinese laborers, but the difficulty of enforcing such a provision would in my judgment render it of little value. It may be humiliating to confess, but the facts are, our commissioners who negotiated the late Chinese treaty were unequal to their task, and failed to properly accomplish, or even to comprehend, the work assigned to them. And I fear, sir, that we of the Pacific coast will yet regret that we ever consented that this treaty might be finally consummated. But, like drowning men who catch at anything which promises the possibility of escape from peril, we were unwilling to make opposition to this treaty, fearing that nothing better might be obtained in any reasonable time, and also hoping that legislation under its provisions might be so framed as to check the tide of Chinese immigration to our coast until such time as the morbid and unnatural, though prevailing, craze about the universal brotherhood of man might in some degree subside and wiser counsels prevail.

Right to Control Immigration

What was needed was the assertion authoritatively of our absolute right to control this immigration in our own way and in our own good time—the assertion of our right to terminate Chinese immigration absolutely and unconditionally when and as we please; and above and over all the assertion of our right as a nation to do just what China has always done under the Burlingame treaty as respects citizens of the United States traveling or residing in China, and that is the right to prohibit Chinese residing or traveling in the United States from engaging in any of the labor avocations of the country. That is what was needed and what should have been insisted upon, and if we had had a foreign policy worthy a nation of fifty million people it is what would have been exacted, not as a concession from China but as a right belonging to us as a people and nation and as inhering to our sovereignty.

It is humiliating to an American to read this later treaty and find from its terms and provisions that the United States is placed in the attitude of a recipient of favors from the hands and by the gracious benignity of the imperial Government of China, as if this country was a dependency. By its terms and provisions we are restricted in the exercise of rights which pertain to our Government as a sovereign State and which are important and necessary to the protection of the interests of our own citizens and to the preservation of the very form and substance of our own Government.

Since the promulgation of the Burlingame treaty the subjects of China have come to the United States and passed freely through every part of it. They have traveled upon our stages, steamboats, and railroads; they have gone singly and in small numbers into any and every part of it without molestation and in perfect safety; they have worked in our mines, as servants, as cooks, as common laborers, as mechanics and artisans, and have been allowed to engage in any business they desired to; and, with rare exceptions, have been unmolested, and always found protection when protection was needed. How has it been during all that time with the citizens of the United States in China? Have they been allowed to enter China at any and all points or to engage in any of the labor avocations of the country? No, sir. Only in certain cities have they been permitted to come, and these have been limited in number, and even in those cities our citizens have been restricted to defined and designated limits, and they are not permitted to engage in any of the labor avocations of the country, but are restricted to commercial business, and not even permitted to engage in the internal trade of the country. If they venture out of the prescribed limits for foreigners in the cities where they are permitted to come, or if they venture into the country beyond the distance allowed, they do it at the peril of their lives.

The Burlingame treaty was very unequal in its terms, and in its practical operation it was still more so. The commission sent to negotiate the new treaty seem to have overlooked these inequalities, and yet the agitation which led to their being sent out ought to have been a sufficient notice to them of these matters. Evidently, however, they and the power that sent them on their mission were so fully imbued with that theory of the modern philanthropist which takes to its embrace "all the world and the rest of mankind" without regard "to previous condition of servitude," and makes but little inquiry as to the degree of development reached by its *protegés* in the process of evolution from lower forms, that the most important part of their mission, the assertion of the inherent right of a nation or people to control in its own way the admission into its own territory and among its own people of foreign elements, incongruous with and dangerous to the peace, happiness, and good order of its own community, was overlooked or subordinated to mere idea.

The advocates and promoters of this bill are met with the objection that the principles upon which it rests are violative of the right of expatriation which we as a people have so long and so persistently proclaimed. Why, Mr. President, this is strange reasoning; the application of these principles can have no kind of application here. The circumstances under which we have so often asserted the fundamental right of every man to sever his relation with his native country does not and cannot apply to the relation the Chinese immigrant seeks to maintain in this country. We have asserted the right of expatriation in behalf of our adopted citizens when and wherever the governments from whence they came sought to enforce upon them obligations supposed and claimed to exist by reason of their having been born within their jurisdiction. We asserted the principle because we had taken upon ourselves the obligation of giving them protection for their allegiance—correlative obligations assumed when we received them into our political community. Certainly, sir; the Chinaman, according to our theories which we have made the basis of our political structure, has a right to expatriate himself from his native country and abjure the authority of his emperor and government, but does that clothe him with the right to demand admission into the social compact of any other country or community without the consent of such community?

Why, sir, the mere statement of such a proposition carries with it its own refutation. No principle is better settled in international law than that aliens can acquire no other or greater right in or among a people to whom they would attach themselves than such people may or will accord them. The very right to come at all is derived not from the alien himself nor yet from the country whence he comes, but from the people with whom he would form new relations.

Again, sir, we are told that in this legislation we are treading backward and forsaking the principles and traditions upon which our fathers one hundred years ago laid the foundations of gov-

Nation Must Protect Its Own

The Congressional Record of March 3, 1882, shows that Senator Thomas Bayard of Delaware argued forcibly against allowing Chinese immigration to continue unabated. He claimed that the Chinese, while not innately inferior to Americans, were harming Americans by their very presence. And, since their cultural and racial differences made them obviously unassimilable, the United States was perfectly right to mandate their exclusion.

Mr. President, I willingly recognize the brotherhood of man, and respond to humanity wherever its voice may be heard; but there is an instinct of self-preservation in nations as well as in individuals. There is an instinct and a duty of justice. A man must be true to himself before he can be true to others; and a nation must be true to its own people before it undertakes to expand its energies in favor of strangers and aliens. There is no inhumanity, there is no injustice in saying, that our duty to republican institutions compels us to consider the character of the population under which such institutions may hopefully be conducted. We consider it in our treaties, we consider it in our laws; we consider the tendencies of treaties and the tendencies of laws; and in the present case, acting under an explicit treaty stipulation, under a statute proposing a remedy confessedly less extreme than the treaty itself obviously would permit, the opportunity, and, it seems to me, the duty for us has arisen to act.

ernment, and the Declaration of Independence is invoked as a sufficient argument and showing of this statement. The right to the pursuit of happiness is asserted as conclusive of the whole question. No one will deny the axiomatic and self-evident truths of the Declaration of Independence respecting human rights, but that they apply in this case may well be denied. The pursuit of happiness is certainly the inalienable right of every human being, but that pursuit must be regulated by human society and by human laws. It might be a great source of happiness to the highwayman to meet the honorable Senator from Massachusetts [Mr. Hoar] upon the highway and forcibly take from his possession his purse. Necessitous hunger and privation might impel to such an act, and the gold or currency that purse might be expected to contain would bring numberless benefits and blessings, not only to the highwayman, but also to those who might be dependent upon him; but the law of society steps in to protect the citizen in his right to go unmolested about his pursuits, and pronounces such acts criminal and affixes severe penalties to their commission.

So it is daily demonstrated in a thousand ways that the pursuit of happiness is circumscribed and limited by the laws and necessities of organized society. What is true of the individual members of a community in this respect is equally true of nations and peoples, and also true of individuals leaving their native land in search of happiness and to better their own condition among another people in another country. They have no right in the pursuit of their own happiness to inflict injury upon the people of other communities. To assert the right of aliens to impose themselves upon or into communities to which they are alien without their consent and to their detriment, is to assert a principle, when carried to its logical consequences, subversive of all human government. Such a principle leads inevitably to anarchy. The law of life and self-preservation is as important and necessary to communities as to individuals, and is as inalienable and inherent in the one case as in the other; and no principle is more firmly imbedded in the ethics of international law than that it is both the right and the duty of the paramount authority in every state, in whatever form that authority may be vested, and however it may be exercised, to protect the state and the people of the state from all and every evil that may threaten its safety or menace the interests, prosperity, or happiness of its people, be they few or many, and herein alone can be found justification for a resort to the arbitrament of war.

Teeming Hordes

Disguise it as we may we cannot longer fail to recognize the fact that western civilization has met the eastern upon the shores of the Pacific. The westward march of the Caucasian has there met the same teeming hordes that generations ago gave a westward direction to his tireless energy by imposing on his east a living wall of Asiatics, impossible to pass or overcome. The Pacific Ocean until recently had proved an impassable barrier and no Mongolian had ever passed to its eastward shore. But recent developments in steamships and the establishment of lines of steam communication between San Francisco and the open ports of China and Japan have practically connected the two continents and bridged the intervening sea. So that for a few dollars a Chinese immigrant can come from any of the ports of China to San Francisco. At first but few came, some returned, and a larger number followed, and in that way the tide of immigrants swelled to considerable proportions. Almost from the first their coming was objected to, and as its effects became more and more apparent this opposition became more and more pronounced, until within the last seven or eight years it has been greatly intensified, and by its universality as well as intensity has served to hold in check and to keep down and diminish the number of Chinese coming to the United States.

From 1850 to 1880 more than 200,000 Chinese landed on the Pacific coast. The census of 1880 shows that there were in that year 105,000 remaining in this country; but persons well informed in the customs and manners of the Chinese affirm that this is far below the correct figures. The smallness of their present numbers as compared to the total population of the country has been strongly contrasted and urged as a reason for discrediting the earnest statements of the people of the Pacific States and Territories that this Chinese population is a menace to good order and good government and the best interest of the people there. But the fact is overlooked that even according to the census there are 75,000 in the State of California, and some ten thousand in the State of Oregon, while the appeal of the Trades Assembly of California, quoted by the honorable Senator from Delaware [Mr. Bayard] on last Friday, estimates, after investigation, the Chinese population of California at 150,000, or 20 per cent. greater than the male whites capable of bearing arms. From this it would seem that the adult Chinese male laboring element in California was very nearly equal to the adult white laboring element. If, however, the census report be taken, then they constitute something like one-half of the male laboring element in that State.

But we are told by the honorable Senator from Massachusetts that the Chinese are the most easily governed race in the world; that every Chinaman in America has four hundred and ninety-nine Americans to control him. But the honorable Senator omitted to state that of the four hundred and ninety-nine Americans four hundred and eighty-seven of them were from one thousand to three thousand miles away from where the evils of Chinese emigration are being felt. Why, sir, in the Pacific States and Territories beyond Utah there are, according to the census reports, one Chinaman to every twelve of the white population, and I have no doubt that if the exact numbers of the Chinese population could be ascertained that the ratio would be one to every eight or ten of the white population. Carry this ratio throughout the United States and there would be a Chinese population of adult male laborers of near 5,000,000 to compete with white labor, to depress and demoralize it by underbidding and bringing it down to starvation prices. Let me bring it a little closer, Mr. President. Massachusetts has a population of 1,758,000. Now let the Senators of that State add to that population 175,000 adult Chinese laborers to compete with and underbid the working classes and they may be able to form some just conceptions of the condition of the poor laboring classes in the Pacific States and Territories. My impression is that there would be a small-sized bedlam in Massachusetts under such a state of facts. Pennsylvania has 4,282,000 population. I ask her Senators what effect it would have upon the laboring population of the great State to send into it 400,000 able-bodied laboring Chinese to depress the labor market in the struggle and competition that would ensue. The State of New York has a population of over 5,000,000; let the Senators of that State reflect what would be the effect of letting in 500,000 Chinese laborers to compete with their laboring population. If Senators will but reflect upon these facts they can readily comprehend how it is that there is such a wonderful unanimity in sentiment in every locality where the blight of this immigration has been felt; they will no longer be surprised at the steady and growing opposition to that class of immigrants, an opposition so universal that in a secret vote by concealed ballots no more than 800 votes were given favoring this immigration to 150,000 against it.

Aliens from an Alien Culture

Mr. President, the honorable Senator from Massachusetts [Mr. Hoar] asked "What argument can be urged against the Chinese which was not heard against the negro within living memories?" I do not suppose that I can satisfy the honorable Senator of the fallacy of his reasoning, but I may call attention to the utter want of any parallelism between the relations of the negro to the people of the United States and that of the Chinese, who desire to come among us as immigrants. The negro was native to the soil, born and bred within our jurisdiction, speaking our language, having, in a large degree, our civilization, and adhering to our religion. He was with us, if not of us; his ancestors were brought here against their will, and the generation with which we had to deal had no land, clime, or country to call their own except the land in which they were born, and no ties with any people or race except those with whom they had been reared. From necessity they were to remain with and of us; the only question, was what should be the relation.

The Chinese are aliens, born in a foreign land, speak a foreign tongue, owe allegiance to a foreign government, are idolaters in religion, have a different civilization from ours, do not and will not assimilate with our people, come only to get money, and return; and they are inimical to our laws, evade them whenever and wherever they can. So numerous are they at home in their own country that existence among the lower orders of their people is, and has been for centuries, a struggle for existence, and through this ceaseless struggle they have developed into a race of people of such character and physical qualities as to be able to exist and thrive where and under conditions the white man would perish and die out. They bring their customs with them, and persistently adhere to and retain them. Having the protection of our laws they systematically evade and violate them. They persistently and secretly maintain a code of laws and a form of govern-

197

ment of their own, which they enforce with seeming certainty and effectiveness. Those who come as immigrants are of the lowest orders of the Chinese population, largely criminal. They bring with them their filth and frightful and nameless diseases and contagions. They bring no families as a general rule, but numbers of their country women are brought for purposes of prostitution, and are bought and sold among themselves as slaves, and our laws and courts are powerless to prevent it. They enhance the cost of government, and increase the burdens of taxation, while they contribute practically nothing in the way of taxes. Their labor is essentially servile, and is demoralizing to every class of white labor with which it comes in competition.

These, sir, are the people for whom the honorable Senator would open wide the door of admission, or, being open, would refuse to close it, but rather invites these hordes of heathens that swarm like rats in a cellar and live in filth and degradation along the sea-coast of China to come and compete with and degrade American labor, and compares them to the colored people born and reared in America. The negro is thoroughly American, if he is not Caucasian; the Chinese are neither Caucasian nor American, but are alien to our race, customs, religion, and civilization. The bill is not directed against those already here, but against the hordes that threaten to come. The terms of the treaty place those here beyond the reach of legislative enactment, and effort is now being made to bring in a large number of Chinese laborers before legislation can be had. Last year's immigration was over 20,000. This fact sufficiently demonstrates their purpose to come.

Mr. President, thirty-two years ago last September I camped on the banks of the Sacramento River, where the city of that name now stands, then a city of tents. There I first met the Mongolian; from that date to the present time I have been familiar with them. I have seen them singly and in crowds as they passed through the country from one section to another, traveling on foot with their bamboo sticks and baggage; have seen them in the mines by tens and by hundreds, and in the towns and cities, where they congregate at times in great numbers; have seen them on the witness stand, in the courts as litigants and criminals; have prosecuted them and have defended them in the courts. From this experience and observation I have formed the deliberate judgment that it will be a serious mistake to allow this tide of immigration to continue without restriction. After careful and thoughtful study of this whole matter I have settled down in the conviction that they should be prohibited from entering the labor avocations of the country, leaving them the right to come for commercial purposes, for travel or curiosity, as the Burlingame treaty left them.

I hope, Mr. President, the bill will pass substantially as reported.

"Nothing is more in conflict with the genius of American institutions than legal distinctions between individuals based upon race."

The Chinese Should Not Be Kept Out of the United States

George F. Hoar (1826-1904)

Senator George F. Hoar of Massachusetts held a strong contempt for the nativists who wanted to exclude foreigners from the United States. He spoke out strongly against the Chinese Exclusion Act. The following viewpoint is taken from his remarks during one of the Senate's debates on the bill in 1882 (*Congressional Record*, vol. XIII, 1882). Hoar eloquently speaks out against the bill as a violation of fundamental human rights.

Despite his eloquence and that of others who spoke against Chinese exclusion, the law was passed and essentially remained unchanged until 1943. This was the first but not the last race-based U.S. immigration law. After the turn of the century, the United States made a series of "gentlemen's agreements" with Japan assuring that Japanese immigration to the United States would be curtailed. As with the Chinese, a major complaint Americans made about the Japanese was that they worsened the plight of white laborers. Like the Chinese, the Japanese were known to be smart, hardworking, and willing to work for low wages. These qualities, said their critics, forced higher-paid Americans out of work.

But labor conditions were not the only basis on which Asians were targeted. Some white people had great fear of the "yellow hordes" overtaking the white population and turning America "Mongolian."

In the course of the speech excerpted here, Senator Hoar speaks out against this fear.

Mr. President, a hundred years ago the American people founded a nation upon the moral law. They overthrew by force the authority of their sovereign, and separated themselves from the country which had planted them, alleging as their justification to mankind certain propositions which they held to be self-evident.

They declared—and that declaration is the one foremost action of human history—that all men equally derive from their Creator the right to the pursuit of happiness; that equality in the right to that pursuit is the fundamental rule of the divine justice in its application to mankind; that its security is the end for which governments are formed, and its destruction good cause why governments should be overthrown. For a hundred years this principle has been held in honor. Under its beneficent operation we have grown almost twentyfold. Thirteen States have become thirty-eight; three million have become fifty million; wealth and comfort and education and art have flourished in still larger proportion. Every twenty years there is added to the valuation of this country a wealth enough to buy the whole German Empire, with its buildings and its ships and its invested property. This has been the magnet that has drawn immigration hither. The human stream, hemmed in by banks invisible but impassable, does not turn toward Mexico, which can feed and clothe a world, or South America, which can feed and clothe a hundred worlds, but seeks only that belt of States where it finds this law in operation. The marvels of comfort and happiness it has wrought for us scarcely surpass what it has done for other countries. The immigrant sends back the message to those he has left behind. There is scarcely a nation in Europe west of Russia which has not felt the force of our example and whose institutions are not more or less slowly approximating to our own. . . .

Racial Distinctions Are Unconstitutional

Nothing is more in conflict with the genius of American institutions than legal distinctions between individuals based upon race or upon occupation. The framers of our Constitution believed in the safety and wisdom of adherence to abstract principles. They meant that their laws should make no distinction between men except such as were required by personal conduct and character. The prejudice of race, the last of human delusions to be overcome, has been found until lately in our constitutions and statutes, and has left its hideous and ineradicable stains on our history in crimes committed by every generation. The negro, the Irishman, and the Indian have in turn been its victims here, as the Jew and the Greek and the Hindoo in Europe and Asia. But it is reserved for us at the present day, for the first time, to put into the public law of the world and into the national legislation of the foremost of republican nations a distinction inflicting upon a large class of men a degradation by reason of their race and by reason of their occupation. . . .

Here is a declaration made by a compact between the two greatest nations of the Pacific [China and the United States], and now to be re-enforced by a solemn act of legislation, which places in the public law of the world and in the jurisprudence of America the principle that it is fit that there should hereafter be a distinction in the treatment of men by governments and in the recognition of their rights to the pursuit of happiness by a peaceful change of their homes, based not on conduct, not on character, but upon race and upon occupation. You may justly deny to the Chinese what you may not justly deny to the Irishman. You may deny to the laborer what you may not deny to the scholar or to the idler. And this declaration is extorted from unwilling China by the demand of America. With paupers, lazzaroni, harlots, persons afflicted with pestilential disease, laborers are henceforth to be classed in the enumerations of American public law. . . .

Chinese Immigration Naturally Decreasing

See also, Mr. President, how this class of immigrants, diminishing in itself, diminishes still more in its proportion to the rapidly increasing numbers who come from other lands. Against 22,943 Asiatic immigrants in 1876, there are but 5,802 in 1880. In 1878 there were 9,014 from Asia, in a total of 153,207, or one in seventeen of the entire immigration; and this includes all persons who entered the port of San Francisco to go to any South American country. In 1879 there were 9,604 from China in a total of 250,565, or one in twenty-six. In 1880 there were 5,802 from China in a total immigration of 593,359, or one in one hundred and two. The whole Chinese population, then, when the census of 1880 was taken, was but one in five hundred of our people. The whole Chinese immigration was but one in one hundred and two of the total immigration; while the total annual immigration quadrupled from 1878 to 1880, the Chinese was in 1880 little more than one-half what it was in 1878, and one-fourth what it was in 1876.

The number of immigrants of all nations was 720,045 in 1881. Of these 20,711 were Chinese. There is no record in the Bureau of Statistics of the number who departed within the year. But a very high anti-Chinese authority places it above 10,000. Perhaps the expectation that the hostile legislation under the treaty would not affect persons who entered before it took effect stimulated somewhat their coming. But the addition to the Chinese population was less than one-seventy-second of the whole immigration. All the Chinese in the country do not exceed the population of its sixteenth city. All the Chinese in California hardly surpass the number which is easily governed in Shanghai by a police of one hundred men. There are as many pure blooded Gypsies wandering about the country as there are Chinese in California. What an insult to American intelligence to ask leave of China to keep out her people, because this little handful of almond-eyed Asiatics threaten to destroy our boasted civilization. We go boasting of our democracy, and our superiority, and our strength. The flag bears the stars of hope to all nations. A hundred thousand Chinese land in California and everything is changed. God has not made of one blood all the nations any longer. The self-evident truth becomes a self-evident lie. The golden rule does not apply to the natives of the continent where it was first uttered. The United States surrender to China, the Republic to the despot, America to Asia, Jesus to Joss.

Base Motives for Exclusion Act

The advocates of this legislation appeal to a twofold motive for its support.

First. They invoke the old race prejudice which has so often played its hateful and bloody part in history.

Second. They say that the Chinese laborer works cheap and lives cheap, and so injures the American laborer with whom he competes.

The old race prejudice, ever fruitful of crime and of folly, has not been confined to monarchies or to the dark ages. Our own Republic and our own generation have yielded to this delusion, and have paid the terrible penalty. I do not mean to go over the ground which Mr. Sumner, with his accustomed industry and learning, so thoroughly traversed in his lecture upon caste. But I wish to plant myself upon the greatest authority in modern science, himself perhaps the most perfect example of the greatness of the capacity of the human intellect under the most favorable conditions. Listen to Alexander von Humboldt, as quoted by Mr. Sumner:

> While we maintain the unity of the human species, we at the same time repel the depressing assumption of superior and in-

ferior races of men. There are nations more susceptible of cultivation, more highly civilized, more ennobled by mental cultivation, than others, but none in themselves nobler than
others.—*Alexander von Humboldt, quoted in Sumner's Works*, volume 13, page 157.

What argument can be urged against the Chinese which was
not heard against the negro within living memory? . . .

The Foolishness of Racism

Who now so bold as to deny to the colored race fitness for citizenship. Twenty years have not passed by since the children of the
African savage were emancipated from slavery. In that brief space
they have vindicated their title to the highest privileges and their
fitness for the highest duties of citizenship. These despised sav-
ages have sat in the House and in the Senate. I have served with
them for twelve years in both branches. Can you find an equal
number, chosen on any principle of selection, whose conduct has
been marked by more uniform good sense and propriety? . . .

It is scarcely forty years since the Irishman, who has been such
a source of wealth and strength to America, began his exodus
across the sea. There are men in this body, whose heads are not
yet gray, who can remember how the arguments now used
against the Chinese filled the American mind with alarm when
used against the Irishman. He comes, said the honest bigotry of
that day, only to get the means of living, and then to return; he
will drive the American to starvation by the competition of his
cheap labor; he lives in squalor and filth; he wants only a few
potatoes for food; he is blindly attached to the Popish religion; he
owes allegiance to a foreign potentate; he is incapable of intelligent citizenship. . . .

Even the humane and liberal John Stuart Mill says:

> If there were no other escape from that fatal immigration of the
> Irish—which has done and is doing so much to degrade the
> condition of our agricultural and some classes of our town pop-
> ulation—I should see no injustice and the greatest possible ex-
> pediency in checking that destructive inroad by prohibitive
> laws.

In the early edition of his *Political Economy*, Mr. Bowen, the
learned and able professor at Harvard, expresses the same fear
for America. He says the annual addition to our population of
400,000 foreigners, of whom one-fourth are Irish, is likely to effect
a general and great depreciation in the price of labor.

> Throw down the little that is left of our protective system—

He proceeds—

> and let the emigration from Great Britain and Ireland to our
> shores increase to half a million annually, and within the life-

time of the present generation the laborer's hire in our Atlantic States will be as low as it is in England. This we should regard as the greatest calamity which the folly of men or the wrath of Heaven could bring upon the land.

These are but temperate expressions of opinions which drove less intelligent persons to frenzy and crime. The streets of Baltimore and of New Orleans ran with Irish blood. A great party was founded, and swept some States, on a platform of opposition to foreigners.

I suppose no person now would like to repeat the arguments which were addressed to the Know-Nothing party in 1855. The Irishman has contributed by his labor to cover our land with railroads, which in their turn create cities, give value to land, and open new opportunities for labor. His sons and daughters are found in large numbers in our factories. He is acquiring land. He is a large depositor in our savings banks. He rendered indispensable service in war. More and more every year he ceases to be the dupe of demagogues, and is learning the higher duties of citizenship. Meantime, the wage of the American workman is higher and not lower for his presence. While he has bettered his own condition he has raised to a higher grade of social life and wealth the American laborer whose place he has taken. . . .

The Chinese Character

An argument is based on the character of the Chinese. You should take a race at its best, and not at its worst, in looking for its possibilities under the influence of freedom. The Chinese are in many particulars far superior to our own ancestors as they were when they first came forth into the light of history. Our British forefathers, at a time far within the historic period, remained in a degradation of superstition and a degradation of barbarism to which China never descended. Centuries after the Chinese philosopher had uttered the golden rule, and had said, "I like life and I like righteousness; if I cannot keep the two together I will let life go; and choose righteousness," the Druids of Britain were offering human sacrifices to pagan deities. We must take a race at its best in determining its capacity for freedom. This race can furnish able merchants, skillful diplomatists, profound philosophers, faithful servants, industrious and docile laborers. An eminent member of the other House told me that he had dealt with Chinese merchants to the amount of hundreds of thousands, perhaps millions, and that they had never deceived him. . . .

One of the ablest of the writers against the Chinese, Mr. James A. Whitney, sums up his opinion thus:

> The Chinese intellect, the Chinese character, is strong, vigorous, patient, and far-sighted. As diplomates, the statesmen of China

Chinese Exclusion Violates Treaty

Senator Orville Platt of Connecticut was one of those who argued against passage of the Chinese Exclusion Act. During the congressional debate on March 8, 1882, he pointed out that the proposed act was a direct violation of the U.S. treaty with China.

Now, Mr. President, what is a treaty? It is a contract between nations. That is all. It occupies the same position between governments that an ordinary contract does between individuals. It is to be kept like every other contract, in the spirit in which it is made. We made this contract which we call a treaty with the Chinese Government, and we must keep it. We must keep it, or stand forever disgraced in the eyes of the world. There is no way in which an individual can so soon and so thoroughly forfeit the respect of the community in which he lives as to be sharp in making a contract and sharp in taking an unfair advantage under the contract which the other contracting party never expected that he would take. There is no way in which a nation can so surely forfeit the respect of all other nations as to make that contract called a treaty in shrewdness, and then as shrewdly take advantage of the technical terms of that treaty to accomplish what the other contracting party never intended should be accomplished.

have held their own with those of every nation in the world.

Indeed, a large part of the argument of the Senator from California is based, not on Chinese inferiority, but on his dread of Chinese superiority in most of the occupations of life. Their civilization, he says, will be too strong for ours, if the two come in conflict in a fair field. . . .

Now I wish to read a sentence or two from the report of Senator Morton, the last dying legacy of this great Senator and lover of human liberty, published since his death and left by him unfinished as his last public work. He says:

If the Chinese in California were white people, being in all other respects what they are, I do not believe that the complaints and warfare made against them would have existed to any considerable extent. Their difference in color, dress, manners, and religion has, in my judgment, more to do with this hostility than their alleged vices or any actual injury to the white people of California. . . .

As a rule, they are industrious, temperate, and honest in their dealings. Some thousands of them are employed as household servants in the cities and in the country. In this capacity the testimony generally concurs in giving them a high character. They very readily learn to perform all kinds of household duty, are devoted to their employment, and soon become exceedingly skillful. The testimony proved that they went to all parts of the

State to serve in that capacity, when other servants or help of that kind could not be obtained from the cities, and that if they were banished it would be very hard, in fact, as many of the witnesses said, impossible to supply their places. As laborers upon the farms and in the gardens and vineyards nearly all of the witnesses speak of them in the highest terms. . . .

In the construction of railroads and other public works of California the Chinese have been of the greatest service and have performed the largest part of the labor. . . .

It is said that two races have been side by side for thirty years and no step taken toward assimilation. It is admitted that they have learned our industries rapidly and intelligently. That they do not incline to become Christians or republicans may perhaps be accounted for by the treatment they have received. They are excluded by statute from the public schools. They have no honest trial by jury. Judge Blake, of the San Francisco criminal court, testifies:

It is true that as a rule when a Chinaman's case goes to a jury there is no help about it, the jury must convict him. . . .

What special inducements have the Chinese to become republicans in a State which has established a constitution which in article 2, section 1, says:

Every native male citizen of the United States, every male person who shall have acquired the rights of citizenship under or by virtue of the treaty of Queretaro, and every male naturalized citizen thereof, who shall have become such ninety days prior to any election, of the age of twenty-one years, who shall have been a resident of the State one year next preceding the election, and of the county in which he claims his vote ninety days, and in the election precinct thirty days, shall be entitled to vote at all elections which are now or may hereafter be authorized by law: *Provided*, No native of China, no idiot, insane person, or person convicted of any infamous crime, and no person hereafter convicted of the embezzlement or misappropriation of public money, shall ever exercise the privileges of an elector in this State. . . .

An eminent and learned judge of the Supreme Court of the United States gave a judgment on an ordinance of the city of San Francisco directing that the head of every person convicted of crime should be shaved, should be "cut or clipped to a uniform length of one inch from the scalp thereof"—an ordinance directed against the Chinese only, intended to impose upon them cruel and degrading punishments. Judge Field says, after pointing out the iniquity of this ordinance:

It is not creditable to the humanity and civilization of our people, much less to their Christianity, that an ordinance of this character was possible. . . .

There is a mass of evidence on this point. I might present many extracts from the report of the Congressional committee of 1876, but I will not, in order to save the time of the Senate. I wish, however, to read one statement of Mr. Pixley, who represented the anti-Chinese side. After summing up the qualities of the men such as he has described, he says:

> In other words, I believe . . . that the Chinese have no souls to save, and if they have they are not worth the saving.

But it is urged, and this, in my judgment, is the greatest argument for the bill, that the introduction of the labor of the Chinese reduces the wages of the American laborer. "We are ruined by Chinese cheap labor" is a cry not limited to the class to whose representative the brilliant humorist of California first ascribed it. I am not in favor of lowering anywhere the wages of any American labor, skilled or unskilled. On the contrary, I believe the maintenance and the increase of the purchasing power of the wages of the American workingman should be the one principal object of our legislation. The share in the product of agriculture or manufacture which goes to labor should, and I believe will, steadily increase. For that, and for that only, exists our protective system. The acquisition of wealth, national or individual, is to be desired only for that. The statement of the accomplished Senator from California on this point meets my heartiest concurrence. I have no sympathy with any men, if such there be, who favor high protection and cheap labor.

But I believe that the Chinese, to whom the terms of the California Senator attribute skill enough to displace the American in every field requiring intellectual vigor, will learn very soon to insist on his full share of the product of his work. But whether that be true or not, the wealth he creates will make better and not worse the condition of every higher class of labor. There may be trouble or failure in adjusting new relations. But sooner or later every new class of industrious and productive laborers elevates the class it displaces. The dread of an injury to our labor from the Chinese rests on the same fallacy that opposed the introduction of labor-saving machinery, and which opposed the coming of the Irishman and the German and the Swede. Within my memory in New England all the lower places in factories, all places of domestic service, were filled by the sons and daughters of American farmers. The Irishmen came over to take their places; but the American farmer's son and daughter did not suffer; they were only elevated to a higher plane. In the increased wealth of the community their share is much greater. The Irishman rose from the bog or the hovel of his native land to the comfort of a New England home and placed his children in a New England school. The Yankee rises from the loom and the spinning-jenny to be the teacher, the skilled laborer in the machine shop, the inventor, the merchant, or the opulent landholder and farmer of the West.

I wish also to read in this connection what Mr. Morton says as his conclusion:

That they have injuriously interfered with the white people of California, or have done them a serious injury, may well be doubted. The great fact is that there is to-day and always has been a scarcity of labor on the Pacific coast. There is work for all who are there, both white and Mongolian, and the State would undoubtedly develop much more rapidly were there more and cheaper labor. There was much intelligent testimony to the fact that the Chinese by their labor opened up large avenues and demand for white labor. The Chinese performed the lowest kind, while the whites monopolized that of a superior character. This was well stated by Mr. Crocker, a very intelligent witness, largely interested in the Central Pacific and Southern California Railroads. In answer to a question as to what was the effect of Chinese upon white labor, and whether it was to deprive white men of employment, or had that effect at any time, he said: "I think that they afford white men labor. I think that their presence here affords to white men a more elevated class of labor. As I said before, if you should drive these 75,000 Chinamen off you would take 75,000 white men from an elevated class of work and put them down to doing this low class of labor that the Chinamen are now doing, and instead of elevating you would degrade the white labor to that extent.

Then again:

For any man to ride through California, from one end of this State to the other, and see the miles upon miles of uncultivated land, and in the mountains millions of acres of timber, and the foothills waiting for some one to go and cultivate them, and then talk about there being too much labor here in the country, is simply nonsense, in my estimation. There is labor for all, and the fact that the Chinamen are here gives an opportunity to white men to go in and cultivate this land where they could not cultivate it otherwise. Other evidence showed that by Chinese labor over 1,000,000 acres of tule lands have been reclaimed. This was work of the hardest and most unhealthy character, requiring them to work for a large part of the time in mud and water; but the lands, when reclaimed, were occupied and cultivated by white men, furnishing a great many homes, and were in fact the richest and most productive in California. They also chiefly performed the work in constructing irrigating canals for farming purposes, and dams and canals for supplying the mines with water, by which a very large extent of country was made exceedingly productive, furnishing homes and employment for thousands of white men, and by which, also, the mines were made profitable, and created a large demand for white labor. The evidence further showed that the railroads, chiefly constructed by these people, were the pioneers in settlement and agriculture; that the settlements followed the railroads; that wherever a railroad was constructed the lands were taken up and converted into farms and homesteads. While there was complaint that the Chinese, by their cheap labor, took it from white people, inquiry failed to show that there was any considerable number of white people in California out of employment, except those who were willfully idle; that there was work, and remunerative work, for all who chose to perform it.

California has a population of 700,000. She can support seventeen million. Will it be claimed that these seventeen million will not be better off by finding there the wealth and the improvements which Chinese labor will prepare for their possession; by finding the railroad built, the swamp drained, the highway smoothed, the harbor dredged?

Will it be maintained that if California could have for nothing what she gets cheaply from Chinese labor, she would not be better off? If the swamp lands had been made prairie lands by nature; if the ravines had been filled and mountains tunneled by nature, so that the road-bed was ready for the rail; if every man, instead of buying shoes from Massachusetts, had a pair left gratis at his door, that the State would not be better off. Is barren land or productive land best for a State? Then surely the laborer who does these things at least cost does most for the community, and gives the people who occupy the State opportunity for better profit in other fields of industry. . . .

The Laws of the Universe

Humanity, capable of infinite depths of degradation, is capable also of infinite heights of excellence. The Chinese, like all other races, has given us its examples of both. To rescue humanity from this degradation is, we are taught to believe, the great object of God's moral government on earth. It is not by injustice, exclusion, caste, but by reverence for the individual soul that we can aid in this consummation. It is not by Chinese policies that China is to be civilized. I believe that the immortal truths of the Declaration of Independence came from the same source with the Golden Rule and the Sermon on the Mount. We can trust Him who promulgated these laws to keep the country safe that obeys them. The laws of the universe have their own sanction. They will not fail. The power that causes the compass to point to the north, that dismisses the star on its pathway through the skies, promising that in a thousand years it shall return again true to its hour, and keeps His word, will vindicate His own moral law. As surely as the path on which our fathers entered a hundred years ago led to safety, to strength, to glory, so surely will the path on which we now propose to enter bring us to shame, to weakness, and to peril.

VIEWPOINT 3

"These facts prove . . . that the exclusion of immigrants unable to read or write . . . will operate against the most undesirable and harmful part of our present immigration."

The Literacy Test Will Preserve America's Natural Superiority

Henry Cabot Lodge (1850-1924)

Senator Henry Cabot Lodge of Massachusetts, Yankee born and bred, was one of those Americans who were deeply concerned by the changing nature of immigration during the latter part of the nineteenth and early twentieth centuries. Lodge, a member of the moneyed, dominant WASP class, feared that the new immigrants—those of southern and eastern European background— would not only adversely affect the working person's wages and contribute to the impoverished conditions of America's cities, but also would dilute the purity of the American race. Lodge supported measures to restrict contract laborers and those with undesirable criminal and medical histories. He was also one of the earliest to support a literacy test as a means of weeding out the worst of the intended immigrants.

Lodge perceived a direct connection between literacy and moral and intellectual character. By insisting that immigrants be able to read and write a passage in their native language, Lodge felt, America could be more certain of getting immigrants able to learn about and ultimately assimilate into American culture. Those who could not read and write, he believed, would be nothing more than foreign paupers and criminals leeching off of American society.

The following viewpoint is excerpted from a speech Lodge gave in the Senate on March 16, 1896. It is one of many speeches and articles he wrote supporting a literacy requirement for immigrants.

Mr. President, this bill is intended to amend the existing law so as to restrict still further immigration to the United States. Paupers, diseased persons, convicts, and contract laborers are now excluded. By this bill it is proposed to make a new class of excluded immigrants and add to those which have just been named the totally ignorant. The bill is of the simplest kind. The first section excludes from the country all immigrants who can not read and write either their own or some other language. The second section merely provides a simple test for determining whether the immigrant can read or write, and is added to the bill so as to define the duties of the immigrant inspectors, and to assure to all immigrants alike perfect justice and a fair test of their knowledge.

Two questions arise in connection with this bill. The first is as to the merits of this particular form of restriction; the second as to the general policy of restricting immigration at all. I desire to discuss briefly these two questions in the order in which I have stated them. The smaller question as to the merits of this particular bill comes first. The existing laws of the United States now exclude, as I have said, certain classes of immigrants who, it is universally agreed, would be most undesirable additions to our population. These exclusions have been enforced and the results have been beneficial, but the excluded classes are extremely limited and do not by any means cover all or even any considerable part of the immigrants whose presence here is undesirable or injurious, nor do they have any adequate effect in properly reducing the great body of immigration to this country. There can be no doubt that there is a very earnest desire on the part of the American people to restrict further and much more extensively than has yet been done foreign immigration to the United States. The question before the committee was how this could best be done; that is, by what method the largest number of undesirable immigrants and the smallest possible number of desirable immigrants could be shut out. Three methods of obtaining this further restriction have been widely discussed of late years and in various forms have been brought to the attention of Congress. The first was the imposition of a capitation tax on all immigrants. There can be no doubt as to the effectiveness of this method if the tax is made sufficiently heavy. But although exclusion by a tax would be thorough, it would be undiscriminating, and your committee did not feel that the time had yet come for its application. The second scheme was to restrict immigration by requiring consular certification of immigrants. This plan has been much advocated, and if it were possible to carry it out thoroughly and to add very largely to the number of our consuls in order to do so, it would no doubt be effective and beneficial. But the committee was satisfied that consular certification was, under existing circumstances, impractical; that the necessary machinery could not be provided; that it would lead to many serious questions with foreign governments, and that it could not be properly and justly enforced. . . .

Literacy Test Will Most Affect Undesirable Aliens

The third method was to exclude all immigrants who could neither read nor write, and this is the plan which was adopted by the committee and which is embodied in this bill. In their report the committee have shown by statistics, which have been collected and tabulated with great care, the emigrants who would be affected by this illiteracy test. It is not necessary for me here to do more than summarize the results of the committee's investigation, which have been set forth fully in their report. It is found, in the first place, that the illiteracy test will bear most heavily upon the Italians, Russians, Poles, Hungarians, Greeks, and Asiatics, and very lightly, or not at all, upon English-speaking emigrants or Germans, Scandinavians, and French. In other words, the races most affected by the illiteracy test are those whose emigration to this country has begun within the last twenty years and swelled rapidly to enormous proportions, races with which the English-speaking people have never hitherto assimilated, and who are most alien to the great body of the people of the United States. On the other hand, immigrants from the United Kingdom and of those races which are most closely related to the English-speaking people, and who with the English-speaking people themselves founded the American colonies and built up the United States, are affected but little by the proposed test. These races would not be prevented by this law from coming to this country in practically undiminished numbers. These kindred races also are those who alone go to the Western and Southern States, where immigrants are desired, and take up our unoccupied lands. The races which would suffer most seriously by exclusion under the proposed bill furnish the immigrants who do not go to the West or South, where immigration is needed, but who remain on the Atlantic Seaboard, where immigration is not needed and where their presence is most injurious and undesirable.

Reduce City Congestion

The statistics prepared by the committee show further that the immigrants excluded by the illiteracy test are those who remain for the most part in congested masses in our great cities. They furnish, as other tables show, a large proportion of the population of the slums. The committee's report proves that illiteracy runs parallel with the slum population, with criminals, paupers, and juvenile delinquents of foreign birth or parentage, whose percentage is out of all proportion to their share of the total population when compared with the percentage of the same classes among the native born. It also appears from investigations which have been made that the immigrants who would be shut out by the illiteracy test are those who bring least money to the country and come most quickly upon private or public charity for support. The replies of the governors of twenty-six States to the Immigration Restriction League show that in only two cases are immigrants of the classes affected by the illiteracy test desired, and those are of a single race. All the other immigrants mentioned by the governors as desirable belong to the races which are but slightly affected by the provisions of this bill. It is also proved that the classes now excluded by law, the criminals, the diseased, the paupers, and the contract laborers, are furnished chiefly by the same races as those most affected by the test of illiteracy. The same is true as to those immigrants who come to this country for a brief season and return to their native land, taking with them the money they have earned in the United States. There is no more hurtful and undesirable class of immigrants from every point of view than these "birds of passage," and the tables show that the races furnishing the largest number of "birds of passage" have also the greatest proportion of illiterates.

These facts prove to demonstration that the exclusion of immigrants unable to read or write, as proposed by this bill, will operate against the most undesirable and harmful part of our present immigration and shut out elements which no thoughtful or patriotic man can wish to see multiplied among the people of the United States. The report of the committee also proves that this bill meets the great requirement of all legislation of this character in excluding the greatest proportion possible of thoroughly undesirable and dangerous immigrants and the smallest proportion of immigrants who are unobjectionable.

I have said enough to show what the effects of this bill would be, and that if enacted into law it would be fair in its operation

Language Unites Nations

The Nation was—and is—a popular journal of commentary on a variety of topics. In 1891, it ran a brief, anonymous article called "The Proper Sieve for Immigrants," which some sources say was written by Henry Cabot Lodge. The article argues for the soundness of a literacy test as a means of weeding out undesirable aliens.

If it be decided that unrestricted immigration, as at present carried on, is dangerous to American institutions and ideals, it is very odd that the value of language as a political and moral test of fitness should be overlooked. Nearly all the really secure or progressive modern States are based on community of language—France, England, Russia, Germany, and Italy. The only two in Europe about whose future there are serious doubts are the polyglot States of Austria and Turkey. All European nationalities have in fact been built up on language. As a cohesive force there is nothing that can compare to language. How a democratic state governed by opinion expressed through universal suffrage could last for any considerable length of time without community of language, it is hard to conceive, for it is through community of language that men are able to feel and think the same way about public affairs, and cherish the same political ideals. Every immigrant who comes to this country speaking or understanding the English language becomes, from the day he lands, exposed to all the moral and social influences and agencies on which we rely for the maintenance and preservation of the American nationality. Everything he hears every hour helps to make him a good citizen. Every man who lands ignorant of English, on the other hand, if an ignorant man generally, is absolutely shielded for an indefinite period against all the instrumentalities of American civilization. No American ideas reach him. American persuasion does not touch him. He remains a foreigner in spite of himself, outside all the great currents of popular thought and sentiment. To feel the pulse or tap the chest of such a man, therefore, in order to ascertain his probable value as a citizen, when he does not know one word of the medium in which the national life, in all fields of activity, is carried on, seems an absurdity on its face. . . .

Taken for all in all, this test would shut out more of the undesirable element in immigration, and would be easier of application, and would have more practical advantages, than any other that could be devised. It is true, it would to a great extent confine immigration to English, Scotch, and Irishmen, but why not, if the restriction be really undertaken in the interest of American civilization? We are under no obligation to see that all races and nations enjoy an equal chance of getting here. This legislation, as we understand it, is to be for the benefit of the United States; and if the United States is desirous of admitting some Europeans, but only those easiest of absorption, the ones to choose are those who, when they land, can at once enter into intellectual relations with the community at large.

and highly beneficial in its results. It now remains for me to discuss the second and larger question, as to the advisability of restricting immigration at all. This is a subject of the greatest magnitude and the most far-reaching importance. It has two sides, the economic and the social. As to the former, but few words are necessary. There is no one thing which does so much to bring about a reduction of wages and to injure the American wage earner as the unlimited introduction of cheap foreign labor through unrestricted immigration. Statistics show that the change in the race character of our immigration has been accompanied by a corresponding decline in its quality. The number of skilled mechanics and of persons trained to some occupation or pursuit has fallen off, while the number of those without occupation or training, that is, who are totally unskilled, has risen in our recent immigration to enormous proportions. This low, unskilled labor is the most deadly enemy of the American wage earner, and does more than anything else toward lowering his wages and forcing down his standard of living. An attempt was made, with the general assent of both political parties, to meet this crying evil some years ago by the passage of what are known as the contract-labor laws. That legislation was excellent in intention, but has proved of but little value in practice. It has checked to a certain extent the introduction of cheap, low-class labor in large masses into the United States. It has made it a little more difficult for such labor to come here, but the labor of this class continues to come, even if not in the same way, and the total amount of it has not been materially reduced. Even if the contract-labor laws were enforced intelligently and thoroughly, there is no reason to suppose that they would have any adequate effect in checking the evil which they were designed to stop. It is perfectly clear after the experience of several years that the only relief which can come to the American wage earner from the competition of low-class immigrant labor must be by general laws restricting the total amount of immigration and framed in such a way as to affect most strongly those elements of the immigration which furnish the low, unskilled, and ignorant foreign labor.

It is not necessary to enter further into a discussion of the economic side of the general policy of restricting immigration. In this direction the argument is unanswerable. If we have any regard for the welfare, the wages, or the standard of life of American workingmen, we should take immediate steps to restrict foreign immigration. There is no danger, at present at all events, to our workingmen from the coming of skilled mechanics or of trained and educated men with a settled occupation or pursuit, for immigrants of this class will never seek to lower the American standard of life and wages. On the contrary, they desire the same

The Illiteracy Test Would Exclude Undesirables

On March 31, 1911, Congressman John L. Burnett entered into the Congressional Record *an outline summary of the arguments in favor of a literacy test as a means of restricting immigration. His "Brief in Favor of the Illiteracy Test" included this table showing that the literacy test would most strongly affect people from southern and eastern European countries and other countries that export "undesirables" to the United States.*

1. It is generally admitted that a large proportion of the aliens coming to us today are not as desirable as the former immigration, which settled the middle and western states.

2. The illiteracy of the various races of immigrants in 1909 was as follows:

Northern and Western Europe (Chiefly Teutonic and Celtic) — Per cent.

	Per cent.
Scandinavian	0.2
Scotch	0.5
Finnish	0.5
English	0.7
Bohemian and Moravian	1.5
Irish	1.5
Dutch and Flemish	2.6
German	6.3
French	8.0
Italian (North)	8.4
Average of above	3.5

Southern and Eastern Europe (Chiefly Slavic and Iberic) — Per cent.

	Per cent.
Spanish	10.6
Magyar	10.8
Slovak	19.7
Greek	26.1
Croatian and Slovenian	28.7
Hebrew	29.2
Polish	39.9
Russian	41.7
Portuguese	42.3
Bulgarian, Servian, and Montenegrin	46.5
Ruthenian	51.3
Roumanian	52.3
Italian (South)	56.9
Lithuanian	58.2
Average of above	42.1

Other Races — Per cent.

	Per cent.
Cuban	2.4
African (black)	22.4
Armenian	22.5
Japanese	28.7
Syrian	52.5
Mexican	64.6
Average of above	42.4

From this appears that the illiteracy of immigrants from southern and eastern Europe is over twelve times as great as that of aliens from northwestern Europe, and that the illiteracy of Armenians, Japanese, and Syrians is also high.

In 1909 over three-fifths of the total immigration was of these illiterate races.

standard for themselves. But there is an appalling danger to the American wage earner from the flood of low, unskilled, ignorant foreign labor which has poured into the country for some years past, and which not only takes lower wages, but accepts a standard of life and living so low that the American workingman can not compete with it.

Foreigners Harm American Race

I now come to the aspect of this question which is graver and more serious than any other. The injury of unrestricted immigration to American wages and American standards of living is sufficiently plain and is bad enough, but the danger which this immigration threatens to the quality of our citizenship is far worse. That which it concerns us to know and that which is more vital to us as a people than all possible questions of tariff or currency is whether the quality of our citizenship is endangered by the present course and character of immigration to the United States. . . .

During the present century, down to 1875, there have been three large migrations to this country in addition to the always steady stream from Great Britain; one came from Ireland about the middle of the century, and somewhat later one from Germany and one from Scandinavia, in which is included Sweden, Denmark, and Norway. The Irish, although of a different race stock originally, have been closely associated with the English-speaking people for nearly a thousand years. They speak the same language, and during that long period the two races have lived side by side, and to some extent intermarried. The Germans and Scandinavians are again people of the same race stock as the English who founded and built up the colonies. During this century, down to 1875, then, as in the two which preceded it, there had been scarcely any immigration to this country, except from kindred or allied races, and no other, which was sufficiently numerous to have produced any effect on the national characteristics, or to be taken into account here. Since 1875, however, there has been a great change. While the people who for two hundred and fifty years have been migrating to America have continued to furnish large numbers of immigrants to the United States, other races of totally different race origin, with whom the English-speaking people have never hitherto been assimilated or brought in contact, have suddenly begun to immigrate to the United States in large numbers. Russians, Hungarians, Poles, Bohemians, Italians, Greeks, and even Asiatics, whose immigration to America was almost unknown twenty years ago, have during the last twenty years poured in in steadily increasing numbers, until now they nearly equal the immigration of those races kindred in blood or speech, or both, by whom the United States has hitherto been built up and the American people formed.

This momentous fact is the one which confronts us today, and if continued, it carries with it future consequences far deeper than any other event of our times. It involves, in a word, nothing less than the possibility of a great and perilous change in the very fabric of our race. The English-speaking race, as I have shown, has been made slowly during the centuries. Nothing has happened thus far to radically change it here. In the United States, after allowing for the variations produced by new climatic influences and changed conditions of life and of political institutions, it is still in the great essentials fundamentally the same race. The additions in this country until the present time have been from kindred people or from those with whom we have been long allied and who speak the same language. By those who look at this question superficially we hear it often said that the English-speaking people, especially in America, are a mixture of races. Analysis shows that the actual mixture of blood in the English-speaking race is very small, and that while the English-speaking people are derived through different channels, no doubt, there is among them none the less an overwhelming preponderance of the same race stock, that of the great Germanic tribes who reached from Norway to the Alps. They have been welded together by more than a thousand years of wars, conquests, migrations, and struggles, both at home and abroad, and in so doing they have attained a fixity and definiteness of national character unknown to any other people. . . .

When we speak of a race, then, we do not mean its expressions in art or in language, or its achievements in knowledge. We mean the moral and intellectual characters, which in their association make the soul of a race, and which represent the product of all its past, the inheritance of all its ancestors, and the motives of all its conduct. The men of each race possess an indestructible stock of ideas, traditions, sentiments, modes of thought, an unconscious inheritance form their ancestors, upon which argument has no effect. What makes a race are their mental and, above all, their moral characteristics, the slow growth and accumulation of centuries of toil and conflict. These are the qualities which determine their social efficiency as a people, which make one race rise and another fall, which we draw out of a dim past through many generations of ancestors, about which we can not argue, but in which we blindly believe, and which guide us in our short-lived generation as they have guided the race itself across the centuries. . . .

Such achievements as M. Le Bon credits us with are due to the qualities of the American people, whom he, as a man of science looking below the surface, rightly describes as homogeneous. Those qualities are moral far more than intellectual, and it is on the moral qualities of the English-speaking race that our history, our victories, and all our future rest. There is only one way in which you can lower those qualities or weaken those characteristics, and that is by breeding them out. If a lower race mixes with a higher in sufficient numbers, history teaches us that the lower race will prevail. The lower race will absorb the higher, not the higher the lower, when the two strains approach equality in numbers. In other words, there is a limit to the capacity of any race to assimilating and elevating an inferior race, and when you begin to pour in in unlimited numbers people of alien or lower races of less social efficiency and less moral force, you are running the most frightful risk that any people can run. The lowering of a great race means not only its own decline but that of human civilization. M. Le Bon sees no danger to us in immigration, and his reason for this view is one of the most interesting things he says. He declares that the people of the United States will never be injured by immigration, because the moment they see the peril the great race instinct will assert itself and shut the immigration out. The reports of the Treasury for the last fifteen years show that the peril is at hand. I trust that the prediction of science is true and that the unerring instinct of the race will shut the danger out, as it closed the door upon the coming of the Chinese. . . .

Mr. President, more precious even than forms of government are the mental and moral qualities which make what we call our race. While those stand unimpaired all is safe. When those decline all is imperiled. They are exposed to but a single danger, and that is by changing the quality of our race and citizenship through the wholesale infusion of races whose traditions and inheritances, whose thoughts and whose beliefs are wholly alien to ours and with whom we have never assimilated or even been associated in the past. The danger has begun. It is small as yet, comparatively speaking, but it is large enough to warn us to act while there is yet time and while it can be done easily and efficiently. There lies the peril at the portals of our land; there is pressing in the tide of unrestricted immigration. The time has certainly come, if not to stop, at least to check, to sift, and to restrict those immigrants. In careless strength, with generous hand, we have kept our gates wide open to all the world. If we do not close them, we should at least place sentinels beside them to challenge those who would pass through. The gates which admit men to the United States and to citizenship in the great Republic should no longer be left unguarded.

"We have been assimilating [illiterates] from the very beginning. . . . For, illiteracy was far more common among the European nations formerly than now."

The Literacy Test Does Not Detect Superior Character

T. J. Brennan

Father T. J. Brennan was one of many people who were against using a literacy test to determine who would be allowed to emigrate to the United States. Brennan, like many Irish Catholics in America in the nineteenth and early twentieth centuries, was personally familiar with the nativist antagonism toward anyone not white, Anglo-Saxon, and Protestant. In this viewpoint excerpted from *Catholic World*, May 1917, Brennan points out that a literacy test does not test a person's character and that in fact many illiterate people are better citizens and workers than many literate people.

I cannot rid myself of the conviction that the literacy test constitutes a radical change in the policy of the nation which is not justified in principle. It is not a test of character, of quality, or of personal fitness, but would operate in most cases merely as a penalty for lack of opportunity in the country from which the alien seeking admission came.—*President Wilson.*

The words quoted are from President Wilson's comments when vetoing the Immigration Bill recently passed over his head. They suggest to us the question of illiteracy in its influence on social and moral life. It is a very big question, and we can give expression to only a few of the thoughts to which it gives rise.

We might, first of all, ask why did Congress bar the illiterates? Was it because it considered illiteracy as incapacitating them for the full discharge of the duties of an American citizen? Or did it consider that illiteracy connotes moral depravity and social backwardness? Or did it judge that an exodus of these unfortunates would create for us a problem of dangerous potentialities? Not having seen the report of the debate on the question we cannot tell; but we can consider for ourselves some aspects of the question.

And first of all we may say that the illiterates, just like the literates, are neither all good, nor all bad. They range over the whole moral scale; there are good and bad and passable. Anyone who would condemn the illiterates as universally bad, is either ignorant or bigoted. Anyone who would laud them as universally guileless and innocent of human weakness, is altogether benighted as to broad facts of human nature and human sinfulness. To be conceived without sin and to live untouched by moral stain is claimed for only one human being, and that claim is made by a society which is divinely guided in its dogmatic statements. The same society has condemned both the idea of universal depravity, and the idea that we can avoid all sin without special divine assistance. Hence, all sweeping assertions either about the goodness or badness of illiterates are based neither on theology nor on common sense.

The same may be said as regards education. For literacy and education are no more convertible terms than illiteracy and ignorance. There are millions absolutely illiterate; there are no rational beings absolutely ignorant. Indeed if you travel through districts or countries where illiteracy prevails, you will be surprised at the skill and ingenuity with which these illiterates manage to support life, and raise large families by the intensive use of their hands and their small gardens. Necessity has been for generations their school and their schoolmaster. It has taught them to limit their wants, and to provide against cold and hunger and nakedness. It has given them secrets about soil and crops and raiment which we seek in vain in the curriculum of our agricultural colleges or social science classes. Education is after all only an equipping of individuals to make the most of environment; and I think you will find that in this respect illiterates are as well equipped as the annual output of our colleges or universities. We often hear, of course, of the starving peasantry of such or such a country, we very seldom hear of the starving college students of our own; the reason being that the aforesaid peasantry are all congregated together and are afflicted at the same time; whereas the starving college men are dispersed throughout the whole country, and are afflicted all the time. If you take any country where illiteracy abounds and compare it with a country where everyone can "read and write," I think you will find that there are as many hungry in the one as in the other. Education indeed increases our efficiency; but at the same time it increases our wants, makes necessities of luxuries, and gives us a distaste for and dissatisfaction with the simple things that were once considered a sufficiency. Illiteracy shuts us off from the world of thought and activity for which reading and writing are prerequisite; but, by way of compensation, it considerably lessens the number of bills and collectors at the end of the month. Literacy has of course its advantages; but advantages always have to be paid for in cash; and, too, after the collector is asked to call again, to find, when he does call, that his debtor has moved and left no address.

You may say, then, that all this merely proves that an illiterate

Illiterate Often Adapt Better

Jane Addams, the renowned social worker and founder of Hull House in Chicago, stood strongly against using a literacy test to judge immigrants. This excerpt is from an editorial she wrote in 1913 for the Survey, *a monthly "Journal of Constructive Philanthropy."*

Literacy is neither a test of character nor of ability; it is merely an index of the educational system of the community in which a man has been reared. The literacy test will always work in favor of the man from the city and discriminate against the man from the country. On the face of it, it would seem safer to admit a sturdy peasant from the mountains of Calabria than a sophisticated Neapolitan, familiar with the refined methods of police graft which have made the Camorra famous. In addition to that, the peasant finds work waiting for him, the educated man "above manual labor" often has a pitiful struggle to keep himself from starvation. Our experience at Hull House is similar to that of the friends of the immigrant everywhere. We recall an Italian editor, a Greek professor, a Russian medical student, an Armenian Master of Arts, for whom it was impossible to obtain anything but manual work which they finally undertook in bitterness of spirit and with insufficiency of muscle. A settlement constantly sees the deterioration of highly educated foreigners under the strain of maladjustment, in marked contrast to the often rapid rise of the families of illiterate immigrants.

population may be, comparatively speaking, as well off at home as a population that is literate; but that when they leave their environment and come into a country like the United States, they create a twofold problem, one for themselves and another for us: they cannot keep up with the procession, and the procession itself is encumbered by their presence. Let us consider this twofold problem for a moment.

And first, the problem of the illiterates. But is it really about that we are worrying? And if so, why *should* we worry? Have not the illiterates sense enough to solve the question for themselves? And the very fact that they are coming and have come is a proof that there is no such problem, or that they have already solved it. After all this coming of the illiterates is not something sudden and unpremeditated. They have been coming from the very beginning. They have formed a portion, though a gradually lessening portion, of every nationality that has peopled our country. They must have done well, and reported favorably, otherwise the supply would have gradually dwindled down to the vanishing point. Men do not continue for centuries to follow a beaten track unless the track leads to something better than they leave behind. They must have found that notwithstanding our school and college-trained population, there is room for those who have known neither school nor college. They must have discovered that there is a big demand for unskilled labor and untrained minds—if these illiterates can be so described. And if we find them pouring in through all our ports, we may safely conclude that they are rushing neither to early graves nor to social annihilation; but that their flight, like the flight of the birds, is guided by a safe if vague instinct. From the point of view of the illiterates, therefore, we need not worry.

However, the other question comes: are these illiterates a problem for us? Are we taking into our system an element that we can neither eschew nor assimilate? This question demands an answer.

We Have Always Had Illiteracy

And first of all we may say that we have been assimilating them from the very beginning; and the farther back you go the more we did it. For, illiteracy was far more common among the European nations formerly than now. A large percentage of the early immigrants knew very little about the three R's. We took them as they came, asking no questions about literary attainments; nor do we find in reading over the history of the country that there was ever any difficulty arising from illiterates. They all seemed to find work and to make a living; and when it came to a question of fighting they lacked neither the will nor the power to use the rifle as cheerfully and intelligently as they used the shovel

"OH, DEAR!! SOME OF THOSE SCRAM-
BLED EGGS ARE A BIT OFF COLOR!!"
—Morris for the George Matthew Adams Service.

or the pickaxe. You will search in vain through the records of our county coroners for a verdict of "death from illiteracy;" and I have never seen a report from any general of the War of Independence or of the Civil War saying that he was defeated because his soldiers could not read or write. One thing seems certain, namely, that this scare about illiterates is something new and has no justification in the history of the country.

Nay, rather, it is based on a false idea of the value of universal education. For universal education is quite a new thing, and like many new things it seems to its devotees to be an absolute necessity. Whereas, the truth is that the more widespread is education, the less commercially valuable it becomes. It ceases to be an asset, and becomes merely a condition. If you had only a few million in the country who could read and write, then reading and writing would become a good investment; but when the number of such runs up to eighty or ninety millions they need other accomplishments ere they can succeed.

Furthermore it is a well-known fact that education gives men an aversion for any kind of work where education is not required. Education is usually acquired for commercial reasons, and we hate to think that all our years in school are to be thrown away for nothing. Hence there is a scarcity of hands for farm work and manual labor; and a superfluity of applicants for clerical positions. It is much easier to get a stenographer than a day laborer; and forty dollars a month in an office is a far more effective bait for a graduate from school or college than two and a half a day with the obligation of using a spade or a hoe.

And here precisely is the value of the immigrant illiterates. We need them and need millions of them for the gardens and the farms; and for the railway tracks, and the city sewers. We cannot run a country by fountain pens and typewriters and tables of logarithms. We need such things indeed; but we need also bone and sinew and muscle; and unless we had the bone and sinew and muscle of these foreign illiterates to draw from, we would soon have very little for the fountain pens and typewriters to do. We have in this country no landed peasantry; for each generation of peasants becomes the parents not of other peasants, but of lawyers and doctors and trained nurses; and unless the supply of peasants is kept up from abroad, our gardens will soon be weed patches, and our sewers choked with dirt.

Of course our illiterates *are* a problem, there is no denying the fact. However, there is this consolation—that they are themselves as willing to help in its solution as we are. And even if the experiment is a little costly, yet we ought to be broad and philanthropic enough to stand the cost. We have been blest in many ways, and instead of sending the multitude away hungry we should say with the Master, "whence shall we buy bread that these may eat." We have boasted much of our broad humanity, of our welcome for the persecuted, of our land of opportunity. But is there much humanity in judging a man by his ability to read and write? Is not illiteracy the greatest of all persecutions? Is it fair to deny an opportunity to a man because of something he never had an opportunity to acquire? Indeed if this present bar had been set up fifty or a hundred years ago, there are many of those representatives and senators who voted "yes" who would now be in European war trenches or concentration camps; for their fathers or grandfathers could not pass the test now raised by their offspring. The Immigration Bill is un-American, and has been so designated by no less an authority than the President of the United States.

"The present laws are inadequate and . . . further selection of immigration is necessary and desirable."

The U.S. Must Restrict Immigration

The Immigration Restriction League

The tremendous influx of immigrants into the United States beginning in 1890 inspired fear and worry in many Americans. They were most concerned by the large numbers of "new" immigrants—those from southern and eastern Europe and Asia. The impact of Asian immigrants was felt primarily in California; the impact of European immigrants was felt primarily in the cities of the East Coast, as well as Chicago and a few other large cities. According to historian Louis M. Hacker, people's worries focused on three primary concerns: job and wage deterioration; the growth of slums with attendant poverty, crime, and low living standards; and eugenic corruption of the white race. That most of the "new" immigrants had dark complexions, spoke in a variety of foreign tongues, and were largely poor and uneducated increased concerns that these people could not be assimilated into the American culture and could only act as corrupting influences.

In 1894 the Immigration Restriction League was formed to combat the increasing arrivals of these "undesirable" immigrants. The IRL was the most prominent of the organizations founded to encourage restriction or elimination of foreign immigration. Its members included many prominent citizens, politicians, and scholars. The pressure of this and other similar groups led the

Congress to pass increasingly restrictive immigration regulations. At first based on qualities such as criminal records, mental and physical health, and ability to pay a head tax, the laws eventually included a literacy requirement and finally a national origin requirement. These latter elements were clearly nationalistic and/or racist in nature; they were devised specifically to favor "desirable" immigrants (from the British Isles, Ireland, and Germany) and to discriminate against "undesirable" immigrants (from Asia and southern and eastern Europe).

The first of these national origin laws, passed in 1921, established a quota system based on 3 percent of the number of residents of a particular nation residing in the United States in 1910. In 1924 the restrictions were increased by reducing the quota to 2 percent and making the base year 1890, just before the large numbers of "new" immigrants began arriving in the United States. The consequence was that only very small numbers of people from these undesirable nations were allowed to immigrate. The law was relaxed somewhat in 1929, making the base year 1920, thereby increasing slightly the proportion of southern and eastern Europeans eligible to immigrate. This law remained in effect until 1965, when a new quota system was devised that significantly decreased the discrimination based on national origin.

The following viewpoint is excerpted from a statement made on October 25, 1910, and presented by the Immigration Restriction League to the Immigration Commission, established by Congress to study and make recommendations on the immigration situation. Its forty-one volumes of reports, published in 1911 (Washington, DC: Government Printing Office), included one volume of statements from a variety of groups invited to present their positions on immigration. The IRL's statement succinctly presents many of the arguments for immigration restriction posed in the thirty-odd years of debate during one of the most important periods of American immigration history.

Boston, Mass., *October 24, 1910.*
To the Immigration Commission:

Gentlemen: The Immigration Restriction League, in response to your courteous invitation of September 26, begs leave to present briefly its views upon the present situation with reference to immigration and the immigration laws of this country.

The league believes that the present laws are inadequate and that further selection of immigration is necessary and desirable from (*a*) the social and moral standpoint, (*b*) the economic standpoint, (*c*) the eugenic standpoint.

The league recommends that—

1. A reading test for aliens of 15 years or over in any language or dialect the alien may choose.

2. An increase of the present head tax to at least $10.

3. Requiring immigrants to be in possession of money for their support while securing employment; say, $50 for single immigrants and heads of families and $25 additional for a wife and each minor child.

4. Abolishing the existing provision for admitting immigrants on bond.

5. Increasing the fines on steamship companies to $500 and extending the system of fines to all cases where the ineligibility of the alien could have been detected at embarkation by careful inspection.

6. Providing for the deportation of aliens without time limit, for causes, other than due to accident, whether arising prior to or subsequent to landing.

Selection Necessary from a Social and Moral Standpoint

(*a*) *Crime.* The census report on prisons (1904) shows that a foreign-born white population 10 years of age and over, which in 1900 was 19.5 per cent of such general white population, furnished 23.7 per cent of the white prisoners; while the foreign-born juvenile white population, which in 1900 was 6.5 per cent of such general white population, furnished 9.4 per cent of the delinquents enumerated June 30, 1904, and 11 per cent of those committed during the year.

Of the total commitments in 1904 those of foreign birth or parentage constituted 39.7 per cent, while those of foreign parentage (practically those of foreign birth or parentage) constituted, in 1900, 27.5 per cent of the total population.

The report of the Commissioner-General for 1908 shows that the foreign-born population, which in 1900 was 13.6 per cent of the total population, furnished 15.6 per cent of all the criminals and over one-half of these had committed serious crimes. It also appears that in the years from 1904 to 1908 the alien criminals increased from 9,825 to 15,323, or over one-half, and twice in serious offenses.

The argument frequently made that these statistics do not allow for the greater proportion of mature aliens in the alien population has two answers: First, the figures given above show an even greater tendency to crime on the part of the juvenile foreign-born population. Second, there is no reason for allowing immigrants of criminal tendency to enter this country and be a burden upon our citizens, even if aliens as a whole can be shown to be no more criminal than natives. The league would approve any arrangements for foreign police or other certificates of good character for immigrants, but as about one-fifth of foreign-born criminals are illiterate and many crimes spring from poverty and a low social standard, it believes the illiteracy test and other legislation recommended would directly tend to weed out the criminal class. General Bingham, when police commissioner of New York City, said:

"There is another very important thing about this crime business. I don't want to say anything that would be indiscreet, but unquestionably the hordes of immigrants that are coming here have a good deal to do with crimes against women and children.

"You will notice that these particular crimes are done by fellows who can't talk the English language. It is this wave of immigration that brings to New York the hundreds of thousands of criminals who don't know what liberty means, and don't care; don't know our customs, can not speak the English language, and are in general the scum of Europe."

The Thirty-second Annual Report of the Board of City Magistrates of New York City (Manhattan and Bronx) shows 12,055 more cases tried in 1905 than 1904, chiefly of Italians, Greeks, and Russian Jews for violation of ordinances and an abnormal increase in serious and higher crimes.

In Elmira Reformatory in 1906, 60 per cent of the inmates were aliens; and in one class of 32, 22 had been in the United States less than one year. Of prisoners in Sing Sing, Clinton, and Auburn prisons in New York State in 1909, 37 per cent were foreign born, the foreign-born population of the State in 1900 being 26.1. (Annual Report of Superintendent of Prisons.)

(b) Insanity and Disease. Census special reports, "Insane and Feeble-Minded in Hospitals and Institutions, 1904," page 20, shows that a white foreign-born population of 10 years old and over, which in 1900 was 19.5 per cent of such general white population, furnished 34.3 per cent of white insane persons in hospitals in 1904, and 29.8 per cent of the admissions to such hospitals during 1904.

The New York lunacy commission (report for 1905) shows an increase of 20 per cent in insanity in the State, largely due to immigration. In 1909 the commission stated that 45 per cent of the insane were foreign born out of a foreign-born population of less than 35 per cent for the State.

Dr. Thomas Darlington, health officer of New York City, states (*North American Review*, Dec. 21, 1906) that over 80 per cent of aliens certified as of poor physique or having physical defects were landed during the year at Ellis Island; that the 40 per cent of foreign-born school children in the city furnished 70 per cent of the defectives; and that of the admissions to the hospitals of New York City from 1885 to 1894, 64 per cent were foreign born.

(c) Pauperism. Census special reports, "Paupers in Almshouses, 1904," pages 16 to 18, shows that a foreign-born white population, which in 1900 was 15.3 per cent of the general white population, furnished 43.2 per cent of the white pauper population December 31, 1903, and 43 per cent of those admitted to the almshouses during 1904.

The native white paupers of foreign or mixed parentage admitted in 1904 were 26.8 per cent of the total paupers as compared with 19.4 per cent among the inmates enumerated December 31, 1903.

The Case for Restriction

Joseph Lee was a frequent writer on the subject of immigration. Many of his articles, including the 1916 article from which this excerpt comes, were published in the Survey, *a "journal of constructive philanthropy."*

The case for restriction in general is first, that it is the only possible way of appreciably raising wages in this country. By restricting immigration we could so greatly increase wages that various methods of outdoor relief, such as health insurance and old-age pensions, would not be needed. People who do not want to restrict immigration do not want wages to rise, or to have the slightest possibility of rising. They may have a pious hope in that direction, but they are averse to the only measure by which such hope can by any possibility be realized.

The other reason for restriction is that upon the whole the illiterate members of the less progressive races—who would constitute the element excluded—are not such good material for citizenship as the average of what we have here now. It is very generous and very modest of Americans to say that the less desirable Sicilians are better folks than we are, but why have they never shown it in Sicily?

In 1890 the foreign whites contributed 2¼ times as many male paupers per million of voting population as the native whites of native parentage, and those of foreign birth or parentage over 3 times as many.

In 1905 there were 50,000 foreign-born paupers in the State of New York alone, costing the State $1,510,506 for their support.

(d) Bonds. The league recommends abolishing or very much restricting the present provisions for admitting aliens on bonds. The State of Massachusetts tried this plan before the United

States took charge of immigration and gave it up as absolutely unworkable. In 1909, of 443 persons certified as mentally or physically defective to such an extent that their ability to earn a living was interfered with, 242, or more than one-half, were admitted on bond.

The Commissioner-General says (report for 1909, p. 115):

"As a general rule, to which there should be only rare exceptions, it should be held unequivocally either that an alien is or that he is not admissible. A bond is by no means a complete protection against an alien's becoming a public charge. Many aliens change their name, rendering identification practically impossible, or remove from their original place of settlement, causing all account of the fact that a bond exists to be forgotten, or the bondsmen are or become irresponsible. Altogether the bonding system is very unsatisfactory."

Inquiries made at various times by the league have failed to discover a single case where a bond has been sued on. Whenever bonds for less than $1,000 are accepted, proceedings would be deemed inadvisable, as the costs and expenses of suit might easily equal the amount of the bond.

Alien Burden

(e) *Generally.* The league believes that, great as is the burden of aliens who fall into the definite classes known as the defectives and delinquents, there is an even greater burden upon and danger to the community from the immigration of large numbers of aliens of low intelligence, poor physique, deficient in energy, ability, and thrift. Many of these have to be supported by public or private charity, are a menace to the public health, and generally lower the mental, moral, and physical average of our population. The league believes that a considerable portion of this class would be excluded by the legislation it proposes, as experience shows that poverty, ignorance, and incapacity in general go together. The statistics given above are but a few of those which might be cited, and which are doubtless well known to you already.

Restriction Needed from an Economic Standpoint

It is likely that this topic will be quite fully treated by others. The league would call attention to the following: (1) That the true wealth of a country consists in the character of its institutions and of its people and not in the number of miles of its railways or the rapid exhaustion of its resources. (2) That what demand there is for free immigration has always come from employers who want to force wages down regardless of the effect upon the community. (3) That the immigration of cheap labor has just this effect, forcing the workman already here to lower his standard of living and often to lose his job. (4) That just so far as immigration of cheap labor injures the status of the native workingmen it prevents the immigration of efficient and desirable foreign workingmen, who will not come here to compete with cheap labor. . . . Labor economically cheap is moreover never socially cheap.

Many Americans wanted to reduce or stop the flow of immigrants into the United States. They felt the overwhelming numbers of newcomers would be a drain on America's human, economic, and environmental resources.

Mr. John Mitchell said recently on this point:

"The standard of wages for both skilled and unskilled labor in the United States has been built up as a result of years and years of energetic effort, struggle, and sacrifice. When an immigrant without resources is compelled to accept work at less than the established wage rate, he not only displaces a man working at the higher rate, but his action threatens to destroy the whole schedule of wages in the industry in which he secures employment, because it not infrequently occurs that an employer will attempt to regulate wages on the basis of the lowest rate paid to any of the men in his employ. Any reduction in wages means a lowering of the standard of living, and the standard of living among a civilized people can not be lowered without lowering in the same ratio the physical standard and the intellectual and moral ideals of that people."

Recent investigations in biology show that heredity is a far more important factor in the progress of any species than environment. Education can develop what is in an immigrant, but can not supply what is not there. Assuming what is by no means proved, that a mixed race is a better race, we should do as we do in breeding any other species than the human, viz, secure the best specimens to breed from. The same arguments which induce us to segregate criminals and feeble-minded and thus prevent their breeding apply to excluding from our borders individuals whose multiplying here is likely to lower the average of our people. We should exercise at least as much care in admitting human beings as we exercise in relation to animals or insect pests or disease germs. Yet it is true that we are to-day actually taking more care in the selection, and in the examination for soundness and for health, of a Hereford bull or a Southdown ewe, imported for the improvement of our cattle and sheep, than we are taking in the selection of the alien men and women who are coming here to be the fathers and mothers of future American children. We do not hesitate to prohibit the importation of cattle from a foreign country where a cattle disease is prevalent. It is only in very extreme cases that we have ever taken such a step in connection with the importation of aliens, yet there are certain parts of Europe from which all medical men and all biologists would agree that it would be better for the American race if no aliens at all were admitted.

We should see to it that the breeding of the human race in this country receives the attention which it so surely deserves. We should see to it that we are protected, not merely from the burden of supporting alien dependents, delinquents, and defectives, but from what George William Curtis called "that watering of the nation's lifeblood," which results from their breeding after admission.

From Backward Countries

A considerable proportion of immigrants now coming are from races and countries, or parts of countries, which have not progressed, but have been backward, downtrodden, and relatively useless for centuries. If these immigrants "have not had opportunities," it is because their races have not made the opportunities; for they have had all the time that any other races have had; in fact, often come from older civilizations. There is no reason to suppose that a change of location will result in a change of inborn tendencies.

The efforts of steamship agents result, moreover, in the immigration of many of the least desirable specimens of these backward races. Many of them would be excluded by the legislation the league proposes, leaving place and creating a demand for members of the progressive Baltic races to whose energy the present prosperity of our country is due.

The Commissioner-General (report for 1909, p. 111) says on this point:

"The bureau has repeatedly called attention to the interesting and important economic problem constituted by this increase in the influx of peoples so different racially from the original settlers of the country—people, who, in their antecedents, ideas, ideals (political and social), and methods of life and thought, are quite distinct from the Teutonic and Keltic stocks, from which our immigration was for so many years derived. What will be the result of a continuance of this preponderance is a question which concerns every thoughtful patriotic American citizen. From one point of view, at least, heterogeneousness in a matter of this kind is undesirable, homogeneousness desirable. There can be but little homogeneity between the people of southern and eastern Europe and the real American. Several generations are required to produce assimilation, even under favorable circumstances.

"What is the explanation of this increased and still increasing influx of Iberic and Slavic people? Several facts may be stated in partial explanation—the poor conditions, political and social, of their native countries, the natural desire to better their condition, and the wish for liberty of thought and conscience that are to some extent inherent with all races of men. But these do not afford what is believed to be the principal, underlying explanation. The truth of the matter is that the peasants of the countries mentioned have for a number of years supplied a rich harvest to the promoter of immigration. The promoter is usually a steamship ticket agent, employed on a commission basis, or a professional money lender, or a combination of the two. His only interest is the wholly selfish one of gaining his commission and collecting his usury. He is employed by the steamship lines, large and small, without scruple, and to the enormous profit of such lines. The more aliens they bring over the more there are to be carried back if failure meets the tentative immigrant, and the more are likely to follow later if success is his lot. Whatever the outcome, it is a good commercial proposition for the steamship line. To say that the steamship lines are responsible, directly or indirectly, for this unnatural immigration is not a statement of a theory, but of a fact, and of a fact that sometimes becomes, indeed, if it is not always, a crying shame."

The Commissioner-General refers (p. 112) to the reports of a special immigration inspector who studied the matter in Europe, and says the Immigration Bureau found "that all of the steamship lines engaged in bringing aliens from Europe to this country have persistently and systematically violated the law, both in its letter and spirit, by making use of every possible means to encourage the peasants of Europe to purchase tickets over their lines to this country."

He also says (p. 113): "It may be asserted as a general rule that stimulated immigration is undesirable. As already stated, a large part of our immigration is known to be of that character."

To the same effect Hon. William Williams, commissioner at New York, says (p. 133):

"I have already adverted to the easy-going character of our exclusion laws and stated that even their strict enforcement keeps out only the very bad elements of foreign countries. Between these elements and those that are a real benefit to the country (as so many of our immigrants are) there lies a class who may be quite able to earn a living here, but who in doing so tend to pull down our standards of living. . . . I wish merely to emphasize, what must be known to every thinking person, that this class is coming here in considerable numbers and that we are making no effort to exclude it.

"Few people are bold enough to claim that we are in urgent need of any more immigrants who will crowd into the congested districts of our large cities. And yet this is where a large percentage of our immigrants now go and stay. At a time when portions of the West are crying for out-of-door labor, congestion in New York City may be increasing at the rate of many thousands per month. Another way of putting this is to say that much of our present immigration is not responsive to the legitimate demands for additional labor in the United States. I think this fact should be made known throughout those sections of our country where many erroneously think that further restrictions of the right kind would increase the difficulties incident to obtaining labor for which there is a real demand. Quite the contrary is the case, for poor immigration tends to deter good immigrants from coming."

The Demand for Restriction

The league would call attention to the fact that those pecuniarily interested in securing low-class immigration are in the nature of the case more inclined to make their wishes known and more insistent in doing so than the general public which does not wish such immigration. It would call attention, however, to the restrictive resolutions printed in the House committee hearings on immigration last winter (1909), representing the wishes of millions of our best and most intelligent citizens. It would also call special attention to the letters from representative men appended to the affidavit of the secretary of its executive committee presented herewith, showing an overwhelming sentiment in favor of more care in selecting our immigrants.

VIEWPOINT 6

"The generous policy of immigration . . . has been in large part the cause of the stupendous growth of the [American] Republic during the last century."

The U.S. Does Not Need to Restrict Immigration

The National Liberal Immigration League

The National Liberal Immigration League was one of several pro-immigration groups that sprang up to protest the anti-immigrant stance taken by many Americans. The following viewpoint, excerpted from a statement presented to the Immigration Commission on November 29, 1910 (*Reports of the Immigration Commission*, vol. 41. Washington, DC: Government Printing Office), includes responses to several of the proposed methods of reducing "undesirable" immigration.

Despite the NLIL's work and that of other groups, they were unable to stop the increasingly restrictive legislation passed during the first two decades of the twentieth century.

I. The Present Law

The National Liberal Immigration League upholds the generous policy of immigration that has been in large part the cause of the stupendous growth of the Republic during the last century. It believes that our present law on immigration is substantially accomplishing the desired result in procuring for us just those classes of citizens that are required for the further upbuilding of the nation. It approves the present law that prohibits the landing of criminals, dependents, habitual paupers, women of bad character, persons afflicted with contagious or loathsome diseases, and similar undesirable classes of immigrants.

On the other hand, the league advocates an amendment of the existing law to give the right of appeal to the courts to all those who feel that they are unjustly debarred from entrance to the United States. The sentence to deportation should, in such disputed cases, be the result of regular judicial procedure and not the decision of officials, who are more liable to error and prejudice.

The league also believes that the present law should be so modified as to permit the free landing of the minor children and the wives of naturalized American citizens, even if they fall within the categories of those who are debarred under existing law, provided, however, that they are not criminals or otherwise morally disqualified.

Furthermore, the league advocates an amendment of the present law making possible the deportation of aliens who are condemned here to a term of imprisonment amounting to a year or over and who are not subsequently pardoned by the proper constituted authorities.

II. Proposed Restrictions

The National Liberal Immigration League is opposed to all of the proposed measures for further restricting immigration, as these are not of nature to keep out objectionable persons, but are adapted simply to cut down indiscriminately the number of immigrants.

Educational Test. Prominent among the restrictive features proposed for a new law is the so-called "Educational test." To such a test in all its forms the National Liberal Immigration League is resolutely opposed. . . .

The league believes that the illiterates who remain among us are not a menace. They are never counterfeiters. They are guiltless of "black hand" letters. In short, there are found among them none of the most dangerous forms of foreign criminals. No educational test yet proposed would give any indication that would be serviceable in judging the character of an applicant for admission. Nor would simple ability to read and write afford any test whatever either of morals or of brains. A concrete instance gives a practical proof. There are more than four times as many illiterates in the general population of the United States as were found among those arrested in Greater New York between January 1 and March 31, 1905; 44,014 persons were arrested; of these only 1,175, or a little over 2.6 per cent, were unable to read or write. The percentage of illiteracy for the entire United States is 10.6 per cent and for that of the native whites alone 4.6 per cent.

And there is a much more important side to the question. The very success of American schools goes far in explaining the mystery of our exorbitant demand for unskilled labor. In proportion as they fulfill their mission they are depriving us of the rough laborer. By our high standards of education we are not fitting our children, nor the children of our foreigners, to do the lower forms of manual labor. We are fitting them all, as far as we possibly can, for different forms of directive work. The boy who is forbidden by the usual state law to leave school until he is 14 years old and has reached the fifth grammar grade, later in life does not join a gang that digs sewers and subways. Such laborers are recruited from the illiterate—those who have failed in the beginning of the struggle in which brains count. For our future supply of the lower grades of labor we must depend more and more upon countries with a poorer school system than ours. . . .

Immigrants Bear Precious Gifts

The Gospel of Fellowship *by Bishop Charles D. Williams, published in 1923, staunchly defended immigrants and urged Americans to recognize the positive qualities the beleaguered foreigners brought to their new country.*

Is it not high time that we, conceited, self-contained, arrogant Americans, should recognize that these strangers that flock to our gates come, many of them, bearing precious gifts, gifts often that we sadly lack and deeply need? I speak not now of the physical contributions of their labor to our industrial production and material wealth, tho where would America be to-day, economically, if it were not for the enormous contributions of so-called foreign labor? But I speak of intellectual, literary, artistic contributions, moral and spiritual values. Often the humblest and commonest of them have gifts in them, gifts in which America is characteristically poverty-stricken. Such recognition would do much to strengthen the foreigner's personal, family and racial self-respect, and upon that foundation rests in large degree the stability of life, homes and personal character.

Inspection at Ports of Embarkation. The proposition that aliens emigrating to the United States should be inspected at the ports of embarkation by surgeons of the United States Public Health and Marine-Hospital Service would place excessive power in the hands of an individual official, from whose decision persons disqualified by him could not appeal.

Increased Head Tax. The league believes that the only purpose of a tax on immigrants should be to create a source of revenue sufficient to defray the expense of the Immigration Service. The present tax of $4 accomplishes this more than adequately, and it should rather be decreased than increased. It would be in conformity with the American spirit to relieve steerage passengers from paying any head tax whatever.

Certificate of Character. The proposition to demand from every immigrant a certificate of good moral character from the home authorities would only result in a new source of extortionate profit for petty foreign officials. Criminals could more easily obtain certificates than simple, honest laborers. Some nations, too, could take advantage of this measure by according certificates to shiftless intending emigrants of whom they wanted to get rid, while withholding certificates from able-bodied and desirable persons.

Physical Test. The league believes that section 2 of the present immigration law enumerates enough classes of persons physically unqualified to be admitted to this country. Immigrants arriving after all the hardships of a journey and the vexations of a steerage passage are likely to suffer under a law providing for the exclusion of aliens of "poor physique"—a very elastic provision, and therefore obviously unreasonable.

Exclusion of Aliens Not Possessing a Stated Amount of Money. Aside from the fact that this provision is utterly opposed to all American traditions, it would shut out many of the most desirable persons. This country needs one workman more than it needs $20 or $100.

III. Constructive Policies Advocated

We are beginning to see that the great body of our immigrants are not only not the scum of Europe, its paupers and criminals, but the very flower of her peasantry, above our average in strength of body; ignorant perhaps, but enterprising, industrious—admirable raw material for our citizenship. Further, it is certain that as far as morals are concerned, these immigrants are fully the equal of any body of American citizens, similarly grouped as to economic conditions. But it is a matter of the highest national importance that our immigrants should become Americans in the shortest possible time. We need a national policy—systematic, simple, practical—of instructing and Americanizing the immigrant. At once after landing we should start to help him to make those social and industrial adjustments that he must make if he is to become an American.

And largely the problem of immigration is a problem of distribution. This motto appears prominently on all the literature of the National Liberal Immigration League: "A stream that is dangerous when unchecked will prove a blessing to the land when well directed."

The most important work of the next decade will be the relief of the congestion in our large cities by aiding the unemployed to go to small towns and to the farming districts—the more distant parts of the country where their services will be more useful to the nation. No excess of population crowds the country. The untilled land forms seven-eighths of the area of the Republic. In the more systematic building-up of American farms the new comer must help more than he has yet done. There, with his almost universal passion for owning land, he will buy farms and speedily come to feel that he is one of us. And on the land and in contented villages his Americanism will be fostered and his welfare assured.

No National or Racial Prejudice

Max J. Kohler, a frequent writer on immigration and the plight of immigrants, in 1913 responded to a congressional proposal for restricting immigration on the basis of national origin. In the Survey, *a monthly journal devoted to consideration of social problems, Kohler called on Americans to remember their liberal heritage when they considered such plans.*

What would be the use of drawing such race and national lines and demarcations in a country which began its career with the Declaration of Independence? Who can safely venture to draw an indictment against whole nations, and declare one race desirable and another undesirable, and exclude a person of one race, while simultaneously welcoming one possibly much less desirable of another race? And where will such fanning of race prejudice and race discrimination end in a land which has heretofore boasted that it frowned upon such a policy? As ex-President Roosevelt well said in his Presidential Message of 1906: "Whether they are Catholic or Protestant, Jew or Gentile, whether they come from England or Germany, Russia, Japan or Italy matters nothing. All we have a right to question is the man's conduct."

A system of free transportation wisely built up through careful experiment is one of the most promising solutions of this problem. The certain advantages to the country far overweigh any difficulties that will be met with in struggling with abuses that are perhaps inevitable on its first adoption. More stringent provisions in the contract labor law could prevent its misuse for supplying strike breakers.

To such a system the progressive republics of South America owe their present advance. Immigration properly directed is rescuing Brazil, Chile, above all the Argentine, from the sloth of those largely tropical and subtropical peoples. In the Argentine Republic the government furnishes the immigrant with liberal and painstaking advice, with one week's hospitality and with free railroad transportation to any part of the country. In the United States it might be sufficient that the railways should carry prospective settlers and laboring men going to work at a long distance at the actual cost of transportation. And this should be greatly to the advantage of the railroads, for they would very soon be carrying back the products of labor, and thus receive rich returns for the first concession of low fare. . . .

We have long insisted that our naturalization laws should be made stricter than they were. We have maintained that citizenship should be made a greater prize and reward. It should not be granted except to those furnishing sufficient proof of good character, as well as knowledge of the language and of American institutions and history beyond that required by present law and practice.

We believe that the law should be strictly enforced to bar criminals from admission to our shores. The regulations should provide for the appointment of additional inspectors at the ports of landing and other points of admission. For the efficiency of the service, these should be of the same nationality as of the immigrants they inspect. By arrangement with the proper authorities of other governments duplicate sets of the records of criminals believed to have emigrated, as well as of their Bertillon and other measurements, should be available for the use of these inspectors. And in this connection it is clearly advisable to establish closer cooperation between the police departments of our large cities and the Commissioner-General and commissioners of immigration, to the end that criminal aliens may more readily be detected and debarred or deported after landing. Such a campaign can not but impress criminals in other countries who are contemplating emigrating to the United States and prevent them from doing so.

IV. Conclusion

The problem is national, and in every way possible the Congress should help in its solution. To this education and cheaper transportation will do most. If the immigrant has offered to him the means of entrance to American life, he will find it easy to become an American and to reach our social and civic standards. Give him the chance to become as efficient a material unit as the native born, and trust the close contact with our general national life to inspire him in the end with the vital principles of our Americanism.

We have at last come to see that immigration is regulated by the economic needs of the nation and follows the workings of regular laws. From the very beginnings of the Republic the proportion of foreign born to native has remained remarkably constant. It has never exceeded one-fifth. And the crisis of 1907 proved conclusively to the whole country that in this new age of transportation the mobility of labor is so great that no matter what may be our temporary need of labor we shall never have a serious problem from the immigrant workman adding in any dangerous measure to the ranks of the unemployed, even in time of panic. That recent crisis came without warning, almost overnight, yet quietly and doing no damage either to our social or economic fabric a half million foreigners promptly returned to their homes abroad.

The National Liberal Immigration League profoundly believes that the United States needs every strong, healthy, moral man and woman who has ambition enough for better living and personal progress to make the long journey from Europe to America. It gives us no concern that our immigrants come to us now, as always, with the idea of bettering their personal fortunes and not for the altruistic purpose of serving the country's good. We need their numbers that our Nation may grow to the first place as a world power as rapidly as possible. We are passing from the age of physical force, but physical force alone will prevent a return to the primitive barbarities of militarism. And for many a day numbers will count. We need their numbers, that by their very swarming define our need for rough workers, which grows with our growth as a nation. We are engaged in tremendous constructive works in building up this Republic to a point of greatness undreamed of in the world's history. There are our railways to be completed, our huge planned municipal improvements—subways and towers and docks—the building of new and better houses, new roads, and this new movement to the farms that is to be the great distinguishing thing of our future. There is the unending demand for armies of men to do the simpler and more disagreeable forms of manual labor—street sweepers and hod carriers, shovelers, and ash men. For all these things we need the strong arms of many workers.

VIEWPOINT 7

"Public opinion in America has upheld a policy of increasing [immigration] restriction."

Quota Acts Carry Out the Will of the American People

Roy L. Garis

By 1924, some Americans felt that the 1921 quota law was not as effective as they wished in restricting the "new" immigrants, those from southern and eastern Europe. Pressure was exerted on Congress to remake the law, tightening restrictions even further. Congress adopted a quota system similar to the one in the 1921 bill, but with different bases for the quotas. Where in 1921 the bases had been 3 percent of the total population of a given nationality in 1910, the 1924 law made them 2 percent of the population in 1890. Since the huge influx of "new" immigrants began in the 1890s, the new figures made the quotas for these "undesirable" groups extremely small while assuring that members of "desirable" groups would be able to immigrate almost unrestricted.

The *North American Review* is a prominent journal of politics and letters, begun in the nineteenth century and still publishing today. In 1924, Roy L. Garis wrote an article for the journal, in which he staunchly defended the 1924 act.

The important provisions of the Immigration Act of 1924, signed by President Coolidge on May 26, are: (1) it preserves the basic immigration law of 1917; (2) it retains the principle of numerical limitation as inaugurated in the act of May 19, 1921; (3) it changes the quota basis from the census of 1910 to the census of 1890; (4) it reduces the quota admissible in any one year from 3 to 2 per cent.; (5) it provides a method of selection of immigrants at the source rather than to permit them to come to this country and land at the immigration stations without previous inspection; (6) it reduces the classes of exempted aliens; (7) it places the burden of proof on the alien to show that he is admissible under the immigration laws rather than upon the United States to show that he is not admissible; and (8) it provides entire and absolute exclusion of those who are not eligible to become naturalized citizens under our naturalization laws.

While it was evident from the beginning that no law would please all, yet it is safe to say that at least eighty per cent. of the American people approve of the new provisions in the Act of 1924. The sources of opposition were and still are:

(1) Those who believe that the law is not sufficiently restrictive. For the most part this opposition was not a stumbling block.

(2) Those who believe that the law does not admit enough common laborers to do the rough work of the United States.

(3) Those who, while pretending to favor restriction, really want anybody and everybody except the insane, the criminal and the diseased, so that they may proceed to reap dividends from their particular lines of endeavor, whether the lines be mills, factories, steamships, newspapers of various languages, or the like, in addition to bondsmen, some lawyers, common crooks, and others who daily exploit the newly arrived alien.

(4) Those of an international mind, who think that migrations should not be impeded, except possibly from China, Korea, Japan and India.

(5) Those who for religious, racial, or family reasons desire more of their own to be residents of the United States.

(6) Those who have been led to believe that the United States can go throughout the world handpicking bricklayers here, plasterers there, gardeners elsewhere and farmers at another place, and bring them, without thought of families, to our States; in other words, selection, distribution and supervision. . . .

Selfish Altruism

A great deal of cant and hypocrisy is being preached at the present day as to the motives that lie back of the attitude of the American Government and the American people toward immigration of the past. "A political asylum," "a haven of refuge," "a welcome to the oppressed," "a home for the persecuted"—these and like phrases are all fine, high-sounding expressions, and we believe in them as did our forefathers. But the fact is, they express a secondary and not the primary cause underlying the action of our people and Government toward the alien.

This primary basis has always been what might be called selfish altruism. We have welcomed the immigrant, not because he was an alien, not because he was escaping religious or political persecution, not because he was down-trodden and oppressed, but primarily and essentially because we believed his coming here was for our own good as a people and as a nation. We have welcomed him only so long as, and no longer than, we believed this. When we had been made to realize that his arrival was dangerous and fraught with injury to us, we objected to his coming and took steps to prevent it—even from colonial times. And once having taken a step forward—once having put up a bar—we have never let it down again or taken a step backward. . . .

American People Oppose Immigration

It [is] evident that from colonial times the American people have opposed the coming of immigrants into this country when they had to associate with them and enter into competition with them; that so long as there was plenty of land—a frontier—and the immigrants were willing to go to it, the problem was not acute; that the young Republic was forced in self-defense to pass drastic laws against the aliens; that with the passing of the years in the last century the opposition to immigrants became more and more crystallized and found expression in one restrictive measure after another until prior to the Act of 1924 less than 400,000 immigrants could enter the United States in any fiscal year under the 3 per cent. law; and lastly but most important of all, that once having passed a restrictive measure, the American people have never repealed it, but have expressed themselves time and time again to be in favor of more severe measures of restriction.

If America can be said to have had a traditional immigration policy, it has certainly not been one upholding free and unrestrictive immigration. On the other hand public opinion in America has upheld a policy of increasing restriction and this, if anything, has been her traditional policy. The American people want restriction, strict, severe restriction. The bars must be put up higher and more scientifically. Practical results are demanded. Does the Act of 1924 take steps in this direction? Does it grant what the public wants in concrete terms?

In the first place and without question, the American people wanted the Act of 1917 excluding certain classes to be continued and strengthened—the most important of these classes being idiots, imbeciles, feeble-minded persons, epileptics, insane persons, paupers, beggars, vagrants, persons afflicted with disease, criminals, polygamists, anarchists, persons likely to become a public charge, illiterates, etc. Such persons as these must be excluded even though they might be eligible for admittance under every other provision of the law. The Act of 1924 continues and strengthens the exclusion of such classes.

Public Opinion and the "New" Immigrants

In the second place and beyond doubt, public opinion is opposed to the so-called "new" immigration and desired its restriction to the lowest possible minimum.

At the present time European immigration to the United States may be divided into two groups, the "old" and the "new." The "old" immigration extended from the beginning of our national

---

Selfish Interests of Anti-Restrictionists

The Cincinnati Times-Star, *a conservative newspaper, editorialized in 1922 that those who are against immigrant restriction are motivated by self-interest.*

It is important that the average American keep the line-up on the immigration question in mind. Those who favor restrictive laws do so for patriotic reasons. The first interest is in preserving their country as a decent place for themselves and their children to live in.

Who are the anti-restrictionists? First, there are certain racial groups, centered chiefly in New York, who insist on looking at the immigration question from the European rather than the American point of view. These groups have money and a kind of fanaticism. They bully politicians when they are able to do so. Maintaining a constant propaganda, they keep many newspapers filled with arguments and "sob stories" aimed to discredit and break down the immigration law.

Next comes the steamship companies, which always maintain a lobby in Washington and which always have a financial interest in the entrance of the largest possible number of immigrants into the United States. And finally there are some employers of labor—people of a selfish and bone-headed type—who want cheap labor and quick profits and don't care how much the country pays for them.

The present immigration law is the first we have ever had that has accomplished important results. It has put a limit on immigration. Perhaps that limit is not as intelligently applied as it should be; perhaps the restrictive principle is not carried far enough. But the law has kept out a considerable proportion of immigrants of the less desirable types, while granting admission to practically all of those who want to come from northern and western Europe.

---

history to about the year 1890 and was derived chiefly from Great Britain and Ireland, Germany, and the Scandinavian countries. Thus practically all the immigrants to 1890 were predominantly Anglo-Saxon-Germanic in blood and Protestant in religion—of the same stock as that which originally settled the United States, wrote our Constitution and established our democratic institutions. The English, Dutch, Swedes, Germans, and even the Scotch-Irish, who constituted practically the entire immigration, were less than two thousand years ago one Germanic race in the forests surrounding the North Sea. Thus being similar in blood and in political ideals, social training, and economic background, this "old" immigration merged with the native stock fairly easily and rapidly. Assimilation was only a matter of time and this was aided by the economic, social and political conditions of the country. Even though those who were already here objected to others coming in, yet once in they soon became Americans, so assimilated as to be indistinguishable from the natives. Furthermore, in comparison with the present-day immigration it was relatively small in volume, while the abundance of free land and our need for pioneers prevented the rise of any serious problem.

In the period centering about the year 1880, and in particular in the decade 1880-1890, there was a distinct shift in the immigration movement. Whereas before 1890 most of our immigrants had been Anglo-Saxons and Teutons from Northern Europe, after 1890 the majority were members of the Mediterranean and Slavic races from Southern and Southeastern Europe. The great bulk of this "new" immigration has its source in Russia, Poland, Austria, Hungary, Greece, Turkey, Italy and the Balkan countries. It is in connection with this "new" immigration that the present immigration problem exists. Its solution challenges our attention.

Separating the Desirable from the Undesirable

As Professor Commons says: "A line drawn across the continent of Europe from northeast to southwest, separating the Scandinavian Peninsula, the British Isles, Germany, and France from Russia, Austria-Hungary, Italy, and Turkey, separates countries not only of distinct races but also of distinct civilizations. It separates Protestant Europe from Catholic Europe; it separates countries of representative institutions and popular government from monarchies; it separates lands where education is universal from lands where illiteracy predominates; it separates manufacturing countries, progressive agriculture, and skilled labor from primitive hand industries, backward agriculture, and unskilled labor; it separates an educated, thrifty peasantry from a peasantry scarcely a single generation removed from serfdom; it separates Teutonic races from Latin, Slav, Semitic, and Mongolian races. When the sources of American immigration are shifted from the Western countries so nearly allied to our own, to Eastern countries so remote in the main attributes of Western civilization, the change is one that should challenge the attention of every citizen."

The racial proportions of incoming aliens having thus undergone a remarkable change since 1890, the result has been "a swift and ominous lowering of the general average of character, intelligence, and moral stamina," with the result now that the situation is "full of menace and danger to our native racial stream and to our long-established institutions." The advocates of free and unrestricted immigration refute such a contention by pointing out that the same has been said time and time again for over a hundred years. They point to members of the old immigration and say that all that these needed was an opportunity. They go to great trouble to compare the present "new" immigration with the types which came to us prior to 1890, in order to establish their contention that the present "new" immigration is no worse than the former. However, I desire to point out in this connection a thought which I have not found expressed in the arguments answering the above contentions of the advocates of free immigration. It is simply this—that the comparison of the present "new" immigration with the lower types which came to us prior to 1890 is wasted energy. The vital thing for us today is not whether the present "new" immigration is equal to, superior to, or lower than the immigration of 35 years ago, but how does it compare with the "old" immigration of *today?* According to every test made in recent years and from a practical study of the problem, it is evident beyond doubt that the immigrant from Northern and Western Europe is far superior to the one from Southern and Eastern Europe.

In the Act of 1924 Congress adopted a suggestion of the writer that a simple and practical solution of the problems created by the "new" immigration—a solution based on scientific and historical facts—would be to adopt the census of 1890 instead of 1910 or 1920 as the basis for permanent legislation and future percentage laws. It is true that the 3 per cent. law based on the census of 1910 was primarily quantitative, but it was nevertheless qualitative to the extent that it kept from our shores millions of undesirables which this country could afford to do without. The 2 per cent. law based on the census of 1890 limits qualitatively to a much higher degree as well as numerically within safe boundaries. It closes the doors to all but a few thousand "new" immigrants each year. It will give us time to educate and assimilate those now here (a task of gigantic proportions, requiring many years). And yet such a plan does not exclude to a detrimental point those immigrants from Northern and Western Europe who

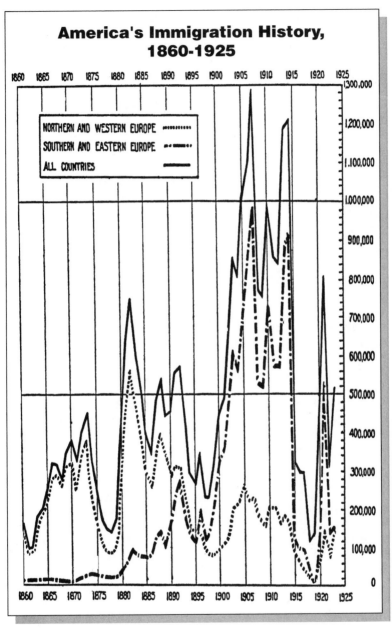

America's Immigration History, 1860-1925

In 1924, The Survey *printed this chart showing America's immigration history broken down by old (northern and western Europe) and new (southern and eastern Europe). The upper line represents total immigration. The lower lines show its two main components—from northern-western and southern-eastern Europe.*

might desire to come and who are easily assimilated. Such a provision is eminently fair and equitable, and yet it raised a storm of protest among the nationals whose quotas it reduced. But this is the invariable effect of any legislative proposals that are frankly framed for the benefit of America and Americans rather than for Europe and Europeans. And yet, as in the case of any bill, the character of the opposition may be the strongest kind of evidence of intrinsic merit.

There are many industries in this country which are dependent upon foreign labor if wage scales and working hours of past years are to prevail. Native American labor will not work twelve-hour shifts when eight-hour jobs can be had. Americans will not be satisfied with the living conditions or the fare that the foreign-born laborer is satisfied with.

The solution of the labor shortage in these industries is either a revised schedule of employment or a free entry of labor from foreign countries. Yet to open the gates again to the common labor of foreign lands would be to surrender much of what we have gained. It would but add to our domestic problems, since the great majority of this class are unfitted for citizenship.

Some industries have not kept pace with other American industries either in working hours or wages. A labor shortage in such industries will probably be a direct result of this condition. The thinking man comes to regard such industries as a place to seek employment only when all other places fail, and to be left as soon as a job can be obtained elsewhere. A revision of standards in some of our industries is what is needed right now. Happily some have seen the handwriting on the wall and are taking such a step. American industries can get all the labor they need if they will give labor a square deal and cease treating it as a commodity.

Cater to Employers No More

Indeed, the time is opportune for Americans to insist on an American policy, regardless of what our employers of cheap labor and our foreign born want. We have catered to them too long already and in consequence have been throwing away our birthright. The vital thing is to preserve the American race, as far as it can be preserved, and build it up with Nordic stock; intelligent, literate, easily assimilated, appreciating and able to carry on our American institutions. The percentage law based on the census of 1890 will in time automatically bring about such a result.

In a recent letter to me, the Hon. Roger W. Babson stated: "Of course I am in favor of an extension of our Immigration Service to the points of embarkation on the other side." Perhaps no other provision in the Act of 1924 has met with such general approval as the one which provides for a form of examination over seas.

For several years it seemed impossible to work out a practical method and one satisfactory to the nations in whose ports such inspection takes place. Under the new law both non-quota and quota immigrants are required to file their written application under oath in duplicate before the United States consul in their country for an immigration certificate. These applications go fully into their past records, their family history, and into their mental, moral and physical qualifications. This process now enables us to weed out in advance those not qualified for entrance into the United States. A satisfactory examination there procures an immigrant certificate for admission here, provided that the quota has not been exhausted. However, the certificate does not exempt the immigrant from a final inspection and medical examination at the port of entry. The immigrant is subject to deportation if he or she fails to measure up to the Act of 1917.

The law provides that not more than 10 per cent. of the total number of certificates allotted to each country may be issued in any one month, and a certificate is void four months after the date of issuance. The counting of these certificates is made abroad. A no more constructive provision could be imagined than this, for it eliminates the racing of steamships into the ports of entry on the first day of each month, it eliminates the necessity of immigrants being forced to return to Europe due to exhausted quotas, and at the same time it gives our consuls the power to prevent obviously undesirable aliens from coming to America.

The provision in the law abrogating the gentlemen's agreement with Japan, and excluding all Japanese laborers from the United States because of their ineligibility for citizenship, has been the subject of world discussion. Under this gentlemen's agreement Japan, not the United States, determined what and how many Japanese laborers could come to America. It was inevitable that this arrangement should be ended and Congress was within its rights in ending it, although it might have accomplished it in a more diplomatic manner.

It has been my purpose to explain briefly those provisions of the new law which have been subject to the most discussion in order to make clear that each provision is but a logical step forward in our traditional policy of increasing restriction of immigration in a more humane, scientific and constructive manner. The Secretary of Labor, Mr. Davis, said in a recent address, "There should be some immigration of the right kind, but we, not Europe, will say who shall come or we will not let any come." Certainly in the Act of 1924 we have taken important steps forward in the right direction toward permanent legislation worthy of the name.

VIEWPOINT 8

"If [the new immigration quota act] becomes law, . . . it is bound to increase the exploitation of immigrants."

Quota Acts Are Inhumane

Edith Terry Bremer (1889-1964)

Edith Terry Bremer was a prominent social service administrator long involved in work with immigrants, particularly immigrant women. She was a special agent for the U.S. Immigration Commission in 1909-1910, and she served on the national board of the YMCA, an organization active in work with immigrants and their Americanization. The following viewpoint, taken from the *Survey* for May 15, 1924, was one of many published in the journal speaking out against the implementation of the proposed 1924 immigration quota bill.

On the same day we read that the Immigration Bill is likely to reach successful adjustment, "if a way can be found to exclude Japanese while maintaining the ordinarily courteous conduct which ought to characterize all the actions of the United States government," we also read that a proposal to establish a graduate school of international relations at Johns Hopkins University is near attainment. The school would "promote" "greater understanding and knowledge of all the branches of international life of a world fellowship, where scientific and economic facts are bringing nations to many forms of interdependency."

American thought is coming to realize the inescapable economic interdependencies. And the day would seem to be drawing nearer when the nation will turn about and embrace the equally inescapable relations of the political realms. But if the Immigration Bill becomes law, we shall have a clear indication of how far we are from perceiving the international character of a great many of our serious human problems.

Immigration and emigration are inherently an international business. No set of immigration laws can be smoothly, justly, and humanely administered, which are not built upon an international philosophy in regard to this vast human phenomenon. The Immigration Bill has no discernible social philosophy. If it becomes law, in spite of its rigidly mechanical devices for execution and its laudable intent to prevent unnecessary distress to immigrants in certain instances, it is bound to increase the exploitation of immigrants, to create new strife among groups already domiciled here, to bring disaster to individuals, and to be as irritatingly difficult to administer exactly as our immigration laws have ever been.

Hope for Presidential Veto

To date of going to press, there is still hope that a courageous President will veto this bill, as on three separate occasions before, other courageous Presidents vetoed the literacy test bill on the ground that a proposal to reduce the number of immigrants to be admitted each year should not, in method, act as a public contradiction of cherished American principles. On every fundamental premise, quite apart from the unnecessary hurt to the sensibilities of the people of Japan, this new bill strikes at important social attitudes upon which our democratic thought and our social institutions have been built. If passed, it will stand before the world as the expression of responsible thought in America upon the controversial theories as to the relative worth of nationalities. It is claimed that the assumptions of the bill are justified by sociological and biological considerations. But upon these premises competent scientists vigorously disagree. The "Nordic superiority" myth which has been floating about the halls of Congress for a long time, for which many congressmen have felt a sneaking friendliness while reluctant to recognize it in public, has suddenly become the basis of the immigration policy of what is still the greatest "receiving country" in the world.

What has happened in Washington, what hitherto opposing views have mysteriously reached a compromise, it is not the purpose of this article to discuss. Nor is it intended to give any detailed analysis of the provisions of the bill. Its diplomatic, political and economic consequences have been widely discussed by the newspapers. The purpose of this article is to show how a law based on assumptions both unscientific and unsocial would also carry vital human consequences. The proposal to admit annually, from each nationality, a number equalling 2 per cent of the number resident in the United States in 1890 would halt the migration from many countries in a mid-way stage. With these, as with all other nationalities for a hundred years, immigration follows a slow process: first the breadwinners come, then the young women, then young families, and finally the older people.

All People Are Equal

The Forward, *a Jewish newspaper published in New York, was adamantly against the proposed changes for the 1924 immigration bill. Long subject to discrimination, Jews would be further handicapped if the changes, a quota system based on the 1890 population, went into effect. This excerpt is from a 1924 editorial.*

"Good" and "Bad" Peoples

The new project makes an attempt to divide the coming immigrants into two different classes: the desirable and the undesirable immigrants. Those who come from England, Norway, Sweden, Finland and Germany, are welcomed guests; those, however, who were born in the eastern and southern part of Europe, should better remain at home. We heard the echo of the spirit when 800 English immigrants were allowed to enter this country above the quota, some thousands of Russians and Jewish immigrants being, however, deported back to Europe at the same time. We must all combat the principle. There ought not to be good and bad nations, good and bad peoples. They must all be equal before the law.

The most serious effect of the bill will not be felt immediately, because it runs back of visible things into men's minds. The ultimate effect upon the structure of international comity, which is held together by what good-will and understanding there is between the "bread and butter" people of the nations, will be positive and deep. The change of feeling will be as vital in Europe as it could possibly be in the Orient, and will be translated into behavior in a greater variety of ways.

Thinly Veiled Discrimination

It is not from the desire of a country like the United States to reduce the volume of its annual human intake, that disillusionment and lasting bitterness will result. Every nation understands that, and more or less sympathizes with it. Representatives of the very countries which the bill now proposes to cut off have repeatedly expressed an understanding of America's rising alarm over the number of immigrants. The resentment—for which, probably, no adequate release will for a long period be found—rises from the thinly veiled discrimination, which fastens the stigma of social incompetence, of cultural inferiority, upon the object of the average individual's most cherished social loyalty: his nationality.

We of the "native American stock" (the white American stock, at least) have never suffered such an attack; most of us have not the sensitive perception to realize what that means. Discrimination—social, economic and political—has been one of the social diseases of Europe. The influence of its adoption into American policy can hardly help working new harm in Europe, and will spread swiftly throughout the several million Europeans domiciled here.

The International Labor Office estimates that the migration of people at the outbreak of the world war amounted to 5,250,000 a year. Two million at least could be said to be leaving home for the first time. The static character of great populations, holding them in traditional localities for centuries, is broken up. The development of great business whose continued profit depends upon getting people to move about, together with profound changes in the economic life of nations, with the spread of industrialism, the contagion of new social ideas, changes in the relative political positions of various nationalities—all have brought the will to venture, and the facilities for doing so, within reach of the humblest folk. In the face of such stupendous social forces, changes in immigration legislation in a single country will neither stop the movements nor for a long period materially hinder them. The recurring springs of emigration will flow in other directions.

Those for whom strong human ties have already been established in America will not, in the main, go elsewhere. It is within this group that the most acute problems of adjustment will arise. That group is relatively large for each of the countries whose emigration has been established since 1890, since it is still in the pioneer or "single immigrant" stage, and has not fully become a migration of families and dependents. The House bill, by providing a non-quota class which would eventually admit wives, minor children and elderly parents of citizens, does offer an ultimate amelioration of this problem, and the conferees wrote this provision into the final draft of the bill.

The fresh emigration of Europe—those groups who have not yet begun migration to the United States—will undoubtedly turn toward South and Central America. Lacking the romantic tradition about these countries which has so long enhanced the lure of America in his mind, the emigrant will probably proceed with greater caution. But if the causes which drive them out of their own homeland continue Italians, Greeks, Armenians, Syrians, Hungarians, Russians and also Germans, will go in increasing numbers to Brazil, the Argentine, Chile, Peru, Uruguay and Paraguay. Colonies of these nationalities are already there, for, in the main, the South American countries are inviting Europeans to come, though each has its own methods for regulation.

Other movements will probably be directed through additional "labor treaties" between European governments themselves, such as those between Italy and France, France and Poland, Czecho-Slovakia and Poland. These are not true "immigration" as the term has been understood in America, but have more of the character of a "contract labor" system, to which American thought is opposed as an anti-social arrangement bound to work against the common welfare of all concerned.

Immigrants' Tragic Plight

The human consequences of a sudden stoppage in any established movement are serious. It is likely to result in personal disaster to the individuals whose lives have been shaped by the expectation of the continuance of the movement. The tragic plight of the half-a-million people caught in mid-migration on August 1, 1914, is an example. They could not go forward, they could not go back, and they had no legal claim to domicile or protection where they were. Exactly that situation, it may be hoped, will never happen again. And yet in the mental confusion and anxiety attendant on being thrown out of normal relations, the stoppage proposed for July 1, 1924, will have comparable results in the lives of a very great number of people. The difficulties created for individuals, even so many, cannot be put forward as a valid argument against restrictive legislation. But there is something wrong in the method and speed by which it is proposed to achieve that restriction.

The absurdly small quotas practically cut away from beneath their feet the foundation for the entire future of thousands of recent immigrants. Their original purpose in coming to America will have been made futile when their right to send home for their relatives is cut off. What will they do?

Even if the non-quota section of the House bill prevails, so that citizens are ultimately provided for, the problem of ruined hopes, defeated expectations, and permanently separated families, will not be greatly helped. A man not now a citizen must wait from three to five years before bringing over his wife. And what assurance has he that the law will not be changed again before that date, once more making all his expectations futile? The single man will, in most cases, have to go back to marry the girl before he can claim the citizen's right to have her admitted. The enormous expense will often prove prohibitive. Too often a girl's best chance to get into America will rest upon marriage with an American citizen; there may be a growing number of "citizens" who make a business of offering themselves for marriage at a good sum to a young woman whose parents try to solve her future by getting her to America where work can be found.

Take a single example. There are about 40,000 Latvians in this country, the majority being young men, for the immigration is comparatively new. How many of them are married and have families in Latvia is not known. A conservative estimate would fix the number of young men as 25,000. Outside of a group of 6,000 in New York, there are no established Latvian communities. The 25,000 are scattered over many states where work can be found. The Latvian quota would be 317 persons a year. Among the 25,000 residents, are several thousand citizens. According to the provision for preferential consular visé, the wives of those citizens would be given first place in the quota even under the Senate plan. How long will it take the 25,000 young men to establish themselves and to form homes here at the rate of 317 women from the old country each year?

Will these men, then, return home? They tell you they would if there was work to be had. Theirs is a new and ambitious country, but there is not enough work for all. Their problem, therefore, resolves itself into this: they cannot get work where their homes could be, and they cannot have homes where their work is. A few may move on to South America. But the world currents have swept this way for a long time, and it is not likely that the young men who have once tried the United States will go elsewhere.

A Choice of Evils

There are three possible solutions for these men: to swell the army of permanently disestablished men; to take out citizenship papers as soon as possible, and become a floating citizenry with ties in two countries, keeping a working residence in the United States while supporting dependents in Latvia and departing on certificated leaves once or twice a year; or to let family ties slip, fall out of the habit of sending money home, save here for a new start, and marry a new wife when and where she can be found. As the line of least resistance, the third choice will probably be the way out for the majority.

A mass of inter-country social problems will develop. In Latvia, there will be deserted families, and non-support, serious enough in a country where the major cause of emigration is economic; a more acute poverty and the psychological ills that attend desertion will follow. In America, there will be the moral collapse of men who meant to be honest and loyal, together with a prevalence of that inner conflict that pursues a mind not at peace with itself, and creates a haunting sense of the insecurity for the future.

A practical difficulty, however, presents itself even here. Where will the young men find these hypothetical "new" wives? All the nationalities of recent immigration are represented here by far more men than women. Successive years of the migration process, following its usual course, would even this up. But those nationalities for whom that natural process is cut short by the new bill have not brought their young women here yet. The Latvian will probably marry German girls, as many speak the German language and the two peoples have a friendly tradition. But what can the Roumanian, the Greek, the Armenian youth do? Will they be able to marry girls of the "second generation?" The girl born and reared in America holds very different ideas from those of the old-country man. And more than that, her social views, bred by "Americanization," lead her to regard such an alliance as a step down. She would rather marry a "smart American fellah" than an old-country man though he may be the more honest and stable.

The Survey, March 15, 1924. Drawn by Hendrik Willem Van Loon

You can't come in. The quota for 1620 is full.

In the great industrial towns where the work is all man's work, such as in the steel cities; where the foreign unskilled worker comes—and moves on as fast as he can; where the immigrant population is fluid, and where the "industry" of the women in the permanently established communities is "keeping boarders," the moral conditions likely to develop will be exceedingly serious. One hesitates to brand any nationality, made up as each is of every variety of character, as more likely to fall into immoral ways than another. But it seems almost certain that those groups most affected by the limitation of immigration, will be forced into situations more unwholesome than those which naturally develop in frontier communities. And, it might be added, this very result of conditions created by American law will ultimately be laid up against the foreigner and his race.

Another social problem arbitrarily created is that of the growing community. The settled foreign community, resulting from an immigration which has long since left its early stages behind, will probably not be disturbed. But those aggregations which are about to take on the characteristics of a community will have their development checked, if not permanently prevented. The Latvians, in another five years, would probably have come together in a number of little nascent communities with a stable group life and interest—thrifty and anxious to get on to that universally desired goal of owning property. How can that happen now?

Restless Singles

Industries know well the restlessness of the "single" immigrant. A high labor turnover decreases as a community grows. Cities which have seen foreigners coming in, at the call of some new factory, view with alarm the crowds of foreign men who don't know what to do with themselves on Sunday. A few months pass and the population mysteriously increases. Women of the new nationality are now and then noticed in the stores. Before Americans realize what has happened a new community has begun, self-respecting, hard-working, buying generous quantities of American furniture, glassware, pots and pans and shoes. There is an agreeable stimulus to local trade. Such processes can no longer come to pass, and American communities will not only be denied real assets of growth and trade, but will face a new problem of continuously unsettled, unsocialized "colonies" of foreign men.

We must not overlook increases in the exploitation to which immigrants are always more or less subject. The bill aims to render the new law more enforceable than the old quota law, by making it rigid. But even a mechanically perfect system cannot nullify the forces that drive people out of their homelands. Efforts at illegal entry will inevitably multiply. Buying up passports (which is known to be going on as a regular business now) to be sold abroad to credulous and anxious immigrants, will be extended to include buying up certificates for temporary absence. The chances are that every sort of paper which an immigrant may need will be offered for sale.

A severe penalty is provided in the bill both for the perpetration of fraud, and for the alien found with fraudulent papers in his possession. Just how the immigrant is to be brought under a sentence of possibly ten thousand dollars or five years in prison before he actually becomes a resident of the United States is not clear. Would he be arrested at the consulate—or imprisoned at Ellis Island instead of being deported?

Perhaps the severest result to America itself will come from the reversal of normal assimilation processes. Assimilation is at bottom a purely psychological thing. Change the attitude of the alien, his desire to become assimilated, and these processes—so long familiar to us that we have failed to value them at their great worth—stop automatically. Among those of French Canadian descent in northern New England, and in the Spanish-speaking stock of Texas, we have a permanently unassimilated, bi-lingual society. Let the feeling of our European stock undergo a severe change, and we may have such groups everywhere.

Freedom leads groups as well as individuals to throw off self-consciousness. Heretofore foreign-language groups have slowly emerged from their intense consciousness of self into the realization that nationality does not matter in America. It neither helps nor hinders. That becomes, in fact, one of the miraculous things to them about America. In so many countries of Europe, no one goes about without carefully wearing his nationality. This immigration bill would throw the wholesome social evolution in America into violent reverse. The United States is made to declare for discrimination. Sensitiveness, rivalry, suspicion are bred by it. And that international good-will which experience in America has, in spite of individual discouragements, stored up for the immigrant—and which he has in turn spread abroad—is also jeopardized.

Understanding and Good Will Are Needed

One wonders whether after all it is worth while to "save the country for posterity"—at the price of making it, for this generation, a much more difficult place to live in. The need of the past, and the hope of the future, is understanding and good-will between the people of the nations. It is the only foundation on which can be built a structure of cooperation for the good of all. This anti-social immigration philosophy will weaken that foundation for a long time to come. This nation may be "saved for posterity," but the rest of the world will go right on having a "posterity" too. It may be that our children will view matters in a different light. Perhaps posterity will not thank us after all.

CHAPTER 5

Immigration in Perspective

Chapter Preface

In the century between 1820 and 1920, some thirty-five million immigrants came to the United States. Most remained and made it their home. While the countries of origin and the characters of the immigrants may have changed over the years, many people would argue that the immigrant experience remained largely the same. The immigrants were changed by America, and they in turn changed America.

In his 1951 book *The Uprooted*, historian Oscar Handlin writes that the impact of the immigrant's experience began with the passage to America:

> The crossing immediately subjected the emigrant to a succession of shattering shocks and decisively conditioned the life of every man [and woman and child] that survived it. This was the initial contact with life as it was to be. For many peasants it was the first time away from home, away from the safety of the circumscribed little villages in which they had passed all their years. Now they would learn to have dealings with people essentially different from themselves. Now they would collide with unaccustomed problems, learn to understand alien ways and alien languages, manage to survive in a grossly foreign environment.

What the consequences were of that shocking passage to a new land is one of the many issues scholars debate when they discuss immigration.

Oscar Handlin is one of the first historians to seriously consider this issue. It is his belief that the cultural shock of immigration was so great that many immigrants never recovered from it. It was for later generations, he says, to reap the benefits of that anguished experience. Handlin believes the immigrants never became fully accepted in American society. In fact, he asserts, the immigrants found themselves alienated from both past and present, alone in a new land, surrounded by strange people, customs, and language. Although they might try to find stability by clinging to the safety of ethnic enclaves, this only alienated them further.

For many years, Handlin's view was the prevailing one. When the 1970s brought an ethnic awakening, however, views of the immigrant experience began to change. No longer did it seem necessary for immigrants to become fully "Americanized" in order to be valid members of American society. The civil rights movement of the 1960s had promoted the idea that "black is beautiful." In the 1970s, other ethnic groups followed suit in asserting pride in their own ethnic traditions. Michael Novak, whose book *The Rise of the Unmeltable Ethnics* is excerpted in the first chapter of this volume, was one of many people who spoke out on the value of maintaining pride in one's ancestral traditions even while maintaining pride in being an American.

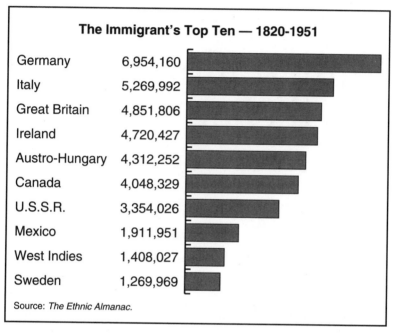

The Immigrant's Top Ten — 1820-1951

Germany	6,954,160
Italy	5,269,992
Great Britain	4,851,806
Ireland	4,720,427
Austro-Hungary	4,312,252
Canada	4,048,329
U.S.S.R.	3,354,026
Mexico	1,911,951
West Indies	1,408,027
Sweden	1,269,969

Source: *The Ethnic Almanac.*

It was perhaps this ethnic movement that first opened scholars' minds to reinterpreting the immigrant experience. John Bodnar is one historian who views the immigrants' efforts to remain in touch with their compatriots as a positive factor in their adjustment to American life. Rather than perpetuating their isolation, he argues, ethnic enclaves and networks eased immigrants' entrance into life in a new land.

Few today would deny that the immigrant experience is a traumatic one. Leaving behind all that is familiar, even for those immigrants fleeing political persecution or economic devastation, cannot be otherwise. But the long-range impact of this trauma continues to be debated.

VIEWPOINT 1

"The history of immigration is a history of alienation and its consequences."

Immigration Was an Alienating Experience

Oscar Handlin (1915-)

Oscar Handlin is one of the most influential American historians, known particularly for his contributions to the study of American immigration and ethnic groups. A professor at Harvard University, he has written more than two dozen books and edited more than a dozen anthologies, many of which have come to be considered classics in his field, including *The Uprooted*, from which the following viewpoint is excerpted. Among his other titles are *The Harvard Guide to American History*, *Race and Ethnicity in American Life*, and *Immigration as a Factor in American History*.

The Uprooted, an evocative examination of the immigrant encounter with and attempts to adjust to the new land, was first published in 1951. Handlin's thesis is that in emigrating from their native lands, people become alienated from both their past and their present. They have cut themselves off from the culture that shaped them, and they do not fit into the culture they have entered. The shock of the dramatic change and of the wealth of choices they must make in shaping their future in the new land, Handlin says, has a deep and lasting impact upon the immigrants themselves and, to a significant degree, upon their descendants as well. The following excerpt focuses on the differences in personal economic systems—jobs and daily living—that immigrants during America's great tide of immigration experienced when they came to America.

Immigration altered America. But it also altered the immigrants. And it is the effect upon the newcomers of their arduous transplantation that I have tried to study.

My theme is emigration as the central experience of a great many human beings. I shall touch upon broken homes, interruptions of a familiar life, separation from known surroundings, the becoming a foreigner and ceasing to belong. These are the aspects of alienation; and seen from the perspective of the individual received rather than of the receiving society, the history of immigration is a history of alienation and its consequences. . . .

In Peasant Europe

The immigrant movement started in the peasant heart of Europe. Ponderously balanced in a solid equilibrium for centuries, the old structure of an old society began to crumble at the opening of the modern era. One by one, rude shocks weakened the aged foundations until some climactic blow suddenly tumbled the whole into ruins. The mighty collapse left without homes millions of helpless, bewildered people. These were the army of emigrants.

The impact was so much the greater because there had earlier been an enormous stability in peasant society. A granite-like quality in the ancient ways of life had yielded only slowly to the forces of time. From the westernmost reaches of Europe, in Ireland, to Russia in the east, the peasant masses had maintained an imperturbable sameness; for fifteen centuries they were the backbone of a continent, unchanging while all about them radical changes again and again recast the civilization in which they lived.

Stability, the deep, cushiony ability to take blows, and yet to keep things as they were, came from the special place of these people on the land. The peasants were agriculturists; their livelihood sprang from the earth. Americans they met later would have called them "farmers," but that word had a different meaning in Europe. The bonds that held these men to their acres were not simply the personal ones of the husbandman who temporarily mixes his sweat with the soil. The ties were deeper, more intimate. For the peasant was part of a community and the community was held to the land as a whole.

Always, the start was the village. "I was born in such a village in such a parish"—so the peasant invariably began the account of himself. Thereby he indicated the importance of the village in his being; this was the fixed point by which he knew his position in the world and his relationship with all humanity.

The village was a place. It could be seen, it could be marked out in boundaries, pinned down on a map, described in all its physical attributes. Here was a road along which men and beasts would pass, reverence the saint's figure at the crossing. There was a church, larger or smaller, but larger than the other structures about it. The burial ground was not far away, and the smithy, the mill, perhaps an inn. There were so many houses of wood or thatch, and so built, scattered among the fields as in Ireland and Norway, or, as almost everywhere else, huddled together with their backs to the road. The fields were round about, located in terms of river, brook, rocks, or trees. All these could be perceived; the eye could grasp, the senses apprehend the feel, the sound, the smell, of them. These objects, real, authentic, true, could come back in memories, be summoned up to rouse the curiosity and stir the wonder of children born in distant lands.

Yet the village was still more. The aggregate of huts housed a community. Later, much later, and very far away, the Old Countrymen also had this in mind when they thought of the village. They spoke of relationships, of ties, of family, of kinship, of many rights and obligations. And these duties, privileges, connections, links, had each their special flavor, somehow a unique value, a meaning in terms of the life of the whole.

They would say then, if they considered it in looking backward, that the village was so much of their lives because the village *was* a whole. There were no loose, disorderly ends; everything was knotted into a firm relationship with every other thing. And all things had meaning in terms of their relatedness to the whole community. . . .

Importance of Family

The family was then the operating economic unit. In a sense that was always recognized and respected, the land on which it worked was its own. The head of the household, it was true, held and controlled it; legally, no doubt, he had certain powers to waste or dispose of it. But he was subject to an overwhelming moral compulsion to keep it intact, in trust for those who lived from it and for their descendants who would take a place upon it. . . .

The seeds of ultimate change were not native to this stable society. They were implanted from without. For centuries the size of the population, the amount of available land, the quantity of productive surplus, and the pressure of family stability, achieved together a steady balance that preserved the village way of life. Only slowly and in a few places were there signs of unsteadiness in the seventeenth century; then more distinctly and in more places in the eighteenth. After 1800, everywhere, the elements of the old equilibrium disintegrated. The old social structure tottered; gathering momentum from its own fall, it was unable to right itself, and under the impact of successive shocks collapsed. Then the peasants could no longer hang on; when even to stay meant to change, they had to leave. . . .

So Europe watched them go—in less than a century and a half, well over thirty-five million of them from every part of the continent. In this common flow were gathered up people of the most diverse qualities, people whose rulers had for centuries been enemies, people who had not even known of each other's existence. Now they would share each other's future. . . .

America as a Foreign Economy

All those who could not immediately move into the interior, purchase at once a farm, and settle down as agriculturists without delay, spent some period as residents of one of the great cities. Here they worked in preparation for the moment when they might leave. Working as they did in a new fashion and in a strange place, it took time to find a way around, to begin to learn the operations of the productive system of which they had become a part.

The difficulty was that a man could live years in an American city without coming to understand the mainsprings of its economy. . . .

What could the peasant do here? He could not trade or do much to help the traders. There was some room for petty shopkeepers; he lacked the training and the capital. Some handicraftsmen supplied clothes and furniture and a variety of other products to the townsfolk; he lacked the skill and tools. Back on the docks at which he had landed were a number of casual jobs with the stevedores. Here and there in the warehouses and stores were calls for the services of porters. But there was a limit to the amount of lifting and carrying to be done. Wandering about in the first days of their arrival, these immigrants learned that beyond these few opportunities there was, at first, no demand for their capacities. . . .

The reservoir of unskilled peasant labor that mounted steadily higher in the cities did not long remain untapped, however. In the 1840's and 1850's came a succession of new inventions that enterprising men of capital used to transform the productive system of the United States. The older industries had disdained the immigrants; but the new ones, high in the risks of innovation and heavy initial investments, drew eagerly on this fund of workers ready to be exploited at attractively low wages. The manufacture of clothing, of machines, and of furniture flourished in the great commercial cities precisely where they could utilize freely the efforts of the newcomers, hire as many as they needed when necessary, lay off any surplus at will. A completely fluid labor supply set the ideal conditions for expansion.

Thereafter, whatever branch of the economy entered upon a period of rapid expansion did so with the aid of the same immigrant labor supply. At midcentury the immigrants went to dig in the mines that pockmarked the great coal and iron fields of Pennsylvania, first experienced Welshmen and Cornishmen, later raw Irishmen and Germans, and still later Slavs—a vague term that popularly took in Bohemians, Slovaks, Hungarians, and also Italians. These people spread with the spread of the fields, southward into West Virginia and westward to Illinois, in a burst of development from which impressive consequences followed.

Coping with America

In this extract from his 1984 revision of his classic Send These to Me: Immigrants in a Strange Land, *noted historian John Higham refers to Abraham Cahan's archetypal novel of an immigrant's life,* The Rise of David Levinsky, *in his discussion of the difficulties of immigrant adjustment to America.*

While illuminating a profound conflict of values in American-Jewish life, Levinsky's story also reflects problems of adjustment that faced immigrants from many lands and backgrounds. They had to cope, in the hurly-burly of an American city, with an unaccustomed tempo of life. Stimulation mingled with confusion, opportunity with exploitation. Success in such a setting depended on assimilation, and this never came easily or automatically. To understand an unfamiliar, unpredictable environment, an immigrant had to distinguish between appearance and reality, between the civic rhetoric he heard in a schoolroom and the behavior he observed outside it. Since his native habits were often an encumbrance, adaptability might damage his inner integrity. Whether he was struggling to keep up with native American slang or, at a more advanced stage, to acquire a proper decorum, he lived insecurely in an ever-shifting milieu. If the immigrant were a woman, shut up in the home, and condemned to learn a new language and new ways from her children while pledging her own happiness to them, the strains of assimilation might become tragically intense. It is no accident that the mother in many an immigrant novel is a doomed figure, and that Cahan's one character of true nobility is Dora, clinging to a boorish husband for the sake of a daughter who proves unworthy of her mother's self-denial.

The wealth of new power extracted from the earth, after 1870, set off a second revolution in American industry. Steam replaced water power. Iron replaced wood in the construction of machines. Factories became larger and more mechanized and the place of unskilled labor more prominent. On the payrolls of new enterprises, immigrant names were almost alone; and the newcomers now penetrated even into the older textile and shoe industries. The former peasants, first taken on for menial duties as janitors and sweepers, found themselves more often placed at machines as the processes of production were divided into ever simpler tasks open to the abilities of the unskilled.

By the end of the nineteenth century the national economy had been transformed. Immigrants then still did the burdensome jobs of commerce. They still toiled in construction and maintenance crews. But they had found a larger usefulness in the mines and factories. In the mill towns and industrial cities the availability of their labor had been instrumental in converting production from its old handicraft forms to the mechanized forms of power.

Immigrants' Pain

This process, so rich in rewards for the country as a whole, paid mostly dividends of pain for the immigrants involved in it. It cost the peasants this to make the adjustment, that the stifling, brazen factories and the dark, stony pits supplanted the warm, living earth as the source of their daily bread. Year after year they paid the price in innumerable hardships of mind and body.

When he reviewed his grievances the man who went to work said that the conditions of his labor were oppressively harsh. His day was long, he pointed out; not until the 1880's was the ten-hour limit an objective seriously to be struggled for, and for many years more that span remained a pleasing ideal rather than a reality. His week was full, he added; seven days, when they could be had, were not unusual. And, he complained, along with the Sunday there vanished that whole long calendar of holidays that had formerly marked the peasant year. Here the demands of industry and the availability of employment alone determined when a man should work and when he should rest.

These were such wrongs as the ache in his muscles recalled. Others were summoned up by an ache of the spirit. For this matter of time reflected an unhuman lack of concern with human needs that was characteristic of the entire system. In these great concerns, no one seemed troubled with the welfare of the tiny men so cheap to come by who moved uneasily about in the service of the immense expensive machines. A high rate of industrial accidents and a stubborn unwillingness to make the most elementary provisions for the comfort of the employees, to the immigrant were evidence of the same penetrating callousness.

In the terms of his own experience, the laborer could come to understand his total insecurity by recollecting the steady decline in the span of the labor contract. In the Old Country, and in the old America, a man was hired for the year or for the season. But that period was altogether out of place under these conditions. Now it was not even by the month or by the week that the worker was taken on, but by the day or by the hour. Such an arrangement released the employer from the compulsion of paying hands when he had no need of them. But it left the hands uncertain, from moment to moment, as to how much work and how much income they would have.

The ultimate refinement was the shift to piecework in which the laborer, rewarded in accord with his output, received payment only for the instants he was actually at his task. The peasant sometimes conceived of this as an attractive alternative, for he hated the idea of selling his time, of taking directions like a servant, of cringing under the frowns of a foreman who judged all performances inadequate. Piecework brought the consolation of independence—one's time was one's own—and the illusion that additional effort would bring additional returns. But, though the immigrants often clung to the illusion as a token of hope, the reality was inescapably different. There was no independence and rewards would not rise. For the employer who set the rates manipulated them to his own interest while the employee had no choice but to accept. The net effect was to shift from the employer to the employee the whole burden of labor insecurity.

Employment Insecurity

These elements of insecurity, the immigrant learned, were not confined to the conditions of the working day; they pervaded the total relationship of the worker to the economy. The fluid labor supply that gave the employer complete liberty to hire as many workers as he wished, when he wished, also gave him the ability, at will, to dismiss those whose toil he no longer needed. Under such circumstances there were always some men without jobs. Each industry came to have its seasons, peaks and troughs in the level of employment dictated either by the weather as in construction, or, more generally, by the convenience of the managers. It was a rare individual who did not go on the bricks for some part of the year, for periodic unemployment was an expected aspect of the laborer's career.

Then there were the years when unemployment deepened and spread out. The intervals of idleness grew longer and were less frequently interrupted until unemployment was no longer intermittent but continuous. More men appeared on the streets during the day; children were seen, pail in hand, on the way to the police station for the doled-out soup. First in the mill and mining towns where there was only one employer or one industry and where a closing had an immediate cataclysmic effect, then in the cities where the impact was delayed by diversity of occupations, but in time everywhere, the laborer knew a depression was upon him.

At such times, the burdens of his economic role became intolerable. The hunger left behind in Europe was again an intimate of the household, and the cold and raggedness. Endurance stretched to the bursting point, and the misery of regret was overwhelming. It was a golden land here in America as long as there was work, but without work it was worth nothing. . . .

Alienation Led to Ethnic Division

Like Oscar Handlin, historian Maldwyn Jones believed that immigrants were faced with terrifyingly alienating experiences when they reached their new country. In his 1960 history American Immigration *he writes that this alienation from the larger American culture led to stronger identification with members of their own ethnic and national backgrounds, development of strong ethnic enclaves within cities, and, consequently, further alienation from the larger culture.*

The persistence of feelings of alienation and isolation could not but stimulate in each ethnic group an awareness of its identity. The strange and often hostile environment in which they found themselves sharpened the nostalgia of immigrants for their homelands, led them to cherish old loyalties, and drove them in upon themselves. The most obvious expression of immigrant yearnings for the familiar was the tendency to congregate in distinct areas. American cities now became agglomerations of separate communities, the ethnic character of which was recognized in such names as Irishtown and Kleindeutschland.

In America bread never came without complications. The peasant, new to the means of earning his livelihood, was also new to the means of spending it. To his misfortune he discovered that he himself added to the difficulties in making ends meet through inability to use efficiently whatever money came to his hands. In his old life, he had thought of objects in their individuality and uniqueness; the chair, the hat, the cow. Here he had to learn to think of them as commodities, subject to a common quantitative standard of price. Without a clear conception of the relationship of money to things, every transaction involved a set of totally new conditions.

What good wife, at home, was so lacking in housewifely skills as to buy food? Only the improvident were incapable of nurturing their families out of their own farms and gardens. But in America every crumb was paid for. The unfamiliar processes of shopping, of purchasing goods from impersonal strangers in stores, led to countless losses and often induced the immigrant, whatever the cost, to deal with peddlers, as in the Old World. Furthermore, lack of funds made it inevitable that these people transact their affairs in a most wasteful manner. There was no margin for stock. They bought bread and potatoes by the pound, rather than by loaf or peck, coal by the basket rather than by ton. (And where would they have put more had they the money to invest in quantity?) Purchasers in such small lots could not choose of whom they should buy, or at what terms. They marketed where they could and were at the mercy of those willing to trouble with their trifling custom.

Frequently, the shortage of cash drove the immigrants into the trap of an expensive credit system. In the bitter intervals between earnings they were compelled to turn to the generosity of the local shopkeeper, who would tide them over to the limit of his own slim resources. (What else could the merchant do when all his customers were in the same miserable condition?) As debts mounted up in the grocer's book, the immigrants lost the freedom to shop and paid, in the price of their food, the interest and more.

For one cause and another, the laborer got pitifully little from his labor. The dollars that seemed large enough from the perspective of Europe shrank with disheartening rapidity under the conditions of America. What was left, every waking hour, was the tormenting need to provide, the nagging need to restrict expenditures. Occasional windfalls, not enough to alter his situation, might be spent in bursts of indulgence—a gold watch, a glittering pin. What difference did that make? Day-to-day existence was still close to the bone.

Losing Dignity and Strength

How could this man, so recently removed from an altogether different life, explain to himself the productive system in which he was enmeshed? Now he was a part of something altogether unnatural. It was that, rather than the length or laboriousness of his work, that was harshest. Indeed the factory was not at all like the field, the field over which he had once bent in piety, the field over which he had once cast forth the sacred seeds that would bring forth God's fruit on a morrow. At best, there was this cardinal fault in the new work, that it was separated from the soil; and, at least, it required this adjustment of the peasant, that he reconcile himself to a life away from the earth, that he cut himself off from the process of birth and death, from the cycle of growth, aging, and regeneration that had once given meaning to his being. Now he was to act within a realm of inanimate things. Senseless iron shapes will everlastingly be about him, and stone will hem him in—on city street, in mill or mine. In his own estimation he would be that much the less a man.

In all matters, the New World made the peasant less a man. Often he toiled at intangibles, labored to produce objects he never would see. In the laborer's perspective, the factory turned out only parts of things: not a shoe, a coat, a plow, a cart—but a sole, a sleeve, a blade, a wheel. Bound to the monotony of a minute task, endlessly repeated, the worker sometimes could not envisage the whole of which his bit would be a part. He through whose hands all of production had then passed, from the dropped seed to the eaten bread, often now could not tell what manner of thing his labor made—its shape, its quality, its function. Such labor was labor for its own sake and meaningless.

Actions no longer related to the rhythms of the soil now seemed related to nothing at all. In the new context, all sorts of old judgments became irrelevant. Formerly the peasant's life had been guided by standards he accepted as fixed and immutable. Now his life made a mockery of those very standards. Could he here, as at home, expect the relationships of reciprocal goodness between master and men, between just employer and true employee? Could he count on neighborly loans, on the mutual help of men working together? Those who thought it were quickly disabused.

As in the crossing, there was a reversal of roles. The loyal dutiful man, faithful to tradition, the man who was the son and grandson of substantial peasants, was reduced to the indignity of hired labor, while shrewd, selfish, unscrupulous upstarts thrived. Clearly the attributes the immigrants held in high esteem were not those that brought success in America. The idea of success was itself strange; to thrust oneself above one's station in life called for harsh competitive qualities the peasant had always despised. Of course there was a satisfaction in the knowledge that even the well-to-do worked here and a man's cap was not worn out from lifting it to the gentry. But the satisfaction was mixed with a sense of impropriety. And to the extent that the immigrant lacked fixity of place, he felt again the less a man for it.

He was not a man at all. Whether he worked or was idle, whether he prospered or starved, was quite unrelated to his qualities as a human being, to his virtues as an individual. The line would move forward by the hiring boss, and then suddenly stop. The rest would be turned away, not through any deficiency of their own, not through lack of skill or will, but because the system operated impersonally. Where the line stopped was unpredictable. Those figures on the line who got in or did not felt part of an entity vast beyond their comprehension, certainly beyond their control. Driven in a helpless alternation of fortunes by the power of remote forces, these were no longer men, not any more men than the cogs spinning in their great machines. . . .

In other forms of enterprise too there were opportunities in contracting for the use of immigrant workers. Within the building and construction trades, the man who could get most out of his fellows could be foreman or boss or padrone. He could take on jobs on his own, become a person of substance. But he did so by climbing on the backs of those whose toil he managed.

A similar situation obtained in commerce. Newcomers could make a start in petty retailing if they drew support from their Old Countrymen by catering to their special needs. Lack of capital and ignorance of English and of business ways were less imposing obstacles if the aspiring businessman stocked the products others did not handle and if he dealt with the immigrants in the familiar forms of the old village market. The essential problem was to establish confidence, to avoid price comparisons. The shopkeeper extended credit, on the book, to those he knew; he bargained in the old manner, dropping a few cents on one article to make them up on another. He spoke to the women in their own language, made his establishment a neighborhood meeting place where gossip and advice passed with each purchase. Against those attractions, the competition of the chain stores was irrelevant.

On this basis, some immigrants became grocers; that trade was entirely with housewives and was conditioned by the persistent habits of particular diets. Restaurateurs and the purveyors of coffee and other liquors, hard and soft, also operated at an advantage; these services had a ceremonial social quality, best indulged in the company of countrymen. Businesses that involved contacts with the Old World were also open to the immigrants' talents. Did you wish to send a steamship ticket to a cousin or money to the old mother, then better to see the man who still knew the Old World, still spoke the old language, yet miraculously had acquired the skill to manipulate drafts and bills, to talk as an equal to the big companies. The notary's seal on his window was a token of government approval, his enterprise was open evenings and Sunday when the worker had time, and he spared you the need of difficult encounters with strangers in the great marble institutions in town. From the confidence of their compatriots such agents and brokers prospered—a few, enough so they could venture into full banking operations.

So, in their various fashions, immigrants became men of business, some to reach ultimate affluence, others to work all their days with effort and heartache, supporting miserable enterprises out of their bodies' spent energy. For all there was a period of hard beginnings, when they toiled long days in the pursuit of the first stake. The peddler's bag, the cart of goods, the uncertain heaped-up wagon, these were the starting points. Here, capital laboriously come at was first invested, added to with pain, and—in some cases—accumulated into the New World's success.

In the pursuit of this fleeting success, the peasant broke with his past. His constant task here was to transform income, no matter how small, into capital. Only with difficulty, if at all, did these people learn to do so who, at home, had conceived only of the land as property and had been accustomed to consuming all their income. To create capital in America meant a miserly scrimping at the expense of day-to-day consumption. It meant also a slighting of traditional obligations, the exploitation rather than the succor of neighbors.

It was, as a result, less often the conventional peasant who got ahead than an outsider not so limited by the peasant past. The most likely to gain by the new situation were the city folk who emigrated with the peasants and who spoke the same language, and such familiar strangers as the Jews who, even in the Old Country, had learned to reckon, to direct earnings toward a purpose.

For those who were themselves not successful the only hope was to transfer hope to the children, to trust that a second generation would find room where the first had not. Given the constant expansion of the American economy, it was not vain to think that the sons of the immigrants might enter the skilled trades, business, and the professions.

But for that hope there was also a cost. For success, whether at first hand or second, put a distance between the immigrant and the ideals of his former life. One way or another he probed this consequence of separation from Europe: that to live in the old way was to court failure and hardship, while success brought the pangs of unsettled, unrooted values.

VIEWPOINT 2

"[Immigrants] were able to remain within the confines of small groups and networks, which assisted them tremendously."

Immigration Was Not an Alienating Experience

John Bodnar (1944-)

John Bodnar teaches history at Indiana University in Blooming-ton and is the author of several books including *Immigration and Industrialization: Ethnicity in an American Mill Town* and *Worker's World: Kinship, Community, and Protest in an Industrial Society*. The following viewpoint is excerpted from his book *The Transplanted: A History of Immigrants in Urban America* (1985). In it, Bodnar argues that the nineteenth- and early twentieth-century immigrants to America moved from one capitalistic society to another and thus were well equipped to compete in the new country. Although most immigrants did not dramatically improve their economic positions in their lifetimes, they were successful in adapting to the conditions of the new land. Bodnar also argues that immigrants were not alienated from both past and present; in fact, most immigrants' decision to emigrate oriented them away from the past and toward the future. In addition, they remained part of large networks of family and acquaintances with similar national backgrounds and with whom they exchanged mutual support.

In every time and place men and women must make some effort to adjust to the economic realities which confront them. Nowhere is this lesson more obvious than in the industrial cities and towns of the United States in the final quarter of the twentieth century. Residents faced with transformations in the labor market which demand skills unlike the ones they possess or industries faced with new forms of competition from abroad all scurry to adjust, adapt, and reorient themselves to new demands and new realities. Young people contemplating their futures must reconsider the value of skills and patterns of life useful to their parents and look in new directions while realizing that even a partial abandonment of all that they previously knew—neighborhoods, values, associations, and even dreams—cannot be accomplished without some pain. Americans coming of age in the 1980s are realizing a lesson their grandparents and great-grandparents knew fully well: The imperatives of capitalism must be served. The continual shift in capital and market conditions stirred by the ceaseless drive for profits and economy still demands a response from ordinary individuals who live under its influence. The fragile link between the generations of the last century and the current one is not necessarily cultural or emotional as much as it is the shared need to respond to an evolving capitalism, the need to choose from available but limited life paths, and the powerful drive to preserve something of one's inheritance even while acquiescing in a changing economic order—a drive which can sometimes influence the larger economic system itself.

The earlier generations, which left behind lessons of confronting American capitalism, were largely immigrants. They were usually young people themselves and their confrontation involved movement over long distances as well as compromises, acceptance of things unfamiliar, and stubborn resistance to change. After the second decade of the nineteenth century and prior to World War II, over 40 million of these individuals left homelands in Asia, North America, Europe and elsewhere to find a place in the new economic order of capitalism. . . .

Most previous descriptions of immigrants assume that the immigrant experience was a common experience shared equally by all; the transition to capitalism is either entirely difficult, conducted entirely within the confines of a traditional but apparently adaptive culture, or entirely rewarding over a given period of time. But even the most cursory glance at an immigrant community or stream will suggest that not all newcomers behaved in a similar fashion, that varying degrees of commitment to an assortment of cultures and ideologies were evident, and that not everyone faced identical experiences. Some individuals pursued modern forms of life and livelihood while others valued more traditional patterns. Workers existed who championed socialism and others died for their attachment to Catholicism. Some immigrants came to America and acquired large fortunes, and many more simply went to work every day with no appreciable gain. What they actually shared in common was a need to confront a new economic order and provide for their own welfare and that of their kin or household group. They all did this but they did so in different ways and with divergent results. . . .

The Structure of Emigration

Most of the immigrants transplanted to America in the century of industrial growth after 1830 were in reality the children of capitalism. They were products of an economic system and, indeed, a way of life which penetrated their disparate homelands in particular parts of the world at various stages throughout the nineteenth century. While the new order of capitalism may have represented an opportunity for surplus and abundance to those possessing the resources to take advantage of its promise, to ordinary farmers and laborers throughout the pre-industrial lands of the world it represented a new dimension to the ongoing challenge of finding a way to sustain the welfare of family, kin, or the small group which formed the boundaries of everyday life. Before promising them opportunity and enhanced material well-being, capitalism presented them with a choice of options. Some would decide to retain traditional, premodern modes of life, others would attempt to adjust to the new realities presented by capitalism in the homelands, and still others would formulate plans to confront changing economic and social demands in industrial regions such as the United States. . . .

Traditionally the impetus for American immigration has been linked to the disparity between an improving standard of living in America and impoverishment of premodern societies throughout the world. . . .

The essential problem with the scholarship which has emphasized the attractiveness of the American economy to the less fortunate of the world, however, is that it badly obscures the complexity of social and economic forces which were affecting emigrants in their homeland. If immigration was caused largely by the lure of America, then we would expect that struggling people everywhere would come here in relatively equal numbers with common intentions and, for that matter, backgrounds. But historical reality suggests a different explanation to this process. Rates of emigration were not the same everywhere. . . .

If the lure of America was an overpowering magnet to the impoverished people of the world, emigration from any country or region would have been essentially a random process draining the lowest elements of society from nearly every geographic area. But emigrants clearly came from some regions and not other. Abundant evidence exists, moreover, to suggest that those departing were not coming from the depths of their respective society but occupied positions somewhere in the middle and lower-middle levels of their social structures. Those too poor could seldom afford to go, and the very wealthiest usually had too much of a stake in the homelands to depart. . . .

Changing Conditions Encouraged Emigration

It was no accident that emigrants tended to come from specific regions and sectors of the social structure. Throughout the nineteenth century the same forces of industrial expansion and urban growth which were transforming America were also affecting the emigrants' homelands. Even in rural lands, where social and economic change was less apparent, the nature of agriculture could be rapidly transformed from an emphasis on subsistence to one on production for export to distant urban markets. Indeed, wherever agriculture tended to become commercial and affect existing patterns of landownership, the beginnings of mass emigration became visible.

Helpful Compatriots

In 1922, Greek-American clergyman J. P. Xenides wrote a short history called The Greeks in America. *In it he comments on the closeness of Greek immigrants to their fellow Greeks and how this association helps the immigrants adjust to life in America.*

People from the same town or village in Greece are usually drawn together in America too. The newcomers find out first of all the whereabouts of their relatives and fellow countrymen. In fact they may come directly to them, having already corresponded with them. Even those of different towns are very helpful to one another in finding work and if need be helping each other financially and otherwise. They room together; work together; frequent the same coffeehouse, club and restaurant. Thus close attachments are formed.

Here people may live in the same neighborhood (even the same house), and not get acquainted with each other. Not so among the Greeks; they easily get acquainted and are friendly and neighborly to one another.

After the late eighteenth century, in much of central and eastern Europe, the old order of nobles and peasants rapidly gave way.

Pushed aside aggressively by the rising power of the state, nobles could no longer count on the loyalty or subservience of the peasantry, who now looked more kindly upon the government and monarch responsible for granting them emancipation from their servile conditions. . . .

Family as Focus of Life

As individuals faced the new demands created by changes in landholding patterns, work opportunities, and population pressures, they usually did not make decisions alone but in the context of a family or household. If emigration was tied to specific regions and social categories, it was also linked to the goals of household groups who sought to adjust to shifting social and economic realities. If an understanding of the emigrant world is to be reached, the pull of familial obligation must be defined.

Families were not only the center of economic production in most preindustrial lands, they were the focus of life itself. In religion, in love, in work, and in all of life, perceptions existed and decisions were made primarily in family terms. As one study of Italian villages concluded, "Le Famiglia" was at the center of Italian life. Families were not only biological arrangements facilitating procreation and socialization but society's basic mode of economic organization in the pre-industrial land.

While the actual structure of family life often differed in the premigration lands, nearly all family forms pursued economic well-being under a particular system of order and authority. In Hungary, power resided, for instance, in the male head. No one was permitted to contradict him. He guarded and managed the money even in households of extended kin and his wife could direct the work of a daughter-in-law. Property, moreover, was nearly always identified with a family unit rather than an individual, and in many regions prohibitions existed against its division not only to insure sufficient land for agriculture but to preserve the integrity of the family production unit. Because of economic conditions, families had to organize hierarchical structures and assign roles and duties on a systematic basis in order to insure the family's existence. . . .

If family units were central to organizing social and economic life for individuals in immigrant homelands, families were also quite familiar with the potential benefits of migration for supplementing household income or even enhancing a household's resources. Traditional views of static and isolated peasant villages in the preindustrial world simply were inaccurate and most rural and town dwellers knew long before they ever heard of America that people frequently had to migrate to meet economic realities. Patterns of temporary and permanent migration had characterized Europe and other lands throughout the eighteenth and nineteenth centuries. The growing connection between industrial and agricultural economies did little to temper this widespread transiency and usually served to intensify it. . . .

Emigrants then were not simply isolated people who had been shaped by long-standing traditions and cultures. They were products of particular social categories, households, and regions who had adjusted their goals and behavior throughout the nineteenth century to meet the changing economic realities induced by factory production, commercial agriculture, and landholding patterns. . . .

Pragmatic Decision to Emigrate

Although the abundant literature which proved emigrants were not originating from the poorest sectors of society has discredited the flight from poverty thesis and recent accounts have shown there was an increase in individual expectations, an easy assumption should not be made that the question of motivation has been satisfactorily answered. Several points still must be considered. First, most emigration took place in village and family networks and not on an individual basis. Second, many who left farms could only go if others agreed to remain behind and perform necessary tasks. Third, sizable amounts of money were sent back to homelands and large percentages of people remained in America only for several years. These points do not support an image of self-interest but one of individuals closely tied to family responsibilities and homeland priorities.

Rather than being bound to tradition or modern notions of achievement, much evidence exists to suggest that immigrants were pragmatic and weighed carefully the original decision to emigrate in the face of contemporary economic and social conditions. They were already formulating ways to confront industrial capitalism prior to moving to urban America. The first to leave were usually artisans and independent farmers who were truly dislocated but not impoverished. They certainly desired to avoid impoverishment, however. Among the mass of landless and marginal owners who eventually formed the bulk of each migration stream, the decision to move usually meant a temporary quest to earn higher wages which alleviated economic pressures at home and often provided additional resources to acquire more land and become self-sufficient in agriculture. Since they were not tied to a distant past or future, their goal was adjustment to the present realities of capitalism as manifested in their homelands. Among Italians, for instance, emigration was not random but tied closely to assessments of economic conditions. Italian emigration was heaviest in years in which harvests were poor. A warm spring which boded well for the winter wheat crop kept many in their villages. They knew an abundant harvest could lead to greater farm employment at home. In the 1880s the residents of one village learned that Pennsylvania coal miners were getting nearly two dollars a day and quickly estimated that in two years they could save enough to return to Italy and purchase sufficient land to support a family. Even among those who stayed in America the dream of returning home to establish independent farms persisted. Some sociologists have described peasants as inhabitants of a culture of poverty which favored immediate gratification over forced savings. But no such culture characterized most emigrants to America who were making realistic decisions about familial and individual survival. . . .

Networks of Migration

Throughout the immigrants' homelands families were forced to select emigration as one possible option in confronting the new order of capitalism. But a multitude of practical problems remained once the decision to move was made. How would information of specific jobs be found? Where could living accommodations be located? How in general did individuals enter sprawling new factories and expanding cities? The answers to these pressing issues emerged not from any long and tedious thought process but largely from familiar patterns cultivated over years of dealing with the vagaries of economic systems, social relationships, and human desires. Work, shelter, and order would be secured in industrial America—as they had been in the pre-industrial and proto-industrial homeland— through an intricate web of kin and communal associations. The immigrant would not enter America alone. The intrusion of capitalism in the premigration lands may have raised the alternative of emigration, but it had not destroyed the essential relationship between family and work that most emigrants, regardless of ethnic background, had nurtured. It was a relationship which would enjoy a rejuvenation in the mills and neighborhoods of American industrial cities.

Because families and friends were in close contact even when separated by wide oceans, immigrants seldom left their homelands without knowing exactly where they wanted to go and how to get there. Relatives and friends constantly sent information back regarding locations to live and potential places of employment. Thousands of Poles were brought from Gdansk to Polish Hill in Pittsburgh by aunts, uncles, brothers, and sisters who sent them passage money and instructions of what to bring and where to make steamship and railroad connections. By 1915, as a result of such patterns, investigators could find heavy clusters of families in city neighborhoods. About three-fourths of the Italians

Immigrants' Choice

Historian Alan M. Kraut agrees with John Bodnar that immigrants were not merely victims of new and alienating circumstances. In his 1982 book The Huddled Masses: The Immigrant in American Society, *he writes that they made deliberate choices and that they acted upon America as much as they were acted on by it.*

Most often, emigrants ventured abroad deliberately, not in a spontaneous somnambulism occasioned by traumatic upheavals. They were not drawn from their homes against their wills, as if by a "distant magnet." Emigration was but one among various choices; not even the most popular in every region of southern and eastern Europe and Asia. . . .

The history of immigration to America can only be understood in light of "what was done" to a newcomer and native alike by this massive migratory movement. Immigrants were confronted with a series of options not even primarily of their own making, options not entirely to their taste. But it was the immigrants themselves who chose how to react; they were not simply the passive victims of large social forces. To portray the newcomers as hapless wayfarers not only robs them of their dignity, but obscures the part they played in creating a new character for America reflective of values, attitudes, and beliefs imported from around the world.

and one-half of the Jews who owned property in Providence, Rhode Island, lived in a building with kin at the same address. One Jewish immigrant explained that her father had bought a three-family house with his cousins. Her family lived downstairs, one cousin on the second floor, and another cousin on the top floor. An Italian working for the Scovill Company in Connecticut brought friends who were "big and strong" from Italy. Women brought their sisters or friends into domestic jobs or gave them references of where to go. Chicanos followed each other along railroad lines into Los Angeles and from there throughout southern California. In the early 1920s Chicanos like José Anquiano were arriving in the Chicago area after hearing about openings at the Inland Steel Company and then sending for friends and kin in Texas and in their home villages in Mexico. In fact, relatives and friends were often responsible for movement to second and third locations in America when employment became slack in areas of first settlement. Thus, Italians from southern Illinois moved to the Italian "hill" in St. Louis when coal mining operations were reduced in the 1920s, and Slavs from mines in western Pennsylvania and northern Michigan moved to Detroit's expanding car industry in the same decade.

It was not unheard of for "middlemen" or labor agents to direct large flows of immigrant workers to particular industries or cities in return for modest fees. Such individuals usually shared a common ancestry and language with newcomers and could effectively gather them for shipment to a waiting industry. Oriental workers were channeled in such a fashion into western railroads for a time. Greeks were brought to firms such as the Utah Copper Company and the Western Pacific Railway by "labor czars," such as Leonidas Khliris; Italian "padrones" funneled their fellow countrymen to railroads and public works projects and into labor turmoil as strike-breakers. Ethnic "bankers," such as Luigi Spizziri, advanced passage to individuals in Italy and then found them work in Chicago. Hungarians were able to get contracts from the agents of Pennsylvania mine owners in the 1880s, which they could break only if they got someone to replace them. In nearly all instances, however, intermediaries functioned only in the early stages of a migration stream. Inevitably the continual and enduring movement of all groups into industrial America would rest on ties and links established in the old world.

Immigrants did not need middlemen in the long run because they received a steady stream of information on labor market conditions and wages from friends and relatives, which allowed them to make reasonably well-informed decisions about where to go and what types of work they could expect to find. Immigrant letters were frequently filled with information on employment prospects, wages, and even the manner in which workers were treated. . . .

Occupational Networks

While immigrants clearly had preferences for work and some advance knowledge of wages and opportunities, however, they were not completely free to move into the industrial economy on an individual basis. Throughout the first century of American industrial expansion both workers and employers experimented with techniques of recruitment and job placement, and no method appeared to be as pervasive or as effective as that of informal familial and ethnic networks. The workplace of early industrial capitalism was a relatively accessible place especially during the six or seven decades after 1850, and kinship ties functioned effectively to provide labor, train new members, and effectively offer status and consolation. Poles, relying on relatives and friends, established occupational beachheads in Pittsburgh at the Jones and Laughlin steel plant, the Pennsylvania Railroad yards in the Lawrenceville section of the city, Armstrong Cork, and H.J. Heinz. As one newcomer recalled, "The only way you got a job was through somebody at work who got you in." . . .

Whether immigrants were recruited directly for their abilities or followed existing networks into unskilled jobs, they inevitably moved within groups of friends and relatives and worked and lived in clusters. Friends and relatives functioned so effectively, in fact, that they invariably superseded labor agents and "middlemen" in influencing the entry of newcomers into the industrial economy and were usually able to create occupational beachheads for those that followed. Scholars who have accepted the "split-labor market" theory and its assumption that "middlemen" affected the placement of migrants in streams possessing a "sojourning orientation" have overlooked the more important role of networks which influenced both permanent and temporary arrivals. . . .

Strength of Immigrant Families

While it is apparent that immigrants were not free to move into the industrial economy wherever they desired, they were able to remain within the confines of small groups and networks, which assisted them tremendously. Such groups could mass around links of friends, villages, or regions but were mostly held together by ties of blood. Kinship formed the stable core of immigrant groups as they flowed into the openings available to them in particular times and places. Ironically, no concept so thoroughly pervaded the older interpretations of the American immigrant experience than the one which linked the growing movement of industrial-urban society to a pattern of family breakdown. This view originated with the belief that the modern capitalist system, especially in its manifestation of the factory system which removed production functions from the traditional family-household unit, simply destroyed the foundation of familial cooperation. Production became compartmentalized in factories and mills and workers began to function as individual components of a factory system and not as integral members of a household. This entire argument rested upon an assumption that families not only became less important in urban-industrial society but that families themselves operated in isolation from the larger economy of industrial capitalism which surrounded them.

The startling discovery of modern historical scholarship, however, has made it quite clear that immigrant families did not wither in their encounter with American capitalism. Immigrant kinship associations not only continued to perform indispensable functions in the industrial city, such as helping to organize the movement of workers into the economy, but actually flourished. At times the relationship between the industrial economy and immigrant families could almost be described as symbiotic, as kinship groups proved very responsive to demands of the workplace, the city, and the individual.

285

The world the immigrant left had exhibited numerous examples of family, in one form or another, as a central focus of organizing life itself. Families were responsible for socialization patterns, the distribution of land and other resources, and even served as a forum to resolve the question of who should emigrate and why. Because they also performed valuable functions in industrial America meant they were not as much cultural baggage as they were institutions which continued to find a relevant role to play in both societies. Family economies were as much a product of industrial capitalism as they were of subsistence agriculture, for in both systems a mediating institution was necessary to stand between economy and society in order to reconcile individual and group demands.

The manner in which the immigrant family remained functional in two economies was its central and enduring attachment to the value of cooperation. Family members were continually instructed in the necessity of sharing and notions of reciprocity were constantly reinforced. Parents, children, boarders, and others who shared particular households were all assigned a series of duties and obligations. By working together, pooling limited resources, and muting individual inclinations, families attempted to assemble the resources sufficient for economic survival and, occasionally, for an improvement in their standard of living. But the first goal was always the most immediate: cooperate and survive. It was not until the era of postindustrialism after 1940, when kinship ties to the workplace were gradually weakened and success was equated with an individual quest, that the underlying system of familial cooperation would be threatened.

The immigrant family economy with its essential ingredients of sharing and reciprocity was found wherever immigrants settled and inevitably shaped their entry into the American economy and society. While not every ethnic group or family behaved in identical terms or pursued exactly the same objectives, an overwhelming majority lived their lives and pursued their goals through familial and household arrangements which often functioned in a similar manner. . . .

Daily Life Strategies and Capitalism

Immigrant adjustment to capitalism in America was ultimately a product of a dynamic between the expanding economic and cultural imperatives of capitalism and the life strategies of ordinary people. Historian Gabriel Kolko wrote that millions of immigrants in industrial America had neither the desire nor the capacity to relate to the social order of capitalism. But . . . this observation was far from accurate. Immigrant people by definition related to capitalism and its attendant social order in complex and often ingenious ways which have often been misunderstood. . . .

Somewhere in time and space all individuals meet the larger structural realities of their existence and construct a relationship upon a system of ideas, values, and behavior which collectively gives meaning to their world and provides a foundation upon which they can act and survive. Collectively their thought and action are manifestations of a consciousness, a mentality, and ultimately a culture. Immigrants, who were after all common men and women, could not completely understand what was taking place as capitalism entered their world. They were not fully aware of the sweeping political and economic decisions and transitions which were altering the nineteenth and twentieth centuries. In lieu of a comprehensive understanding of social and historical change, they fashioned their own explanations for what they could feel and sense. To give meaning to the realities and structures which now impinged upon them, they forged a culture, a constellation of behavioral and thought patterns which would offer them explanations, order, and a prescription for how to proceed with their lives. This culture was not a simple extension of their past, an embracement of the new order of capitalism, or simply an affirmation of a desire to become an American. It was nurtured not by any one reality such as their new status as workers but was produced from whatever resources were at hand: kinship networks, folklife, religion, socialism, unions. It was a product of both men and women, believers and non-believers, workers and entrepreneurs, leaders and followers. It was creative yet limited by available options. It drew from both a past and a present and continually confronted "the limits of what was possible." The demands of economic forces, social structures, political leaders, kin, and community were real and could not be ignored. Life paths and strategies were informed by knowledge from the past and estimates about the future but largely from the specific options of the present. Immigrants were free to choose but barely. . . .

Ultimately, then, the mentality and culture of most immigrants to urban America was a blend of past and present and centered on the immediate and the attainable. Institutions from the past such as the family-household were modified but retained; the actions of landed elites at home and industrial capitalists abroad forced them to confront a new market and social order which they accepted but somewhat on their own terms. They would move, several times, if they had to, and become wage laborers or even small entrepreneurs. They did so not because they were victimized by capitalism or embraced it but because they pursued the immediate goal of family-household welfare and industrial jobs which were very accessible.

Chronology

Editor's note: This chronology highlights important events in American immigration history primarily during the time period covered by this book, 1820-1924.

1565 First permanent European settlement in the United States is established at St. Augustine, Florida, by the Spanish.

1598 Spanish immigrants settle in what is now Texas and New Mexico.

1619 First shipment of African slaves arrives in Virginia.

1751 Benjamin Franklin worries about German immigrants, writing, "This Pennsylvania will in a few years become a German colony; instead of [their] learning our language, we must learn theirs, or live as in a foreign country."

1776 The Declaration of Independence charges the king of England with obstructing migration to British North America, thereby indirectly indicating that the colonies were greatly interested in recruiting new settlers. In fact, most colonies are in active competition with other colonies for these prospective settlers.

In his pamphlet *Common Sense* Thomas Paine writes that "Europe, not England, is the parent country of America," thereby offering early evidence that America's very heterogeneity is intimately connected with its character.

1789 Jedidiah Morse uses the word "immigrant" in his patriotic textbook *American Geography*, making mention of the "many immigrants from Scotland, Ireland, Germany, and some from France" living in New York. Previously, writers had referred only to "emigrants," but after 1789 the American language identified newcomers with the country they were entering rather than the country they had left.

1795 Congress passes the Naturalization Act, requiring for citizenship a five-year residence in the United States and the renunciation of all former allegiances.

1798 Alien and Sedition acts give President John Adams

arbitrary power to seize and expel resident aliens suspected of subversive activities. The laws expired after two years and were not renewed.

1812 The War of 1812 brings immigration to a complete halt as hostilities prevent transport across the ocean.

1820-1880 The first great wave of immigration to the United States. Over ten million immigrants arrive with northern and western Europeans (mostly British, Irish, and German) predominating. Many settle in the rural Midwest.

1835 Scottish-born journalist James Gordon Bennett founds the *New York Herald*, thus beginning the long history of immigrant pioneers in the fertile field of the production of mass culture in the United States.

1839 Pennsylvania passes a law enabling public schools to provide instruction in the German language when at least 30 percent of the parents request such instruction.

1841-1850 First decade in American history in which immigration to the United States exceeds one million. (The total for the decade is 1,713,251.)

1848 Lajos Kossuth tours the United States in search of support for the Hungarian revolution against the Hapsburg Empire. He fails to gain official governmental support and returns to Europe, but many Hungarians choose to remain in or migrate to the United States nonetheless.

Treaty of Guadalupe-Hidalgo ends Mexican-American War and allows the United States to acquire Colorado, Arizona, New Mexico, Texas, California, and parts of Utah and Nevada from Mexico for $15 million. Mexican residents of the newly acquired territory are allowed to remain. They are subjected to serious discrimination but become the heart of labor for the American Southwest.

1848-1849 Failed revolutions in Europe spur migration to the United States from what will be Germany and what was the Austro-Hungarian Empire.

1849 Significant Chinese migration to the United States begins in the aftermath of the California gold rush.

In the Passenger cases the Supreme Court rules that state laws, such as head taxes on arriving immigrants, are unconstitutional because only Congress has the power to regulate immigration under the commerce clause of the Constitution.

1850 As of this census the Roman Catholic church becomes the largest religious denomination in the United States, due primarily to Irish and German immigration. It remains the largest single religious denomination today.

1851-1860 The peak decade for Irish migration to the United States. (The total for the decade was 914,199.)

1854 The California Supreme Court bars Chinese immigrants from testifying in any trial involving a white man.

The Know-Nothing movement wins sweeping victories in Congress and state legislative elections. The Know-Nothings objected to the increasing numbers of Roman Catholic immigrants from Ireland and other countries. They called for limits on immigration and a twenty-one-year period before immigrants could become voting citizens. The Know-Nothing movement ceases to be a national force by 1860, although nativists (those who stand up for the "native" Americans) continue to lobby against immigrants in the succeeding decades.

1864 Congress enacts legislation to help stimulate immigration by authorizing employers to pay for the passage of prospective immigrants. This legislation is repealed in 1868.

1868 The Burlingame Treaty is ratified. The treaty pledges to China the right of unrestricted immigration of Chinese citizens to the United States.

1869 Japanese begin to migrate to the United States. The first arrive in California as political refugees. Racial tensions grow between Asians and other Californians.

The Knights of Labor is founded by Philadelphia garment cutters. Under the leadership of Irish-American Terence V. Powderly the Knights recruit immigrant workers previously excluded from craft unions.

1870 The Naturalization Act is passed, limiting American citizenship to "white persons and persons of African descent," thereby discriminating against Asian immigrants.

1875 The Supreme Court, in *Henderson v. Mayor of New York,* rules that the administration of immigration is a federal matter and not a concern for state and/or local government.

1880 Polish National Alliance is founded with the idea of promoting middle-class, secular Polish-Americans.

1880-1920 The second great wave of immigration to the United States. Over 23.5 million immigrants arrive, predominantly from southern and eastern Europe. Many settle in cities and become factory workers.

1881-1890 The peak decade for German migration to the United States. (The total for the decade is 1,452,970.)

The peak decade for Scandinavian migration to the United States. (The total number of migrants from Sweden, Norway, and Denmark for this decade is 656,494.)

1882 The Chinese Exclusion Act is passed. The first serious prohibition of free immigration in all of American history, this legislation bans Chinese migration to the United States for ten years. It was renewed in 1892 and again in 1902 when the Congress moved to make the ban permanent.

1883 Hungarian-American Joseph Pulitzer purchases the *New York World*, continuing the connection between the American immigrant and the American mass popular culture.

1885 Josiah Strong publishes *Our Country*, which is a strongly nativist statement against the encroachment of the immigrant from central and southern Europe.

Congress moves to place a ban on contract labor. Passed largely to please organized labor, this law was seldom enforced.

Bohemian and Polish workers strike the Cleveland Rolling Mill Company after facing repeated wage cuts. Armed with guns and clubs, they forced their way into the mill and shut it down. But their efforts failed when they received no support from the skilled native workers.

1885-1886 Anti-Chinese riots engulf the city of Seattle.

1886 The Statue of Liberty is dedicated in New York Harbor.

Hull House opens in Chicago. Under the leadership of Jane Addams this settlement house will become a model for reformers working among working-class immigrants in many American cities.

1886-1887 The Haymarket riot occurs in Chicago in May of 1886. German-American anarchists are among those indicted for inciting the riot and killing police officers. Four German-American anarchists are executed in November of 1887 for their role in the riot even though none of the four was present at the time of the riot itself.

1887 The American Protective Association is founded by Henry F. Bowers. It was essentially an anti-Catholic organization that appealed to midwestern middle-class white Americans. The APA was the most noteworthy anti-Catholic organization between the Know-Nothings of the 1850s and the second Ku Klux Klan of the 1920s.

1889 Daniel DeLeon, who was born in Curaçao, takes control of the Socialist Labor party and gives it a solidly Marxist direction.

1890 Wisconsin passes the Bennett Law, which becomes a model for other states. It required public school instruction in English for at least sixteen weeks a year.

Ignatius Donnelly reveals the divided mind of American populism on the subject of the Jewish immigrant. His utopian novel *Caesar's Column*, published in 1890, portrays the Jew as an evil revolutionary, but also regards the Jew as a "noble race" perverted by Christian persecutions.

1891 Several leading citizens of New Orleans lead a lynching party into a local prison and kill eleven Italian immigrants who had just been found not guilty of a murder charge.

Congress bans the immigration of "all idiots, insane persons, paupers or persons likely to become a public charge, persons suffering from a contagious or loathsome disease, persons who have been convicted of a felony or other infamous crime or misdemeanor involving moral turpitude, and polygamists."

1892 The federal government opens its new immigration reception center on Ellis Island, which had been the site of a naval arsenal in New York Harbor. Over the next forty years some twelve million immigrants passed through it.

1893 The Pennsylvania Slovak Catholic Union is formed by immigrant miners to ease the financial burden on injured fellow workers and the families of miners killed while on the job.

1894 The Immigrant Restriction League is founded in Massachusetts by a group of Harvard graduates. In short order Senator Henry Cabot Lodge becomes its leader and its reason for being becomes the passage of a literacy test for entering immigrants.

1897 Abraham Cahan founds the *Jewish Daily Forward*. A Yiddish newspaper with socialist inclinations, it became the largest foreign language newspaper in the United States prior to World War I.

1899 Fourteen Jewish societies in Brooklyn declare that "no Jew can go on the street without exposing himself to the danger of being pitilessly beaten."

1901 Pres. William McKinley is assassinated by a young Polish-American anarchist.

1901-1910 The decade during which the largest number of immigrants arrived in the United States. (The total for the decade is 8,795,386.)

The peak decade for Italian migration to the United States. (The total for the decade is 2,045,877.)

1902 A riot occurs in New York City when a Jewish funeral procession is attacked by Irish immigrants.

1903 Congress passes the Anarchist Exclusion Act in response to the assassination of President McKinley. This is the first time that Congress demands to examine the political opinions of prospective immigrants.

1905 For the first time in American history more than one million immigrants arrive in the United States in a single year.

An anti-Japanese movement begins to gather steam in the United States. It is centered on the West Coast, especially California.

The Industrial Workers of the World (IWW) is organized. Though it grew out of the struggles of western miners, it immediately moved to include immigrant workers from the cities of the East Coast of the United States.

1906 The American Jewish Committee is founded. It was the first national Jewish organization that claimed to speak for all American Jews.

The National Liberal Immigration League is founded, largely under Jewish auspices. Its central purpose was to fight against literacy tests for prospective immigrants.

1907 Congress passes the Expatriation Act of 1907, which provides that an American woman, naturalized or native born, loses her citizenship upon marrying a foreigner.

1907-1908 President Theodore Roosevelt negotiates the Gentlemen's Agreement with Japan. This effectively ends the migration of Japanese laborers to the United States by having the Japanese government refuse to issue passports to them.

1907-1911 The Dillingham Commission (officially the United States Immigration Commission) works to record the migration of the so-called "new immigrants" from Italy and Russia, as well as central, eastern, and southeastern Europe. The result of its work is a forty-two-volume report on immigration to the United States.

1908 Israel Zangwill's play *The Melting Pot* opens in New York City. For the first time the notion of the United States as a melting pot is asserted. Previously, the process of assimilation was thought to be more effortless and spontaneous than the result of the heat generated within a fiery crucible.

1910 Croats, Serbs, and Slovenes come together to create a tenuous alliance named the Yugoslav Socialist Federation. But ethnic divisions are so serious that the alliance publishes three newspapers in three separate languages.

Mexican Revolution sends thousands of Mexicans to the United States. Over the next twenty years, nearly a million enter the United States, seeking work.

1911 The Triangle Factory Fire rages through the garment district of New York City killing 145 young immigrant working women.

1912 A strike breaks out in the textile mills of Lawrence, Massachusetts. IWW organizers quickly move to bring unity to the various immigrant strikers, including Italian, Irish, and French-Canadian workers.

1913 Epic (and partially successful) strike of immigrant workers in Paterson, New Jersey, is organized by the IWW.

1914-1918 World War I interrupts mass immigration to the United States.

1915 The American Jewish Congress is founded by American Zionists who draw their greatest support from eastern European Jews.

Louis Brandeis becomes the first Jewish-American to sit on the Supreme Court.

1916 Madison Grant writes *The Passing of the Great Race*, which warns Anglo-Saxon Americans that they had better prepare to make their last stand against the inferior races pouring into the United States from southeastern Europe.

Fiorello La Guardia is elected to Congress from a partially Italian district on New York City's Upper East Side. La Guardia will become the first Italian-American to play a significant role in national politics.

1917 A literacy test for incoming immigrants finally becomes law. Such legislation had previously secured congressional approval only to fall to vetoes by three different presidents. In this instance the bill was passed over the veto of President Woodrow Wilson. With its passage Congress for the first time enacts a general restriction of immigrants. In this case the legislation excluded any adult unable to read some language. The legislation also ordered the deportation of aliens who preached revolution or sabotage any time after their entry into the United States.

1918 Socialist party member Victor Berger is elected to Congress from a largely Polish-American district in Milwaukee. However, he is denied his seat in Congress during the Red Scare of the following year.

1919 Two years after the Russian Revolution succeeds, many Americans panic, believing that the nation is threatened by a communist menace. Thousands of immigrants are seized and hundreds deported for their anarchist or communist beliefs.

1921 Congress passes immigration restriction legislation. A quota of 350,000 is established. Under this legislation European immigration is limited to 3 percent of the number of foreign-born of each nationality present in the United States as of the last available census, that of 1910.

1922 Congress passes the Cable Act which nullifies the so-called Expatriation Act of 1907 except as it applies to those American women who married "aliens ineligible to citizenship" (meaning Asians).

1924 Congress passes the National Origins Act, which reduces the total number of potential immigrants to 300,000 annually and sets 1890 as the base year for determining the quota of those eligible. The quota itself is reduced from 3 to 2 percent of those migrants from any given country living in the United States as of 1890.

Horace Kallen publishes *Culture and Democracy*, a pioneering statement of cultural pluralism.

1928 Governor Al Smith of New York is the Democratic nominee for president of the United States. For the first time in American history the son of immigrant parents is the candidate of a major political party.

1943 The Chinese Exclusion Act is repealed.

1965 The Immigration Act of 1965 removes the national origins quota system. It establishes a ceiling of 270,000 immigrants per year with no more than 20,000 from any one country. It creates a system of preferences, with highest priority given to family reunification.

Annotated Bibliography

Edith Abbott, *Historical Aspects of the Immigration Problem: Select Documents*. Chicago: University of Chicago Press, 1926. Invaluable collection of periodical articles, essays, and government documents relating to emigration conditions, the economic impact of immigration, assimilation problems, social problems, and public attitudes toward immigrants, primarily relating to the nineteenth century.

Edith Abbott, *Immigration: Select Documents and Case Records*. Chicago: University of Chicago Press, 1924. Invaluable collection of documents relating to immigrant transport, admission, and restriction; essays, government documents, and social workers' case records.

Jane Addams, *Twenty Years at Hull House*. New York: Macmillan, 1910. The memoir of one of the leading settlement house workers and her life among the immigrants of Chicago.

Glenn C. Altschuler, *Race, Ethnicity and Class in American Social Thought, 1865-1919*. Arlington Heights, IL: Harlan Davidson, 1982. Brief but very readable intellectual history of the response to post-Civil War immigration.

H. Arnold Barton, *Letters from the Promised Land*. Minneapolis: University of Minnesota Press, 1975. Collection of letters from Swedish immigrants to their families during the height of Scandinavian immigration, 1840-1914.

Ronald Bayor, *Neighbors in Conflict: The Irish, Germans, Jews, and Italians of New York City*. Baltimore: Johns Hopkins University Press, 1978. An excellent study of the tensions among immigrant groups in an urban setting.

Ray Allen Billington, *The Protestant Crusade*. New York: Macmillan, 1938. A history of American reform and American nativism, especially its anti-Catholic dimension.

Theodore Blegen, *Norwegian Migration to America, 1825-1860*. Northfield, MN: Norwegian-American Historical Association, 1931. The authoritative history of the early migration of Norwegians to the United States.

Paul Boyer, *Urban Masses and Moral Order in America, 1820-1920*. Cambridge, MA: Harvard University Press, 1978. A history of efforts to reform both the immigrant and the cities in which many immigrants lived.

John W. Briggs, *An Italian Passage: Immigrants to Three American Cities, 1890-1930*. New Haven, CT: Yale University Press, 1978. A study of immigrant life as lived in Utica, New York; Rochester, New York; and Kansas City, Missouri.

David M. Brownstone, Irene M. Franck, and Douglass L. Brownstone, *Island of Hope, Island of Tears*. New York: Penguin, 1986. The story of Ellis Island, the gatepost to America for most of the millions of immigrants entering the United States from Europe, told in the words of people who passed through there.

Abraham Cahan, *The Education of Abraham Cahan*. Philadelphia: Jewish Publication Society of America, 1969. The memoir of the founder and editor of the *Jewish Daily Forward*.

Robert Carlson, *The Quest for Conformity: Americanization Through Education*. New York: Wiley, 1975. A revisionist history that seeks to argue that public education has been used to create a homogeneous America rather than a melting pot America.

Dennis Clark, *The Irish in Philadelphia*. Philadelphia: Temple University Press, 1973. A history covering three hundred years of Irish immigration and focusing on mechanisms that helped ease their path to becoming Americans.

Kathleen Conzen, *Immigrant Milwaukee, 1836-1860*. Cambridge, MA: Harvard University Press, 1976. Primarily a history of German immigration and secondarily a history of Irish immigration and Irish efforts to build communities within the city.

Roger Daniels, *Asian America: Chinese and Japanese in the United States Since 1850*. Seattle: University of Washington Press, 1988. A comparative history that studies living communities of immigrants. It offers brief profiles of individual immigrants and does not shy from chronicling racial prejudice.

Roger Daniels, *Coming to America*. New York: HarperCollins, 1990. A superbly readable general history of American immigration from the seventeenth century to the 1980s.

Philip Davis, ed., *Immigration and Americanization: Selected Readings*. Boston: Ginn & Company, 1920. Aimed at students and participants in Chautauquas, the lecture programs popular in the early part of this century. Includes readings both supportive and critical of immigrants by Jane Addams, Edward Everett, Henry Cabot Lodge, and many others.

Robert Divine, *American Immigration Policy, 1924-1952*. New Haven, CT: Yale University Press, 1957. A history of congressional debates and legislation beginning with the severely restrictive laws of the 1920s.

Jay P. Dolan, *The American Catholic Experience*. Garden City, NY: Doubleday, 1985. Social and religious history of Catholic immigration through the Mexican-American migration of this century.

Jay P. Dolan, *The Immigrant Church: New York's Irish and German Catholics, 1815-1865*. Baltimore: Johns Hopkins University Press, 1975. A history of parishes and preaching, but also a history of the conflicts between these two immigrant groups.

Albert B. Faust, *The German Element in America*. New York: Houghton, 1909. A history of German immigrants and influence in the United States.

David Gerber, *The Making of an American Pluralism: Buffalo, New York, 1825-1860*. Urbana: University of Illinois Press, 1989. A history of pluralism and nativism, of class and ethnic tensions.

Louis Gerson, *The Hyphenate in Recent American Politics and Diplomacy*. Lawrence: University of Kansas Press, 1964. A history that focuses primarily on the early 1920s and the years just before and just after World War II.

Nathan Glazer and Daniel P. Moynihan, *Beyond the Melting Pot*. Cambridge, MA: MIT Press, 1963. An early study emphasizing the permanence of ethnicity and stressing the interactions among the Irish, Jews, Italians, and Puerto Ricans of New York City.

Emma Goldman, *Living My Life*. New York: Macmillan, 1931. The memoir of one of the leading American anarchists, a Jewish immigrant to the United States.

Madison Grant, *The Passing of the Great Race*. New York: Charles Scribner's, 1916. A potent statement of turn-of-the-century American nativism.

Victor Greene, *American Immigrant Leaders, 1800-1910*. Baltimore: Johns Hopkins University Press, 1987. A history that includes portraits of thirty immigrant leaders and that stresses their defense of separate ethnic communities and their development of an American identification.

Oscar Handlin, *Boston's Immigrants*. Cambridge, MA: Harvard University Press, 1941. An early study of patterns of migration to and acculturation within a single American city.

Marcus Lee Hansen, *The Atlantic Migration, 1607-1860*. Cambridge, MA: Harvard University Press, 1940. Pioneering survey of the general history of immigration prior to the Civil War.

Will Herberg, *Protestant, Catholic, and Jew*. Garden City, NY: Doubleday, 1955. A restatement of the melting pot notion in religious and ethnic terms.

John Higham, *Send These to Me: Immigrants in Urban America*. Baltimore: Johns Hopkins University Press, 1984. A collection of the author's own essays and reviews on issues concerning the late nineteenth and early twentieth centuries. The focus is on the Jewish-American experience and the history of anti-Semitism.

John Higham, *Strangers in the Land*. New Brunswick, NJ: Rutgers University Press, 1955. A thorough survey of the history of American nativism from the Know-Nothings of the 1850s to the restrictive legislation of the 1920s.

Irving Howe, *World of Our Fathers*. New York: Harcourt Brace Jovanovich, 1976. An encyclopedic history of the Jewish immigrant experience in the aftermath of the onset of the mass Jewish migration of the 1880s.

Edward P. Hutchinson, *Immigrants and Their Children, 1850-1950.* New York: Wiley, 1976. Examines the migration and occupational patterns of immigrant populations across the United States and across a number of generations.

Joseph Huthmacher, *Senator Robert Wagner and the Rise of Urban Liberalism.* New York: Atheneum, 1968. A history of the new immigrants that argues that the immigrants themselves, not the politicians, were the major source for urban reform.

Kenneth Jackson, *The Ku Klux Klan in the City, 1915-1930.* New York: Oxford University Press, 1967. A general history of the urban Klan; as such, it is concerned with their anti-immigrant activities.

Maldwyn Jones, *American Immigration.* Chicago: University of Chicago Press, 1960. A general survey of the history of American immigration that downplays the differences among various immigrant groups and eliminates the distinction between the "old" and "new" immigrant.

Maldwyn Jones, *Destination America.* New York: Holt, Rinehart and Winston, 1976. Describes the hardship of turn-of-the-century migration to the United States and compares it to that experienced by earlier immigrants.

Thomas Kessner, *The Golden Door: Italians and Jewish Immigrant Mobility in New York City, 1880-1915.* New York: Oxford University Press, 1977. A comparative history of the problems of and opportunities for ethnic minorities.

James H. Kettner, *The Development of American Citizenship, 1607-1870.* Chapel Hill: University of North Carolina Press, 1978. A legal, political, and constitutional history of the idea of citizenship.

Harry H. L. Kitano, *Japanese Americans: The Evolution of a Subculture.* Englewood Cliffs, NJ: Prentice-Hall, 1969. A history of Japanese-American acculturation written by a Japanese-American.

Alan M. Kraut, *The Huddled Masses: The Immigrants in American Society, 1880-1921.* Arlington Heights, IL: Harlan Davidson, 1982. The best single-volume survey of turn-of-the-century immigration.

Fiorello La Guardia, *The Making of an Insurgent.* Philadelphia: J. B. Lippincott Co., 1948. The autobiography of the colorful Italian-Jewish-American reform politician.

Salvatore J. LaGumina and Frank J. Cavaioli, *The Ethnic Dimension in American Society.* Boston: Holbrook Press, 1974. Incorporating many excerpts from primary sources, this book theorizes that the American social fabric can best be understood through studying its immigrants and ethnic minorities.

Emil Lengyel, *Americans from Hungary.* Philadelphia: J. B. Lippincott Co., 1948. A popular survey of Hungarian migration to the United States.

Allan J. Lichtman, *Prejudice and the Old Politics.* Chapel Hill: University of North Carolina Press, 1979. A history of the 1928 presidential election and the impact of the immigration question on its outcome.

Helen Z. Lopata, *Polish Americans: Status and Competition in an Ethnic*

Community. Englewood Cliffs, NJ: Prentice-Hall, 1976. A fine overview of the Polish-American experience with special emphasis on the social structure of Polish-American communities in the United States.

Samuel Lubell, *The Future of American Politics.* New York: Harper and Row, 1952. An early example of the study of immigrant voting behavior.

Frederick C. Luebke, *Bonds of Loyalty: German-Americans and World War I.* Dekalb: Northern Illinois University Press, 1974. A history of the wartime treatment of German-Americans in the United States and of their response to that treatment.

Delber L. McKee, *Chinese Exclusion Versus the Open Door Policy.* Detroit: Wayne State University Press, 1977. A history of the methods and nature of exclusion as practiced during the administration of Theodore Roosevelt.

Carey McWilliams, *North from Mexico.* New York: Monthly Review Press, 1961. History of Mexican immigration to the United States.

Ande Manners, *Poor Cousins.* New York: Coward, McCann and Geoghegan, 1972. A history of the differences between German-Jewish immigrants and the later Jewish immigrants from Eastern Europe and Russia.

Kerby Miller, *Emigrants and Exiles: Ireland and the Irish Exodus to North America.* New York: Oxford University Press, 1985. The best single-volume history of the Irish migration to the United States.

Randall Miller and Thomas Mazrik, *Immigrants and Religion in Urban America.* Philadelphia: Temple University Press, 1977. A collection of essays concerning the relationships between immigrant groups and American religious organizations.

Stuart C. Miller, *The Unwelcome Immigrant.* Berkeley: University of California Press, 1969. A study of prejudice toward the Chinese immigrant.

Joan Morrison and Charlotte Fox Zabusky, *American Mosaic: The Immigration Experience in the Words of Those Who Lived It.* New York: E. P. Dutton, 1990. An oral history of twentieth-century immigration.

Robert Murray, *Red Scare: A Study in National Hysteria.* Minneapolis: University of Minnesota Press, 1955. A history of the anti-radical and anti-immigrant attitudes and activities of the post-World War I period.

Victor G. Nee and Brett de Barry, *Longtime Californ'.* New York: Pantheon Books, 1973. A documentary study of an American Chinatown.

Cecyle S. Neidle, *America's Immigrant Women.* Boston: Twayne Publishers, 1975. Essays on contributions of immigrant women in all aspects of American life.

Humbert Nelli, *The Business of Crime: Italians and Syndicate Crime in the United States.* New York: Oxford University Press, 1976. A thoughtful treatment of the delicate issue of Italian-Americans and organized crime.

Humbert Nelli, *Italians in Chicago: A Study of Ethnic Mobility.* New York:

Oxford University Press, 1970. A study applying social science methodology to the question of occupational mobility within a single ethnic group.

Thomas Pitkin, *Keepers of the Gate: A History of Ellis Island.* New York: New York University Press, 1975. A history of the main immigrant depot, Ellis Island.

George E. Pozetta, ed., *American Immigration and Ethnicity*, 20 vols. New York: Garland Publishing, 1991. Each volume contains two dozen or so "classic" essays relating to particular aspects of immigration and ethnicity in America. Excellent source of historical and historiographical materials from the 1950s on. Volume titles include *Themes in American History; Assimilation, Acculturation, and Social Mobility; Nativism, Discrimination, and Images of Immigrants*; and others.

Jacob Riis, *How the Other Half Lives.* Cambridge, MA: Harvard University Press, 1910. A muckraking reformer looks at the lives of ghetto immigrants.

Moses Rischin, *Immigration and the American Tradition.* Indianapolis: Bobbs-Merrill, 1976. A general account of the fit between the practice of immigration and the American experience.

Moses Rischin, *The Promised City: New York's Jews, 1870-1914.* Cambridge, MA: Harvard University Press, 1962. The history of the Jewish immigrants of the Lower East Side.

Peter Roberts, *The New Immigrants: A Study of the Industrial and Social Life of Southeastern European Immigrants in America.* New York: J. S. Ozer, 1912. A sociological study of the new immigrants and an argument for their rapid assimilation.

Andrew Rolle, *The Immigrant Upraised: Italian Adventurers and Colonists in an Expanding America.* Norman: University of Oklahoma Press, 1968. A study examining the lives of Italian-Americans who settled in rural America.

Gerald Rosenblum, *Immigrant Workers: Their Impact on American Labor Radicalism.* New York: Basic Books, 1973. A history of the Old World fears that the author thinks were at the root of the immigrants' hesitation to adopt radicalism.

Theodore Saloutos, *The Greeks in the United States.* Cambridge, MA: Harvard University Press, 1964. The most authoritative study of Greek migration to the United States.

Alexander Saxton, *The Indispensable Enemy.* Berkeley: University of California Press, 1971. Case study of anti-Chinese movement.

Arnold Schrier, *Ireland and the Emigration.* Minneapolis: University of Minnesota Press, 1958. An analysis of the impact of Irish immigration on the United States.

Maxine S. Seller, ed., *Immigrant Women.* Philadelphia: Temple University Press, 1981. A collection of immigrant memoirs, oral histories, and diaries.

James P. Shannon, *Catholic Colonization on the Western Frontier.* New

Haven, CT: Yale University Press, 1957. A history of the efforts of Archbishop John Ireland to recruit Irish immigrants from the cities on the eastern seaboard to a life in the rural Midwest.

Dorothy Skardal, *The Divided Heart.* Oslo: Universitetsforlaget, 1974. A literary history of Scandinavian-American writers.

Josiah Strong, *Our Country.* New York: Baker and Taylor, 1885. The classic nativist attack on post-Civil War immigration.

Philip Taylor, *The Distant Magnet.* New York: Harper and Row, 1971. A study focusing on the immigrant's journey rather than arrival and settlement.

William Tefft and Thomas Dunne, *Ellis Island.* New York: Norton, 1971. A portrait of immigrant inspection procedures at the main point of entry in New York.

Leslie Tentler, *Wage-Earning Women: Industrial Work and Family Life in the United States, 1900-1930.* New York: Oxford University Press, 1979. A history that places the problems facing immigrant women in the larger context of industrialization.

Stephan Thernstrom, ed., *Harvard Encyclopedia of American Ethnic Groups.* Cambridge, MA: Harvard University Press, 1980. A superb collection of sources and essays by the leading American historians of specific immigrant groups. Also includes general essays on such topics as assimilation, pluralism, and U. S. immigration leglislation.

Stephan Thernstrom, *The Other Bostonians: Poverty and Progress in the American Metropolis, 1880-1970.* Cambridge, MA: Harvard University Press, 1973. A history tracing the mobility of immigrants over several generations.

Henry Shih-shan Tsai, *The Chinese Experience in America.* Bloomington: University of Indiana Press, 1986. A general survey of the history of the Chinese-American immigrant from the nineteenth century to the present.

Rudolph J. Vecoli and Suzanne M. Sinke, eds., *A Century of European Migrations, 1830-1930.* Urbana: University of Illinois Press, 1991. Historians explore a range of immigration topics, from the general ("Migration from Europe Overseas in the Nineteenth and Twentieth Centuries") to the specific ("Migration Traditions from Finland to North America").

Mack Walker, *Germany and the Emigration, 1816-1885.* Cambridge, MA: Harvard University Press, 1964. A history that focuses on German immigration through German-Americans themselves and their organizations.

David Ward, *Cities and Immigrants.* New York: Oxford University Press, 1971. A general survey of the phenomenon of the congregation of immigrant groups in urban places.

Thomas C. Wheeler, ed., *The Immigrant Experience: The Anguish of Becoming American.* New York: Penguin, 1971. Nine personal accounts from people of different ethnic groups recounting their experiences as immigrants or children of immigrants.

For Discussion

Chapter One

1. J. Hector St. John de Crèvecoeur and Marcus Eli Ravage were both immigrants to the United States, Crèvecoeur in the eighteenth century and Ravage in the twentieth. What different conditions did the two men face that may have affected their views about becoming American?
2. Two authors in this chapter suggest that America is a "melting pot"; the other two suggest that it is difficult, if not impossible, for immigrants to truly "melt" into American society. Consider what you know of American society today. Which view do you think is more accurate? Why?
3. In general, what do you think of the melting pot metaphor for America?

Chapter Two

1. After reading the viewpoints by the Native American party, L. C. Levin, and the *New York Mirror*, list what you think were the primary concerns Americans of the early and mid-nineteenth century had about immigrants. List some of the facts these three authors used to validate their concerns.
2. List the main facts presented by Thomas L. Nichols, Martin J. Spalding, and *Putnam's Monthly* to refute the idea that immigrants endanger American society.
3. What threats to America does Rena Michaels Atchison perceive in immigrants' continued use of their native tongue? For what reasons does Waldemar Ager think it is essential that they do so?

Chapter Three

1. One argument against immigrants, stated succinctly by Prescott F. Hall, centers around the value of racial purity. What commonsense arguments does Percy Stickney Grant use to counter this idea?
2. One continuing fear of people already established in the United States was that immigrants would impair the earning power of "native" Americans. Who do you think addresses this issue

more convincingly, John Mitchell or Harris Weinstock? Why? What elements of each writer's personal life may have influenced his viewpoint?

3. What forces in American life does Grover G. Huebner say help immigrants assimilate? Do you think his ideas or those presented by Henry P. Fairchild are more convincing on the issue of immigrant assimilation? Why?

4. Considering all the viewpoints in this chapter, what seem to be the main concerns of Americans about immigrants during this late nineteenth- and early twentieth-century period? Do you hear any of the same concerns being voiced by Americans today? If so, list some specific instances.

Chapter Four

1. From your reading of this chapter, what seem to be the main reasons some Americans wanted to place restrictions on immigration?

2. From your reading of this chapter, were the reasons of those who were against immigration restriction altruistic or self-serving? Explain.

3. Several different kinds of restrictive legislation are discussed in this chapter. In your opinion, do they all have a common basis, or are they all different? That is, are all to some degree based on racist attitudes, limitations of the country's resources, or another common idea? Explain your answer.

4. What do you think about immigration restriction today? Do you believe immigration must be restricted or not? If you believe restriction is necessary, what limitations would you establish? Why?

Chapter Five

1. Oscar Handlin and John Bodnar agree that immigration is a difficult experience, but Handlin's viewpoint emphasizes the negative consequences of that experience and Bodnar suggests that what at first appears negative may in actuality be positive. With which historian do you agree more? Why?

General

1. Talk to someone who is an immigrant or a child of immigrants. If this immigration occurred after 1930, how did conditions compare to those during the nineteenth and early twentieth centuries? Overall, does this person believe immigration was a beneficial or a harmful experience? Why?

2. Imagine yourself emigrating to another country. What things do you think would be most difficult for you? Least difficult? Why?

3. Historians have said that American history is the story of its immigrants. Do you agree with this idea? Explain.

4. Many people have pointed out the contradiction between the welcome represented by the Statue of Liberty (and Emma Lazarus's poem inscribed there: "Give me your tired, your poor . . .") and the way the country has actually treated immigrants. How would you respond to someone who pointed out this contradiction?

Index

201-2
as teeming (yellow) hordes, 195-97, 199
Chinese Exclusion Act (1882), 190, 199, 205
church
  as assimilation barrier, 180-81
  as assimilation factor, 171
Cincinnati Times-Star, 246
civil rights movement and ethnic identity, 49
Claghorn, Kate Halladay, 143
Clark, Walter E., 178
College of St. James, 27
Colonial Dames, 148
Commissioner-General of Immigration, 114, 157, 228, 231, 234-35, 241
Commons, John Rogers, 114, 247
Congress of Races, 122
contract-labor laws, 153, 215, 241, 256
Cook, Joseph, 134
Coolidge, Calvin, 243
Cooper, James Fenimore, 77
Crèvecoeur, J. Hector St. John de, 24-31
crime, immigrants and, 134, 145, 228-29, 237-38
Crocker, Charles, 208
Cromwell, Oliver, 80
Curtis, George William, 115, 233

D'Angelo, Pascal, 37
Darlington, Thomas, 229
Darwin, Charles, 101, 112, 118
Davenport, Charles B., 120
delinquency and immigrants, 132-34
deportation, 228, 237, 251
Deutscher Liederkranz, 100
disease, immigrants and, 229-30
domestic service and immigrants, 161-62
Dumas, Alexandre, 122
Du Maurier, George Louis, 123

economic indications for restrictions, 231-33
education and immigration
  compulsory language education, 93-96, 97-101
  see also schools
Eliot, Charles W., 111
Ellis Island, 47, 117, 229
emigration
  conditions encouraging, 279-80
  from Europe in World War I, 255-56
  flight-from-poverty theory of, 281
  networks of migration, 282-85
  pragmatism and, 281-82

structure of, 278-79
Emigration and Immigration: A Study in Social Science (Mayo-Smith), 173
Emmet, Robert, 69
employers
  as assimilation factor, 172-74
  impact on immigrants, 246, 250
employment insecurity and immigrants, 270-72
English language
  compulsory education in
    arguments against, 97-101
    arguments for, 93-96
  non-English speakers, percent by areas, 94-95
Esoteric Anthropology . . . (Nichols), 66
ethnic groups
  civil rights movement and, 49
  distrust of intellectuals, 53-54
  failure to assimilate, 49-55
  Vietnam War and, 49
  white, 50
  women's movement and, 49
eugenics, 119
Europe, southern and eastern
  immigrants from, 34-35, 54, 142-47, 243, 247-48
  illiteracy of, 216, 249

Fairchild, Henry P., 40, 175-84
Fair Play and the Workers, Socialism and Christianity (Grant), 116-27
family
  as assimilation barrier, 181
  as focus of life, 280-81
  importance in Europe, 266-67
  kinship networks, 285-86
  property and, 280
Finch, Earl, 122
Finot, Jean, 120
Flannigan, Edward, 91
Forward, 254
Foundations of the XIXth Century (Chamberlain), 106
Fulton, Robert, 69
Future of American Wage Earners (Mitchell), 149

Gallatin, Albert, 70
Galton, Francis, 118
Garibaldi, Giuseppe, 132
Garis, Roy L., 243-51
Garrison, William Lloyd, 115
Gavit, John Palmer, 119
German immigrants, 95-96, 100
  early prejudice against, 142
germ-plasm theory of heredity, 118